P9-CQN-252

ULTIMATE COMICS

X-MEN

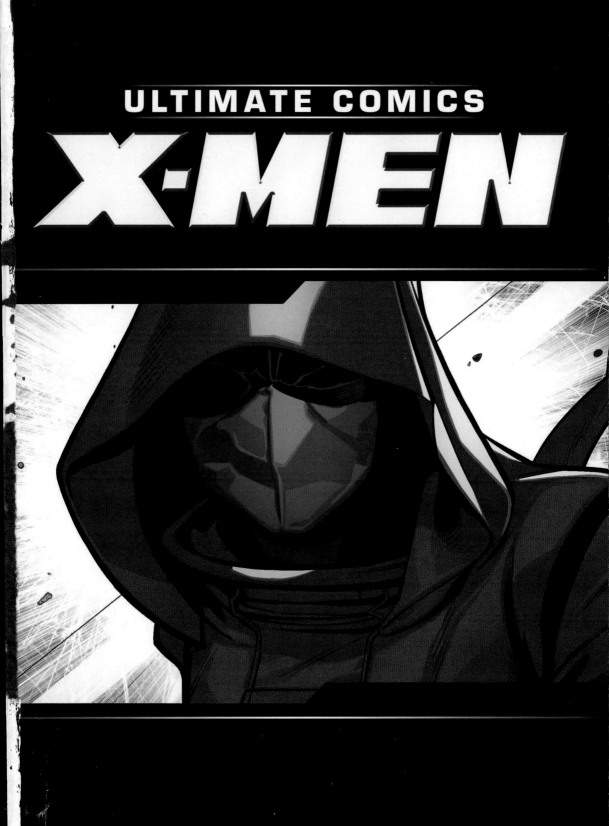

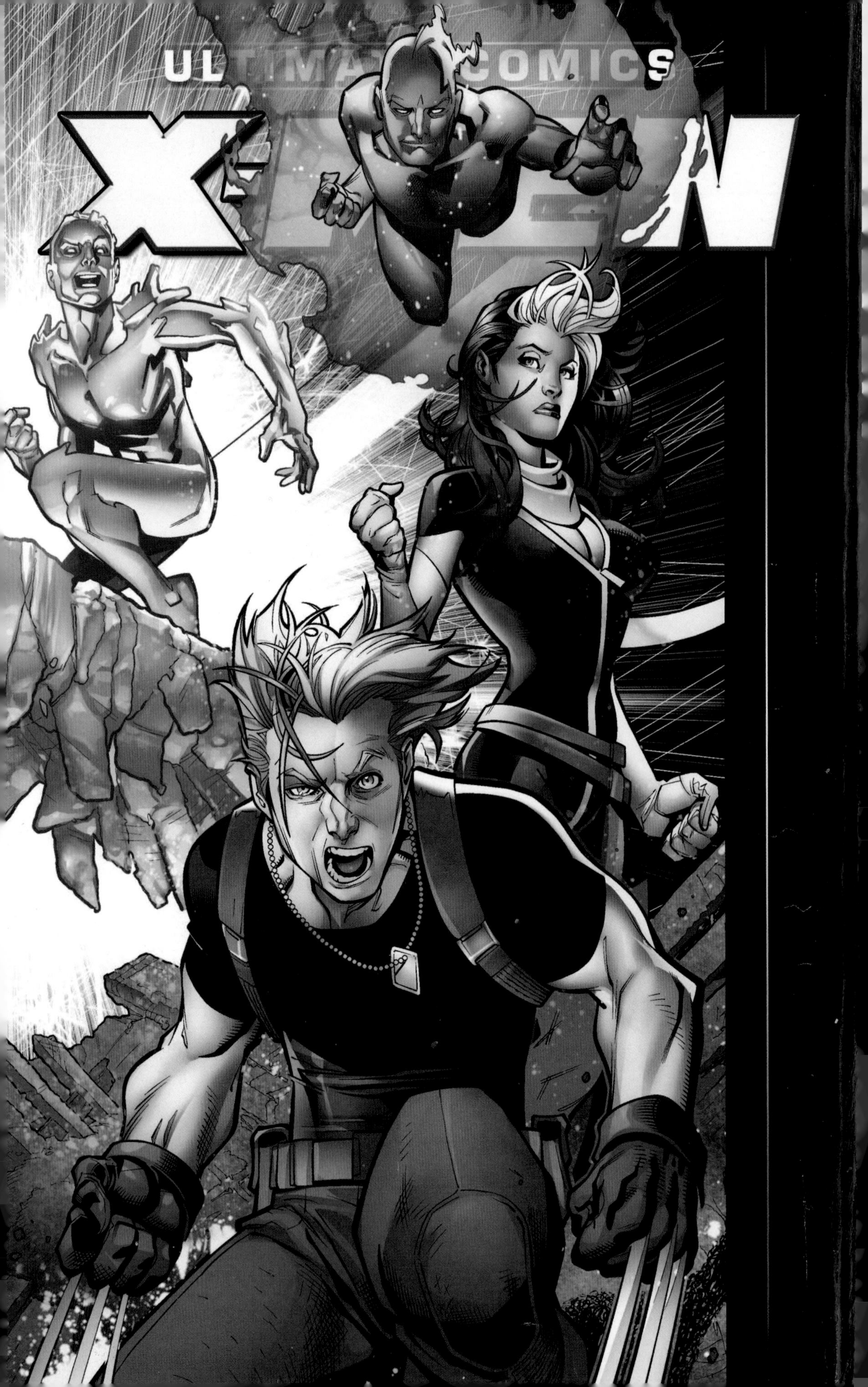
COMICS

WRITER: **NICK SPENCER**

PENCILER: **PACO MEDINA** WITH **CARLO BARBERI** (#6)

INKER: **JUAN VLASCO**

COLORISTS: **MARTE GRACIA** (#1-4),

DAVID CURIEL (#5) & **REX LOKUS** (#6)

COVER ART: **KAARE ANDREWS**

LETTERER: **VC'S JOE SABINO**

ASSISTANT EDITOR: **JON MOISAN**

ASSOCIATE EDITOR: **SANA AMANAT**

EDITOR: **MARK PANICCIA**

COLLECTION EDITOR: **JENNIFER GRÜNWALD**

ASSISTANT EDITORS: **ALEX STARBUCK** & **NELSON RIBEIRO**

EDITOR, SPECIAL PROJECTS: **MARK D. BEAZLEY**

SENIOR EDITOR, SPECIAL PROJECTS: **JEFF YOUNGQUIST**

SENIOR VICE PRESIDENT OF SALES: **DAVID GABRIEL**

SVP OF BRAND PLANNING & COMMUNICATIONS: **MICHAEL PASCIULLO**

BOOK DESIGNER: **RODOLFO MURAGUCHI**

EDITOR IN CHIEF: **AXEL ALONSO**

CHIEF CREATIVE OFFICER: **JOE QUESADA**

PUBLISHER: **DAN BUCKLEY**

EXECUTIVE PRODUCER: **ALAN FINE**

ULTIMATE COMICS X-MEN BY NICK SPENCER VOL. 1. Contains material originally published in magazine form as ULTIMATE COMICS X-MEN #1-6. First printing 2012. Hardcover ISBN# 978-0-7851-4015-3. Softcover ISBN# 978-0-7851-4102-0. Published by MARVEL WORLDWIDE, INC., a subsidiary of MARVEL ENTERTAINMENT, LLC. OFFICE OF PUBLICATION: 135 West 50th Street, New York, NY 10020. Copyright © 2011 and 2012 Marvel Characters, Inc. All rights reserved. Hardcover: $24.99 per copy in the U.S. and $27.99 in Canada (GST #R127032852). Softcover $19.99 per copy in the U.S. and $17.99 in Canada (GST #R127032852). Canadian Agreement #40668537. All characters featured in this issue and the distinctive names and likenesses thereof, and all related indicia are trademarks of Marvel Characters, Inc. No similarity between any of the names, characters, persons, and/or institutions in this magazine with those of any living or dead person or institution is intended, and any such similarity which may exist is purely coincidental. Printed in the U.S.A. ALAN FINE, EVP - Office of the President, Marvel Worldwide, Inc. and EVP & CMO Marvel Characters B.V.; DAN BUCKLEY, Publisher & President - Print, Animation & Digital Divisions; JOE QUESADA, Chief Creative Officer; DAVID BOGART, SVP of Business Affairs & Talent Management; TOM BREVOORT, SVP of Publishing; C.B. CEBULSKI, SVP of Creator & Content Development; DAVID GABRIEL, SVP of Publishing Sales & Circulation; MICHAEL PASCIULLO, SVP of Brand Planning & Communications; JIM O'KEEFE, VP of Operations & Logistics; DAN CARR, Executive Director of Publishing Technology; SUSAN CRESPI, Editorial Operations Manager; ALEX MORALES, Publishing Operations Manager; STAN LEE, Chairman Emeritus. For information regarding advertising in Marvel Comics or on Marvel.com, please contact John Dokes, SVP Integrated Sales & Marketing, at jdokes@marvel.com. For Marvel subscription inquiries, please call 800-217-9158. **Manufactured between 2/6/2012 and 3/5/2012 (hardcover), and 2/6/2012 and 9/10/2012 (softcover), by R.R. DONNELLEY INC., SALEM, VA, USA.**

10 9 8 7 6 5 4 3 2 1

1

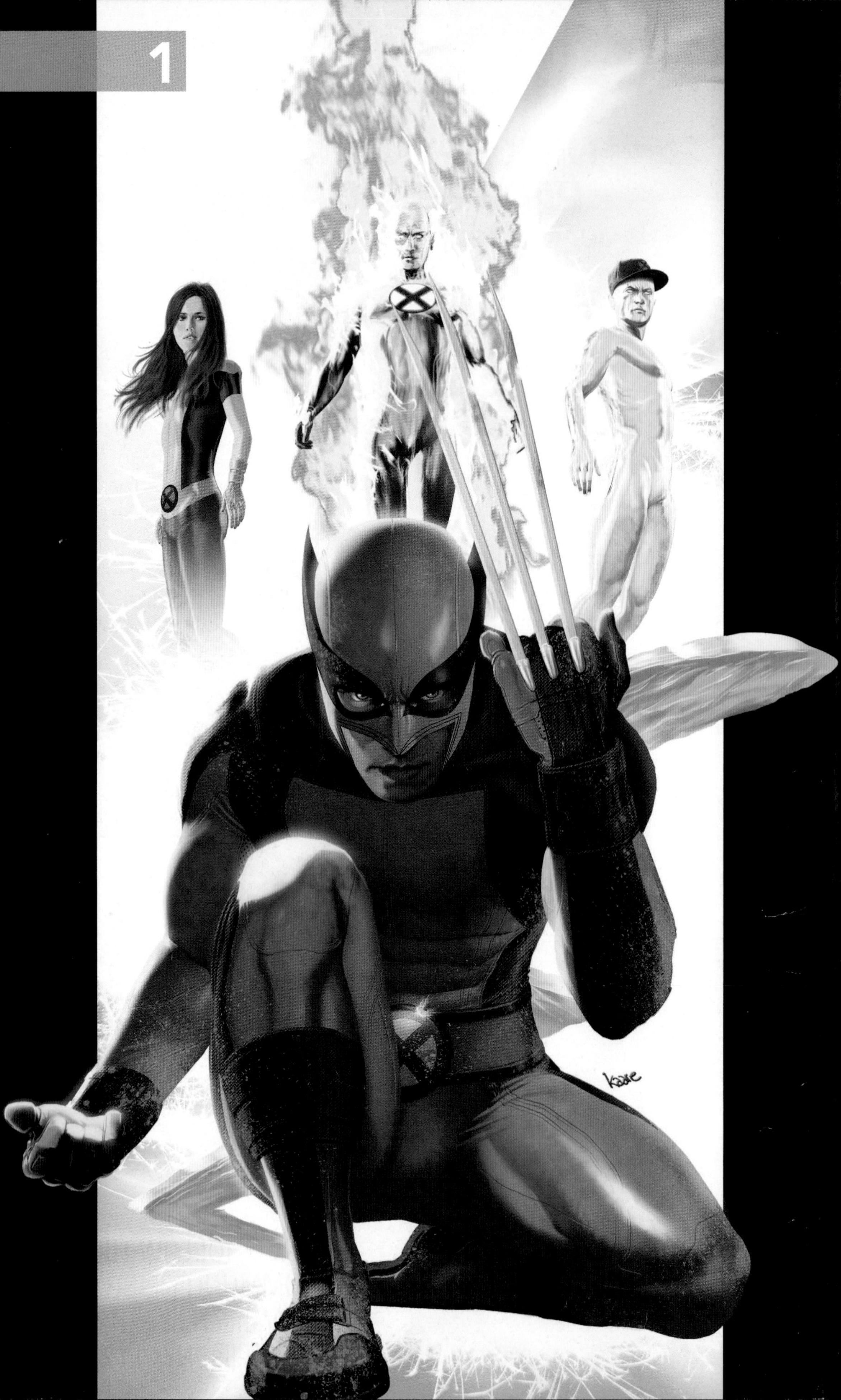

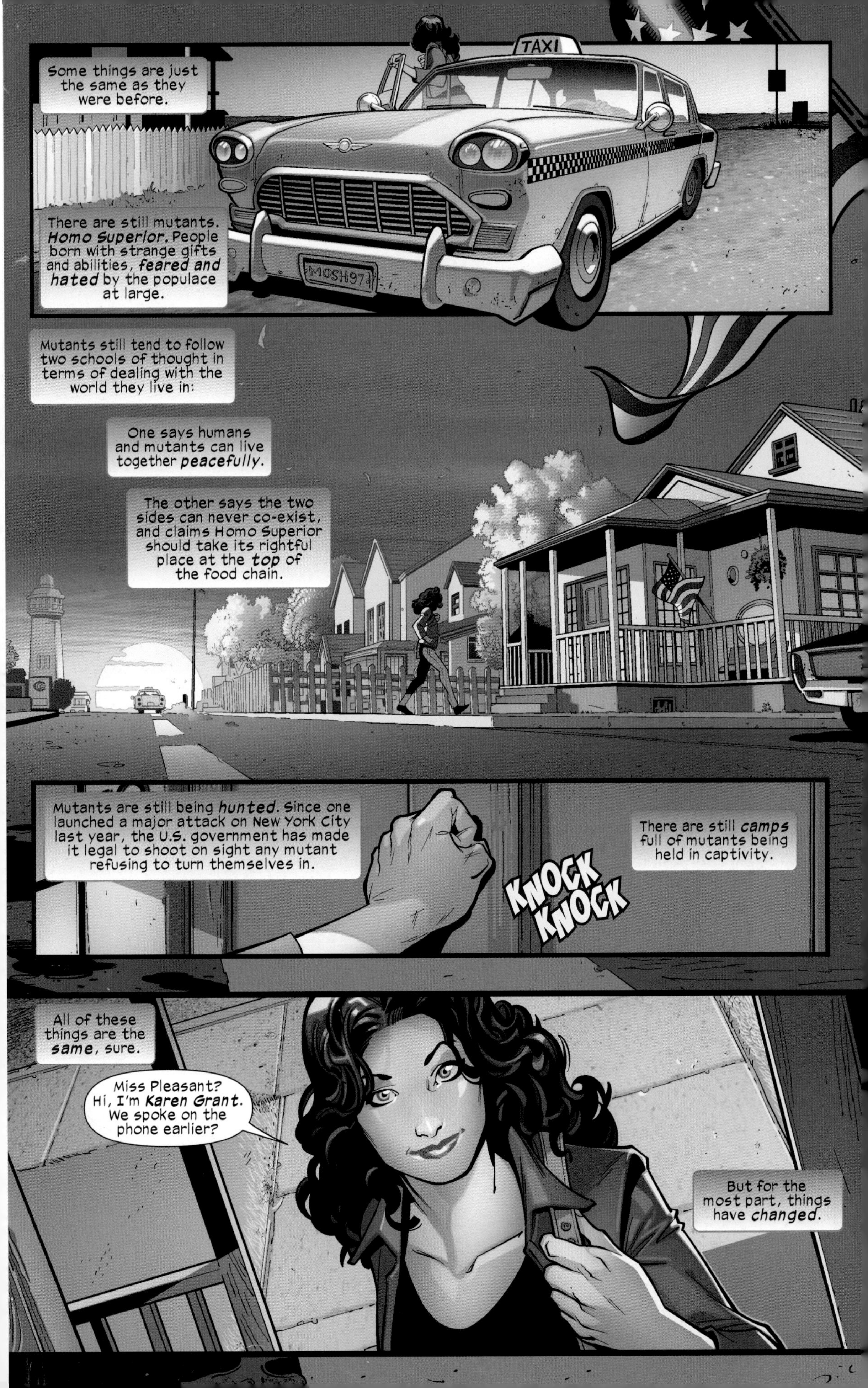

Some things are just the same as they were before.
TAXI
MOSH97
There are still mutants. *Homo Superior.* People born with strange gifts and abilities, *feared and hated* by the populace at large.
Mutants still tend to follow two schools of thought in terms of dealing with the world they live in:
One says humans and mutants can live together *peacefully*.
The other says the two sides can never co-exist, and claims Homo Superior should take its rightful place at the *top* of the food chain.
Mutants are still being *hunted*. Since one launched a major attack on New York City last year, the U.S. government has made it legal to shoot on sight any mutant refusing to turn themselves in.
There are still *camps* full of mutants being held in captivity.
KNOCK KNOCK
All of these things are the *same*, sure.
Miss Pleasant? Hi, I'm *Karen Grant*. We spoke on the phone earlier?
But for the most part, things have *changed*.

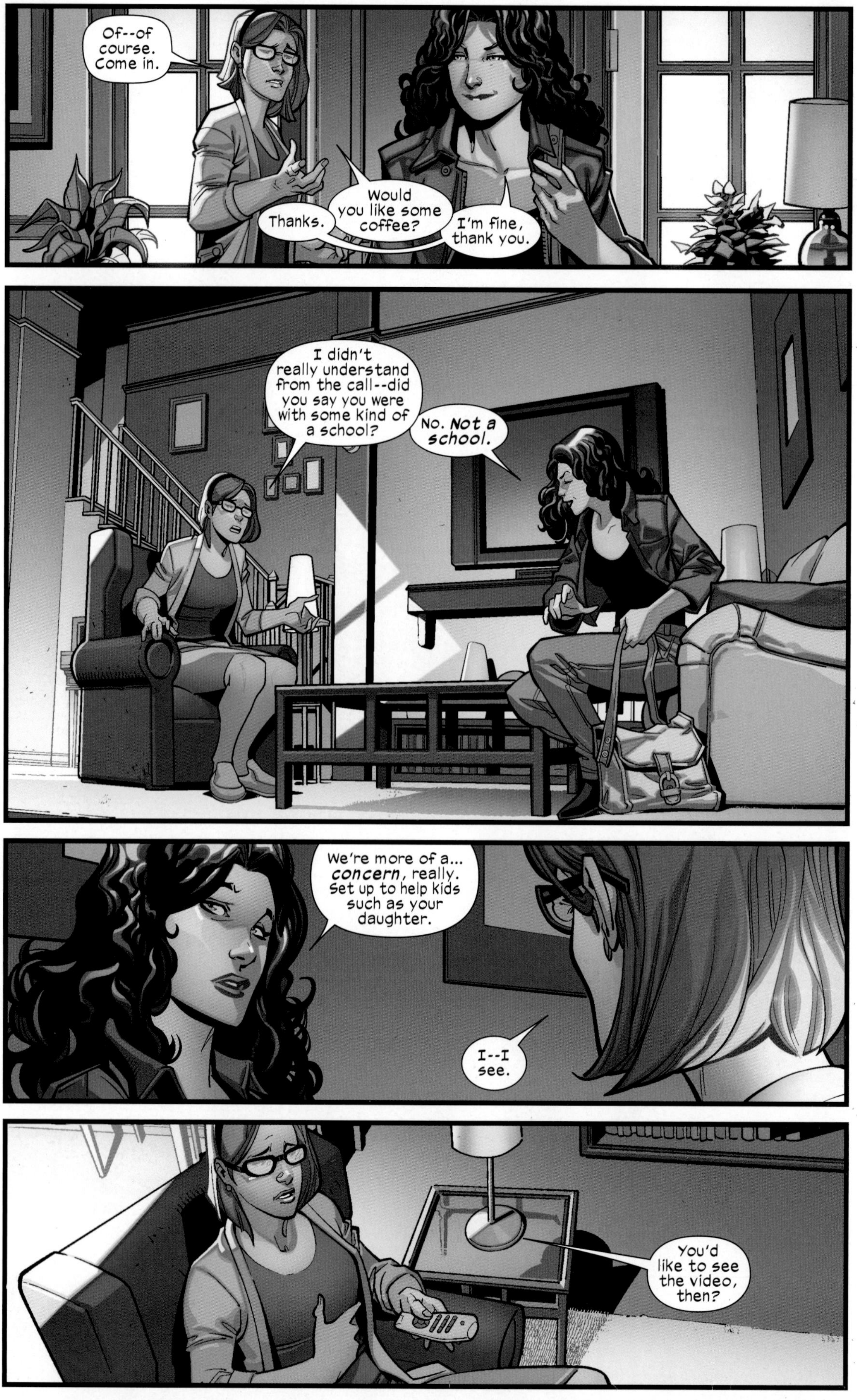
Of--of course. Come in.
Would you like some coffee?
Thanks.
I'm fine, thank you.
I didn't really understand from the call--did you say you were with some kind of a school?
No. *Not a school.*
We're more of a... *concern*, really. Set up to help kids such as your daughter.
I--I see.
You'd like to see the video, then?

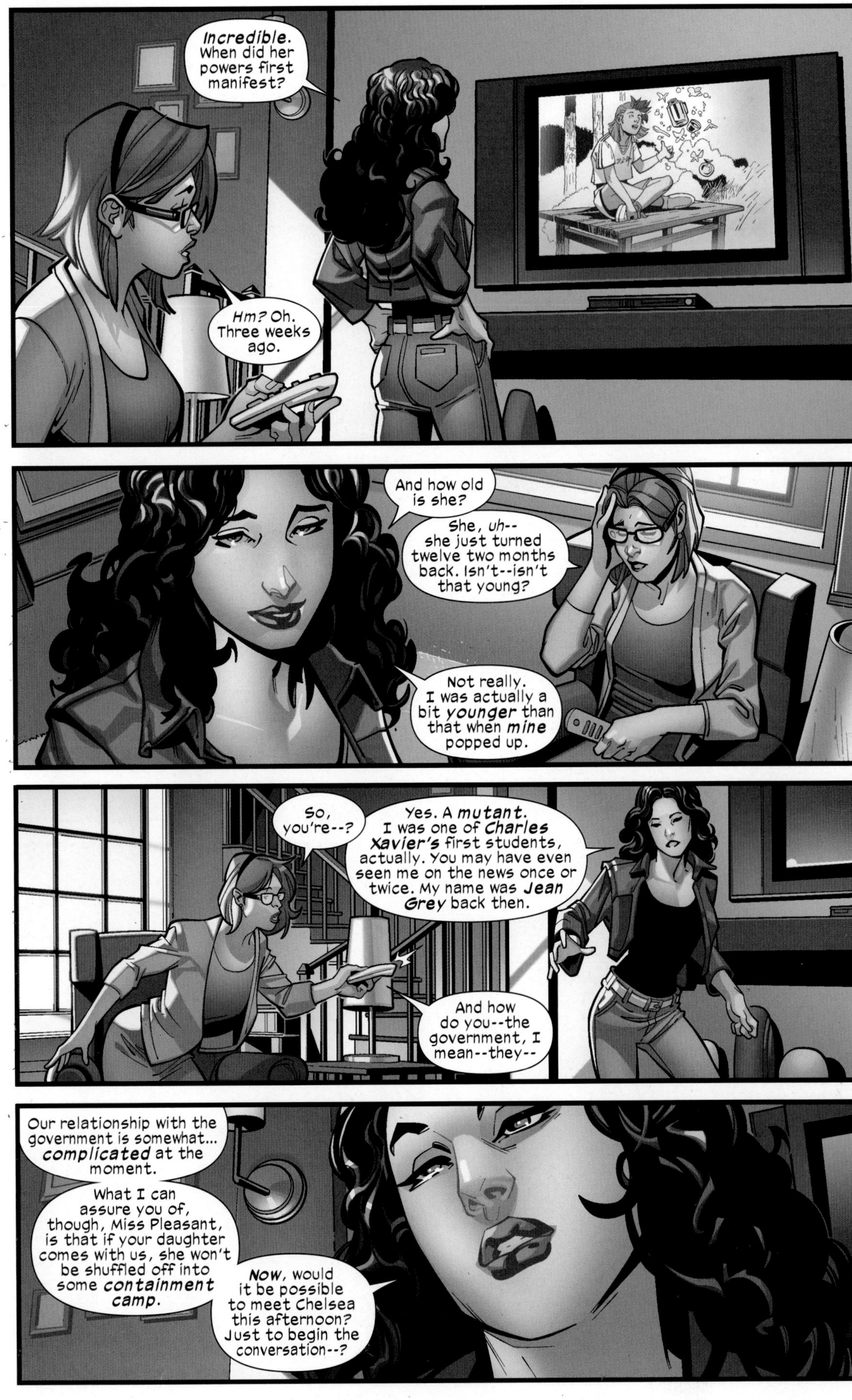
Incredible. When did her powers first manifest?
Hm? Oh. Three weeks ago.
And how old is she?
She, uh-- she just turned twelve two months back. Isn't--isn't that young?
Not really. I was actually a bit younger than that when mine popped up.
So, you're--?
Yes. A mutant. I was one of Charles Xavier's first students, actually. You may have even seen me on the news once or twice. My name was Jean Grey back then.
And how do you--the government, I mean--they--
Our relationship with the government is somewhat... complicated at the moment.
What I can assure you of, though, Miss Pleasant, is that if your daughter comes with us, she won't be shuffled off into some containment camp.
Now, would it be possible to meet Chelsea this afternoon? Just to begin the conversation--?

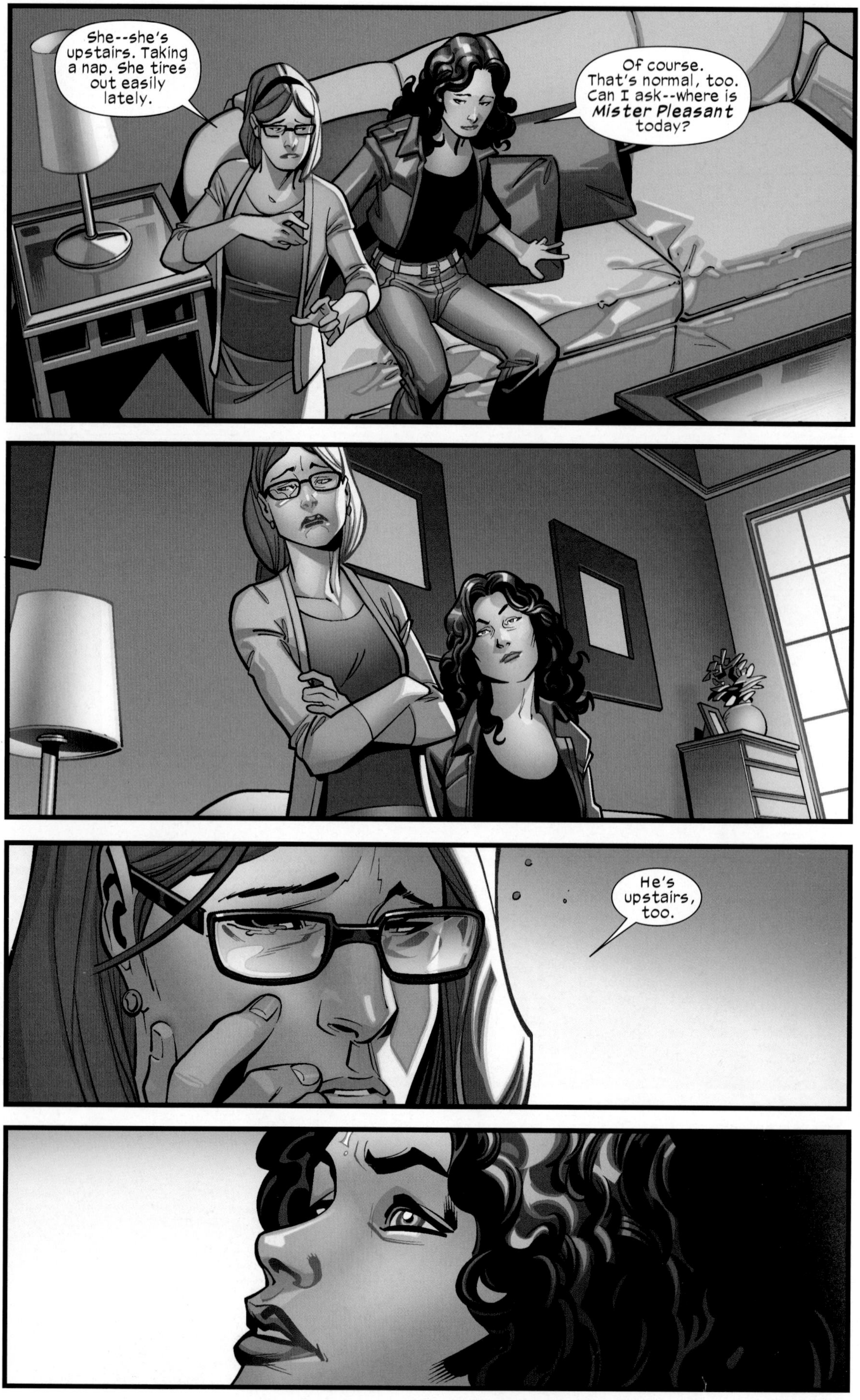
She--she's upstairs. Taking a nap. She tires out easily lately.
Of course. That's normal, too. Can I ask--where is *Mister Pleasant* today?
He's upstairs, too.

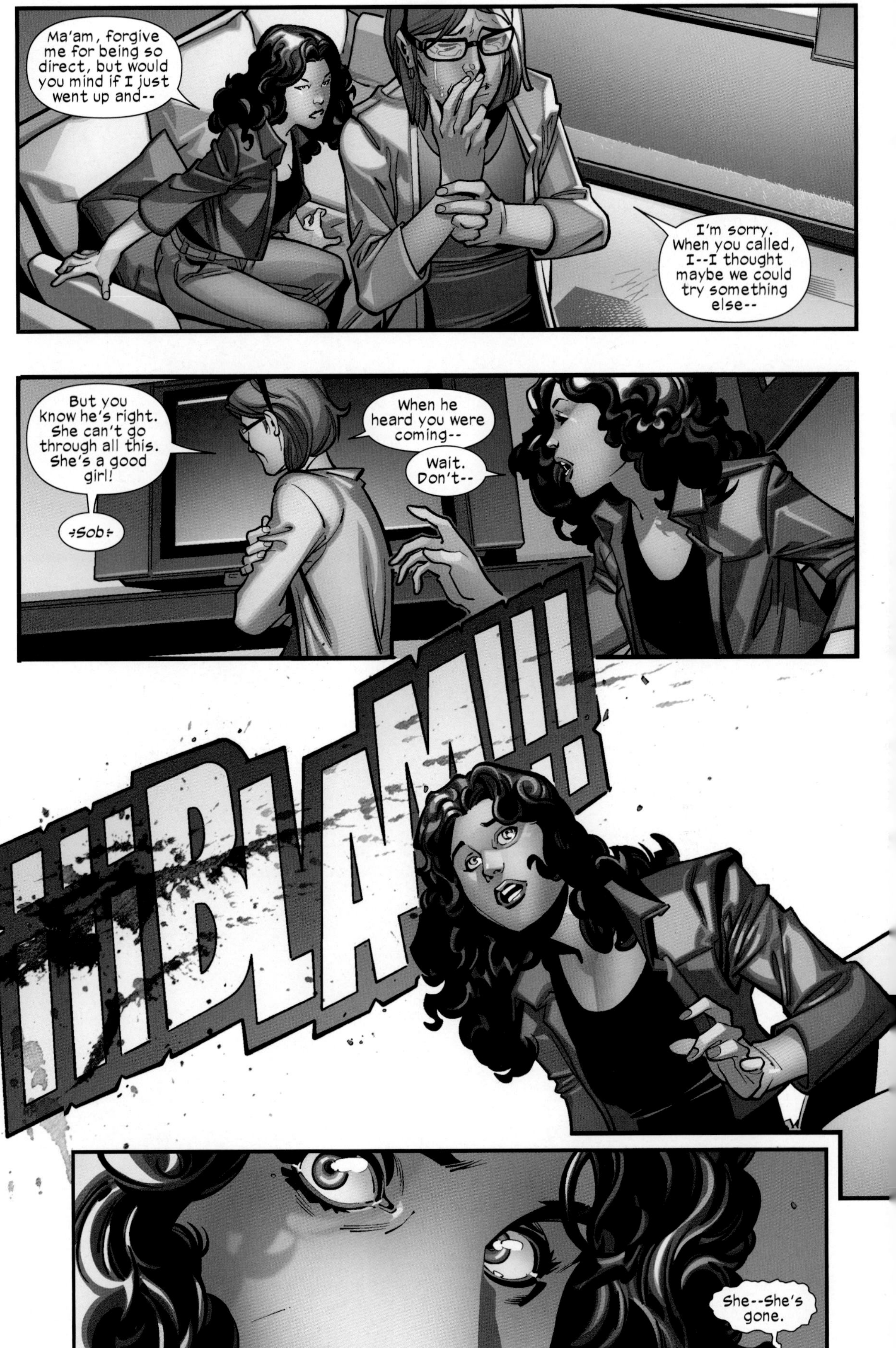
Ma'am, forgive me for being so direct, but would you mind if I just went up and--
I'm sorry. When you called, I--I thought maybe we could try something else--
But you know he's right. She can't go through all this. She's a good girl!
-Sob-
When he heard you were coming--
Wait. Don't--
THBLAM!!!
She--She's gone.

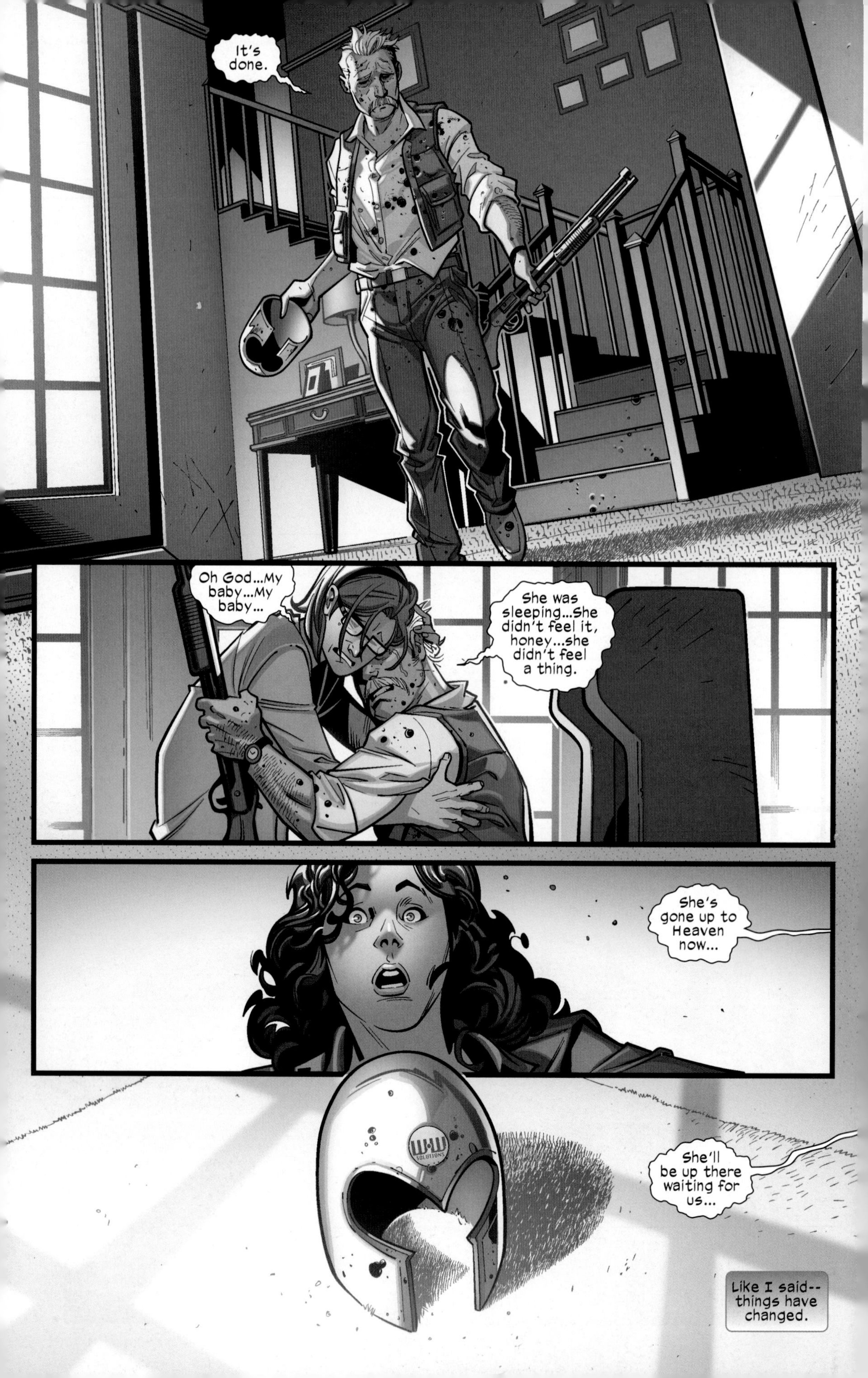
It's done.
Oh God...My baby...My baby...
She was sleeping...She didn't feel it, honey...she didn't feel a thing.
She's gone up to Heaven now...
W·W SOLUTIONS
She'll be up there waiting for us...
Like I said--things have changed.

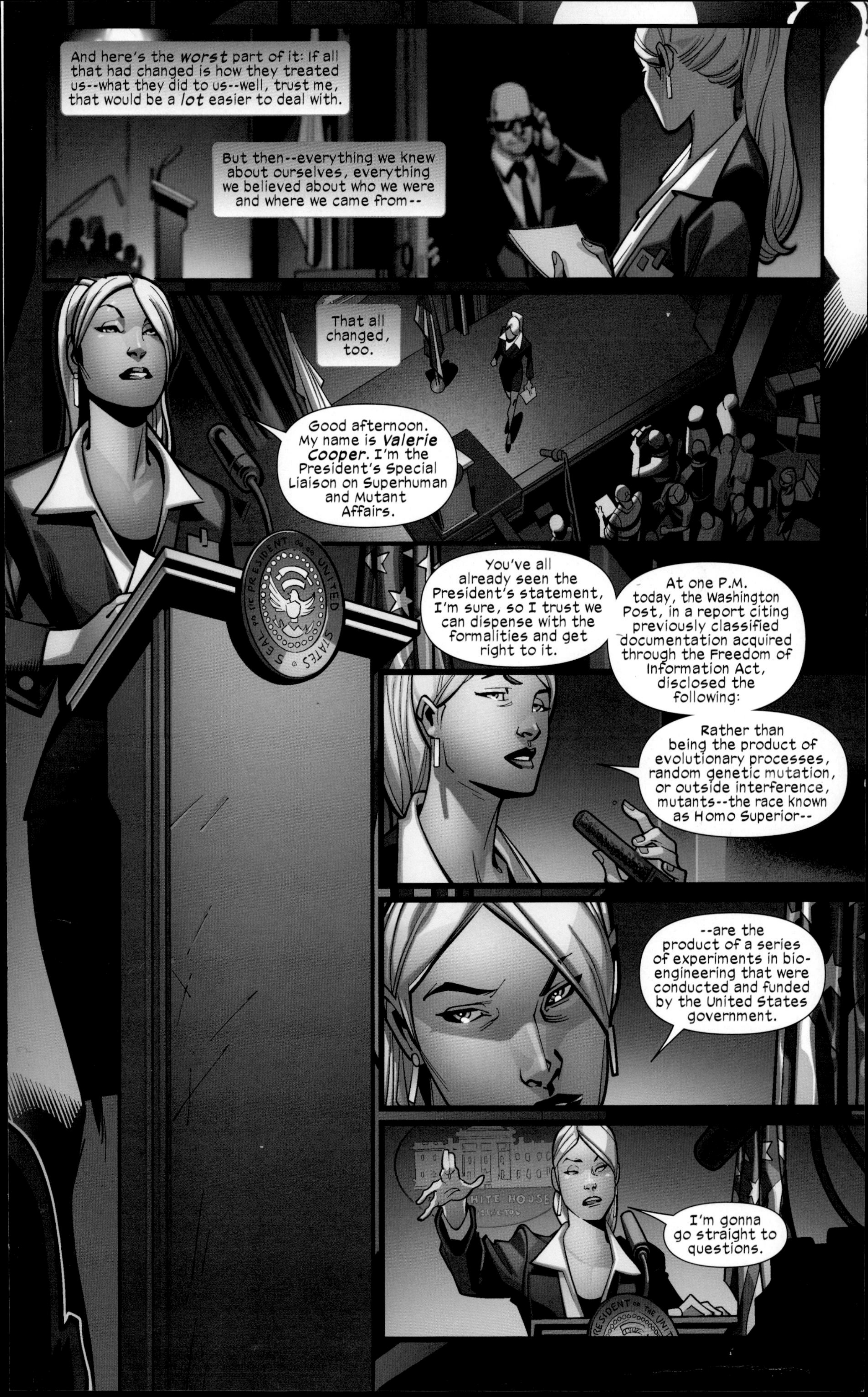
And here's the *worst* part of it: If all that had changed is how they treated us--what they did to us--well, trust me, that would be a *lot* easier to deal with.
But then--everything we knew about ourselves, everything we believed about who we were and where we came from--
That all changed, too.
Good afternoon. My name is *Valerie Cooper*. I'm the President's Special Liaison on Superhuman and Mutant Affairs.
You've all already seen the President's statement, I'm sure, so I trust we can dispense with the formalities and get right to it.
At one P.M. today, the Washington Post, in a report citing previously classified documentation acquired through the Freedom of Information Act, disclosed the following:
Rather than being the product of evolutionary processes, random genetic mutation, or outside interference, mutants--the race known as Homo Superior--
--are the product of a series of experiments in bio-engineering that were conducted and funded by the United States government.
I'm gonna go straight to questions.

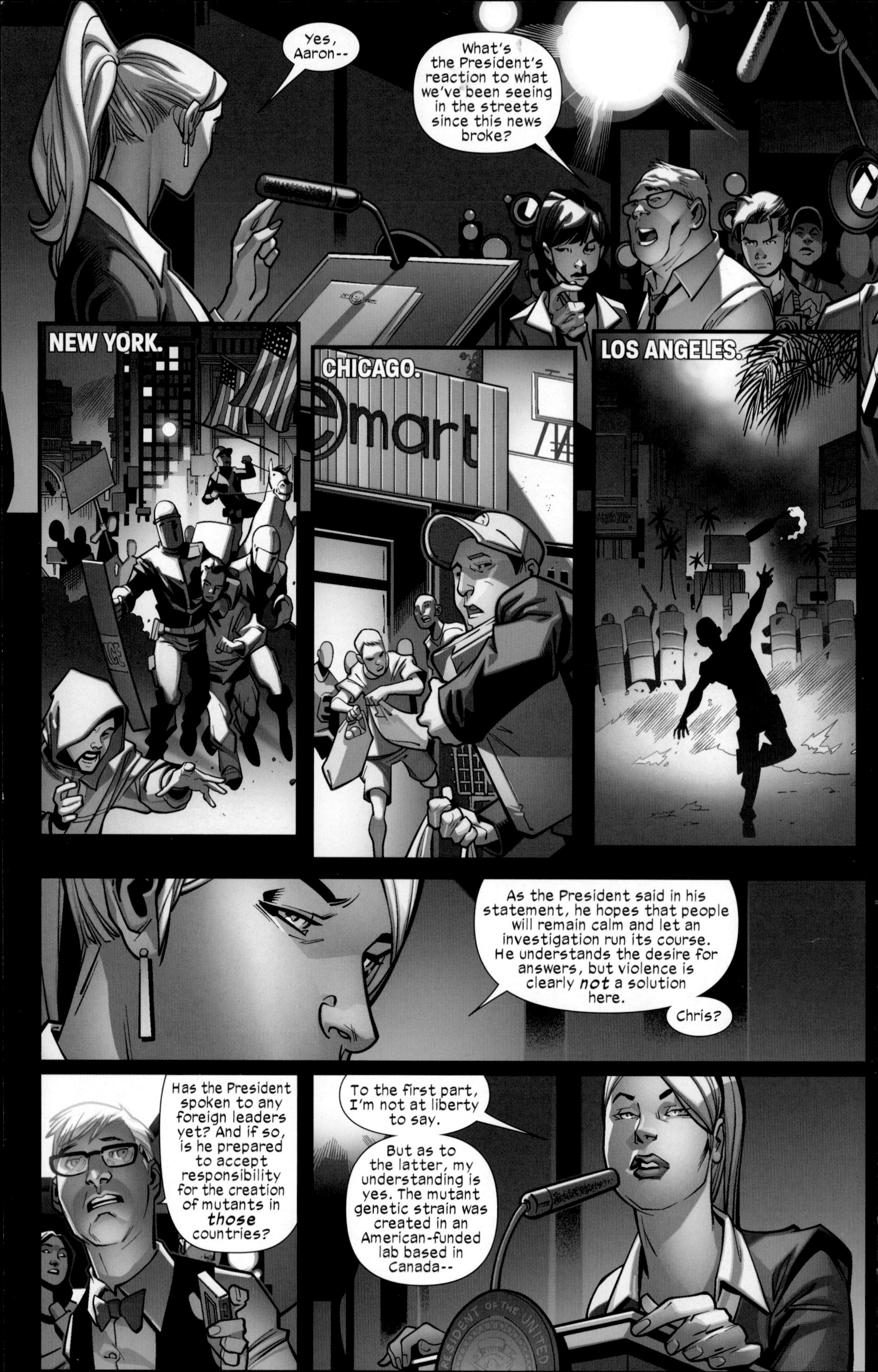
Yes, Aaron--
What's the President's reaction to what we've been seeing in the streets since this news broke?
NEW YORK.
CHICAGO.
mart
LOS ANGELES.
As the President said in his statement, he hopes that people will remain calm and let an investigation run its course. He understands the desire for answers, but violence is clearly *not* a solution here.
Chris?
Has the President spoken to any foreign leaders yet? And if so, is he prepared to accept responsibility for the creation of mutants in *those* countries?
To the first part, I'm not at liberty to say.
But as to the latter, my understanding is yes. The mutant genetic strain was created in an American-funded lab based in Canada--

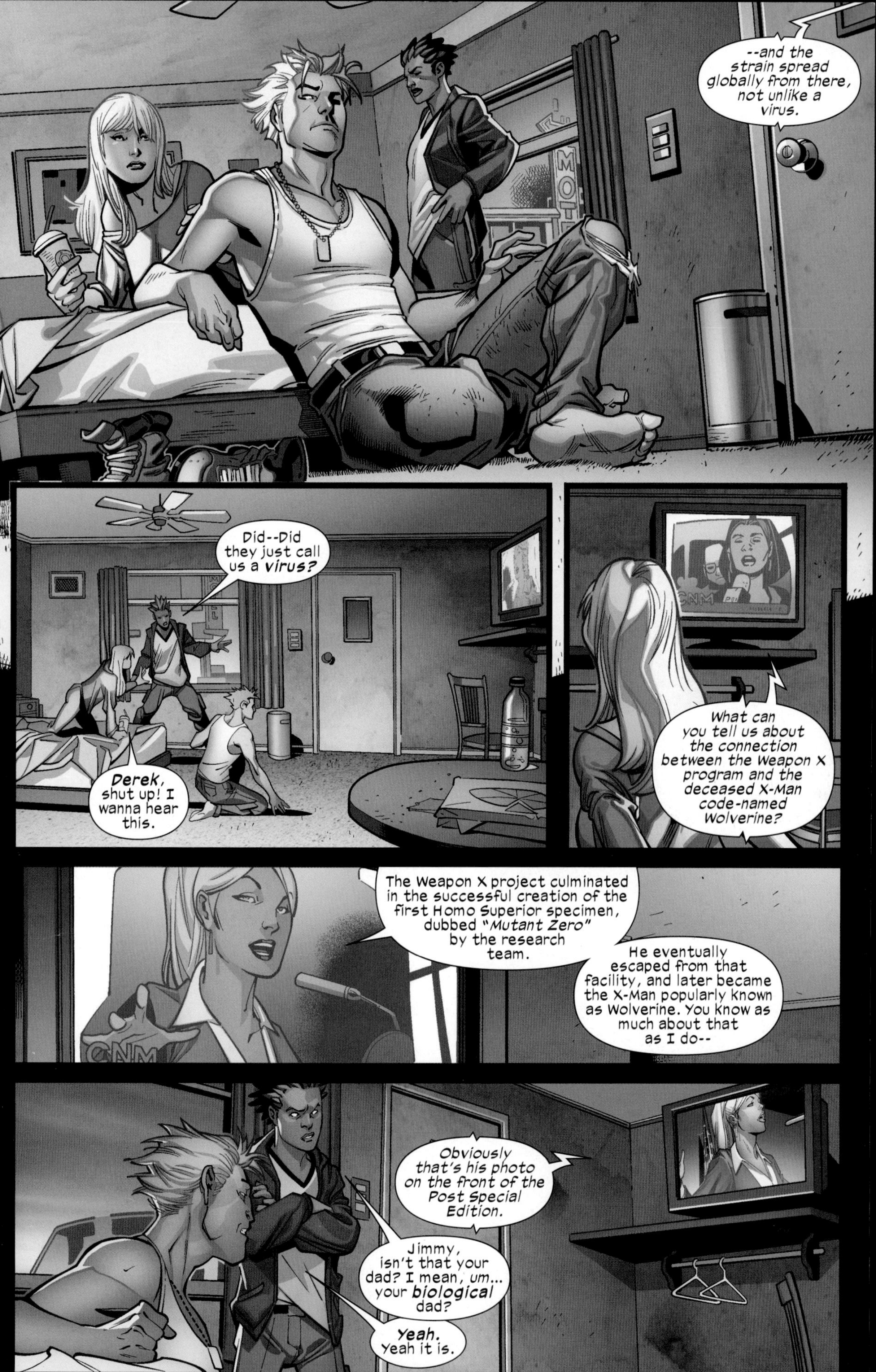
--and the strain spread globally from there, not unlike a virus.
Did--Did they just call us a *virus?*
Derek, shut up! I wanna hear this.
What can you tell us about the connection between the Weapon X program and the deceased X-Man code-named Wolverine?
The Weapon X project culminated in the successful creation of the first Homo Superior specimen, dubbed *"Mutant Zero"* by the research team.
He eventually escaped from that facility, and later became the X-Man popularly known as Wolverine. You know as much about that as I do--
Obviously that's his photo on the front of the Post Special Edition.
Jimmy, isn't that your dad? I mean, *um*... your ***biological*** dad?
Yeah. Yeah it is.

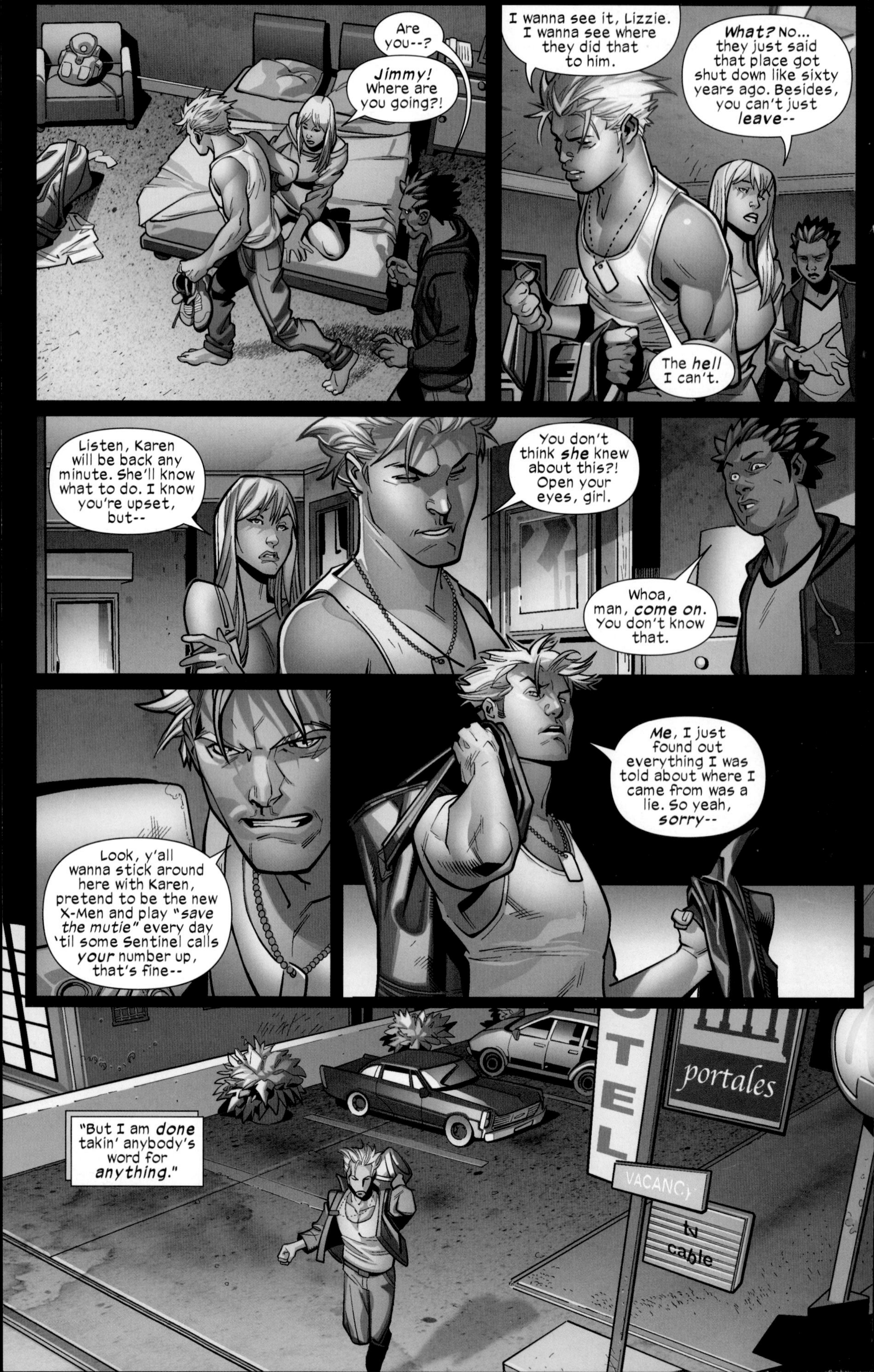
Are you--?
Jimmy! Where are you going?!
I wanna see it, Lizzie. I wanna see where they did that to him.
What? No... they just said that place got shut down like sixty years ago. Besides, you can't just leave--
The hell I can't.
Listen, Karen will be back any minute. She'll know what to do. I know you're upset, but--
You don't think she knew about this?! Open your eyes, girl.
Whoa, man, come on. You don't know that.
Look, y'all wanna stick around here with Karen, pretend to be the new X-Men and play "save the mutie" every day 'til some Sentinel calls your number up, that's fine--
Me, I just found out everything I was told about where I came from was a lie. So yeah, sorry--
"But I am done takin' anybody's word for anything."
portales
TEL
VACANCY
cable

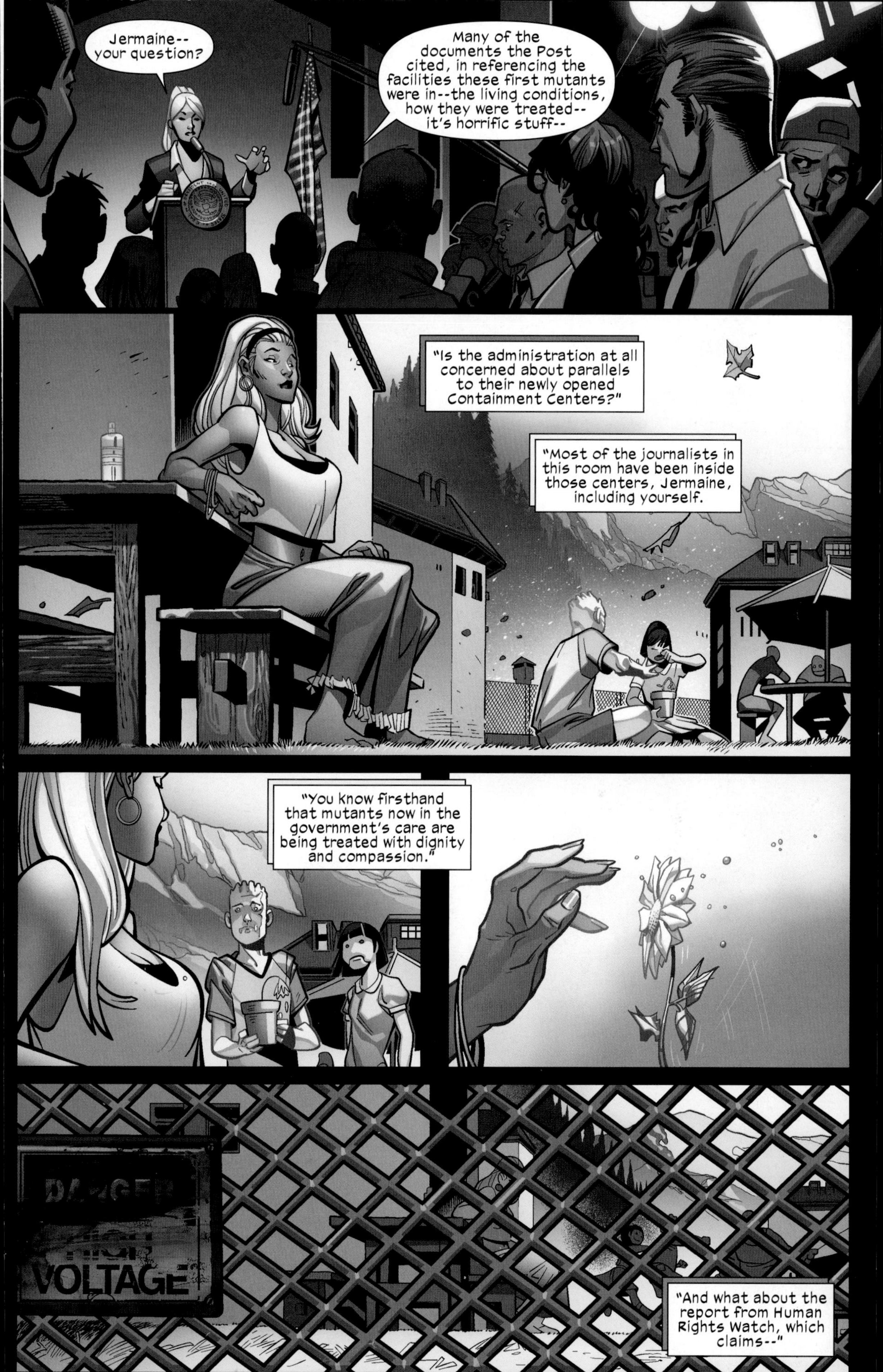
Jermaine--
your question?
Many of the documents the Post cited, in referencing the facilities these first mutants were in--the living conditions, how they were treated--it's horrific stuff--
"Is the administration at all concerned about parallels to their newly opened Containment Centers?"
"Most of the journalists in this room have been inside those centers, Jermaine, including yourself.
"You know firsthand that mutants now in the government's care are being treated with dignity and compassion."
VOLTAGE
"And what about the report from Human Rights Watch, which claims--"

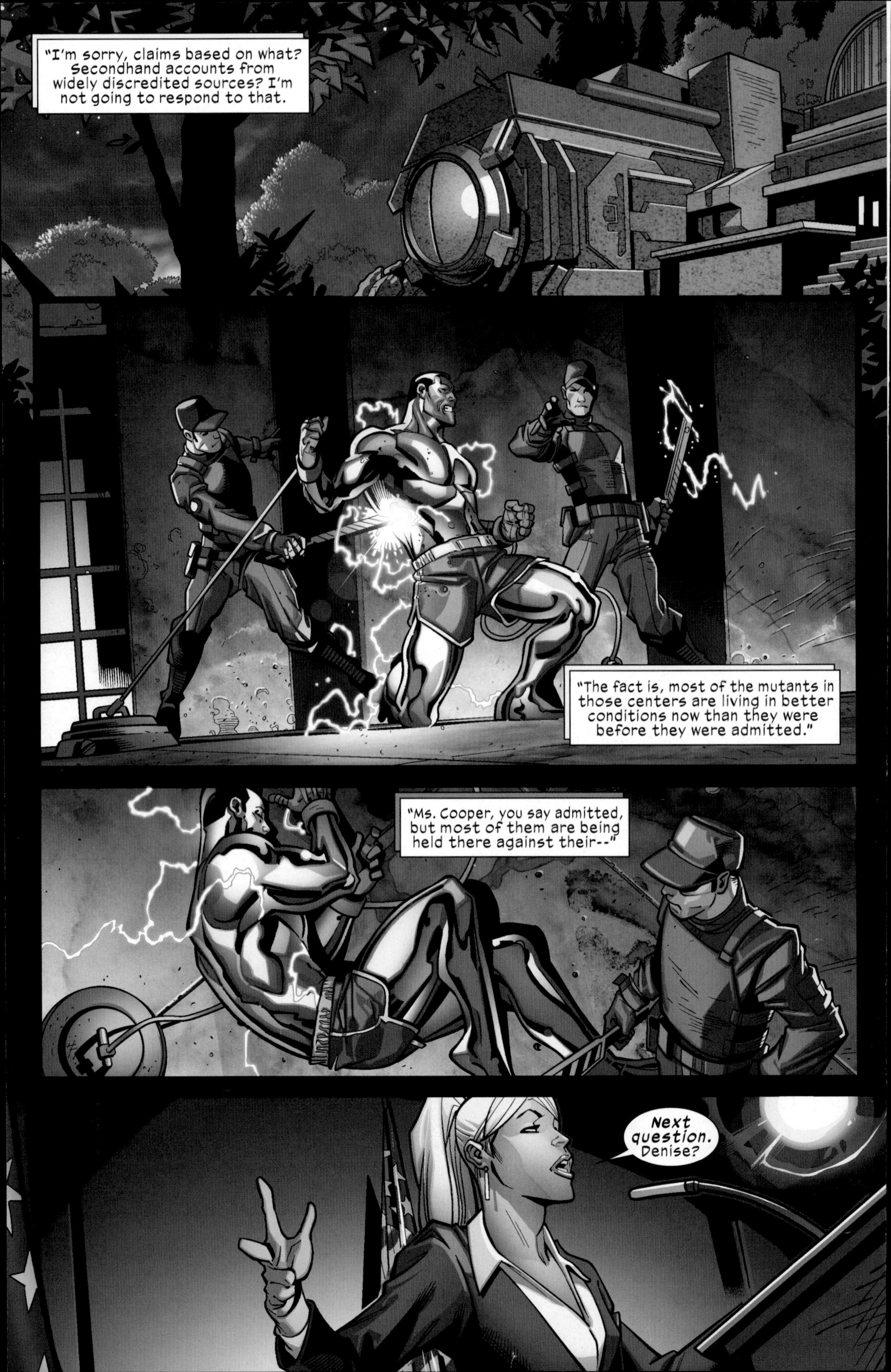
"I'm sorry, claims based on what? Secondhand accounts from widely discredited sources? I'm not going to respond to that.
"The fact is, most of the mutants in those centers are living in better conditions now than they were before they were admitted."
"Ms. Cooper, you say admitted, but most of them are being held there against their--"
Next question. Denise?

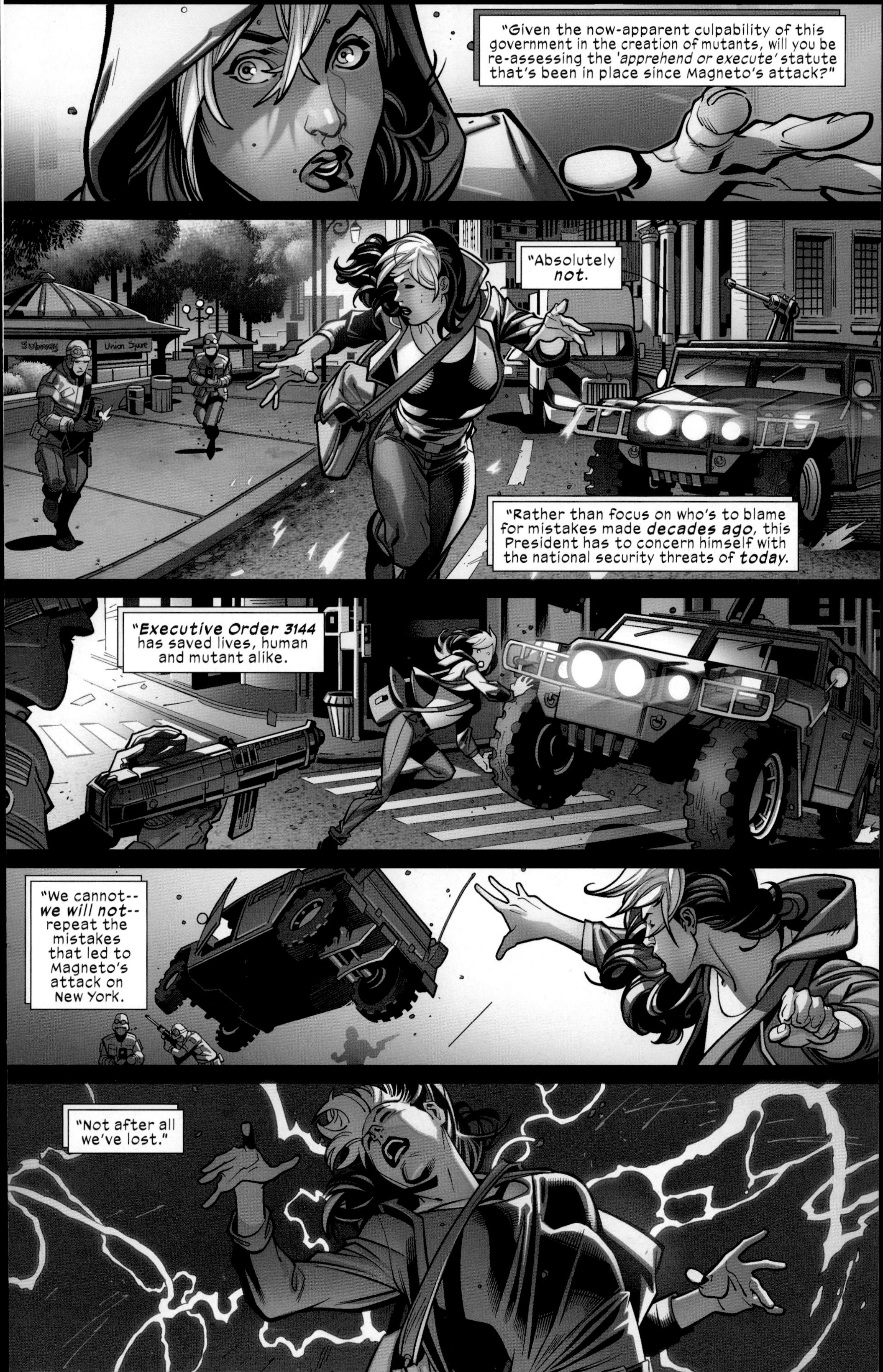
"Given the now-apparent culpability of this government in the creation of mutants, will you be re-assessing the *'apprehend or execute'* statute that's been in place since Magneto's attack?"
Subway
Union Square
"Absolutely *not*.
"Rather than focus on who's to blame for mistakes made *decades ago*, this President has to concern himself with the national security threats of *today*.
"*Executive Order 3144* has saved lives, human and mutant alike.
"We cannot-- *we will not*-- repeat the mistakes that led to Magneto's attack on New York.
"Not after all we've lost."

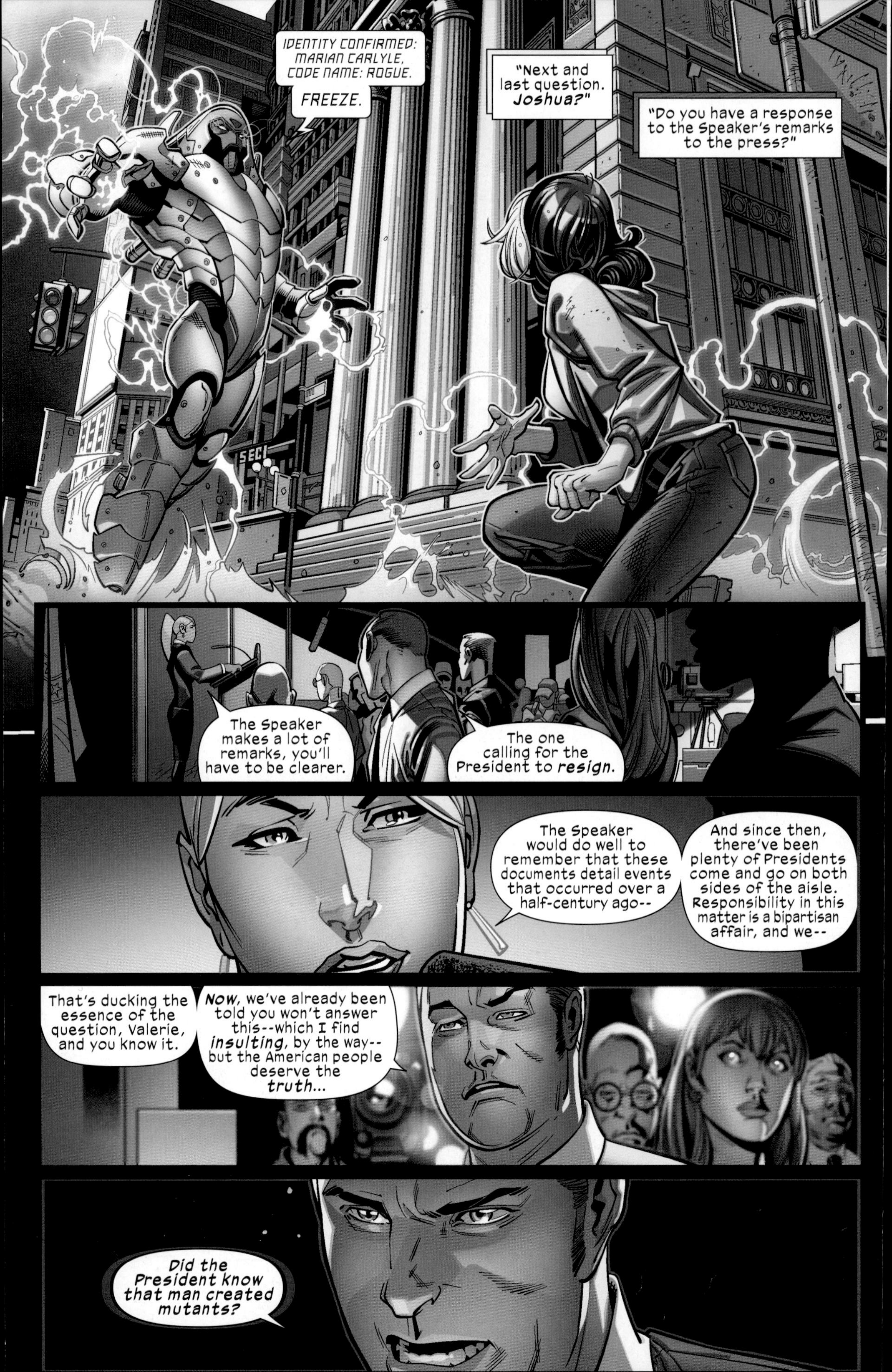
IDENTITY CONFIRMED: MARIAN CARLYLE, CODE NAME: ROGUE.
FREEZE.
"Next and last question. Joshua?"
"Do you have a response to the Speaker's remarks to the press?"
The Speaker makes a lot of remarks, you'll have to be clearer.
The one calling for the President to resign.
The Speaker would do well to remember that these documents detail events that occurred over a half-century ago--
And since then, there've been plenty of Presidents come and go on both sides of the aisle. Responsibility in this matter is a bipartisan affair, and we--
That's ducking the essence of the question, Valerie, and you know it.
NOW, we've already been told you won't answer this--which I find insulting, by the way--but the American people deserve the truth...
Did the President know that man created mutants?

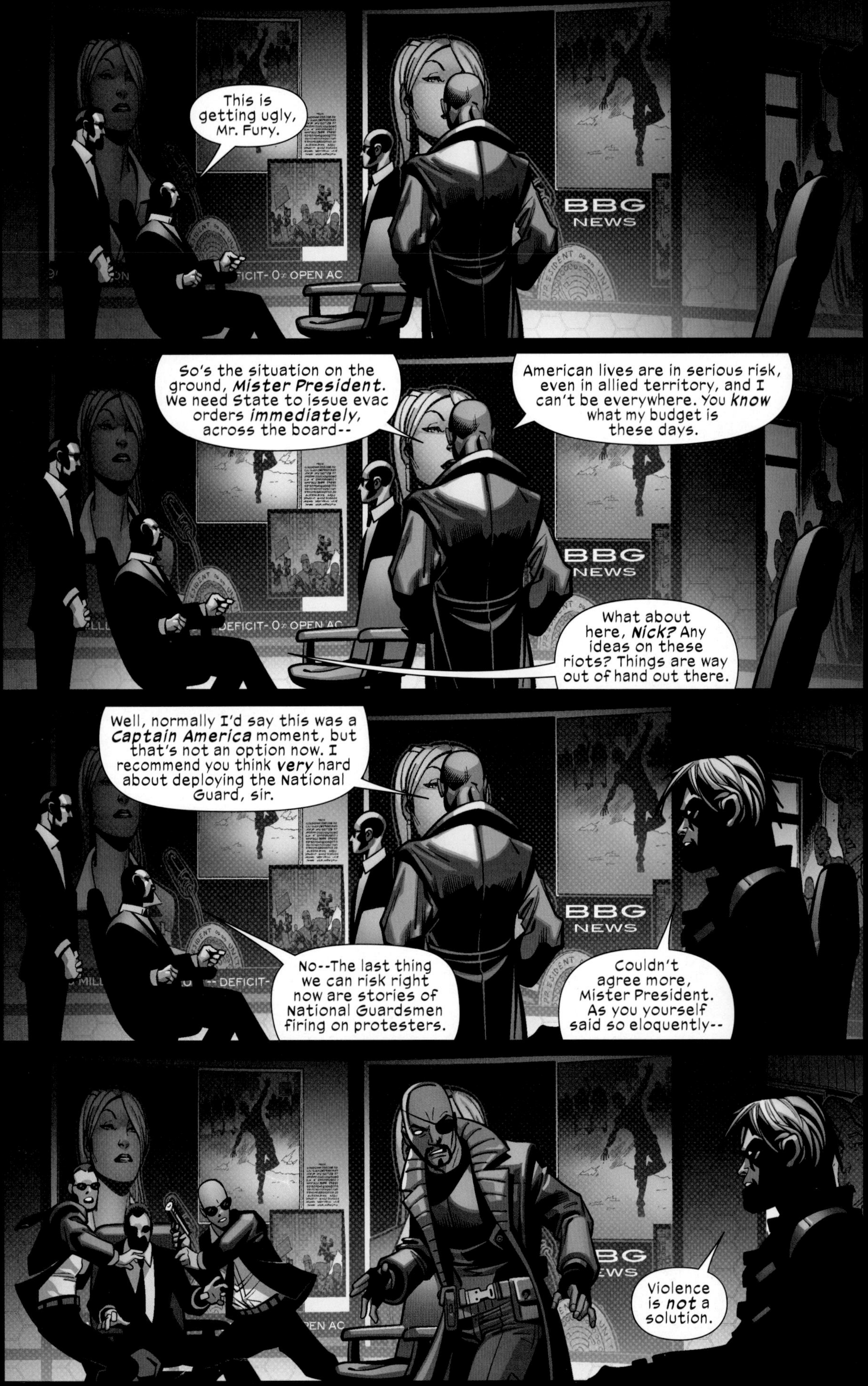

This is getting ugly, Mr. Fury.
BBG NEWS
DEFICIT- 0% OPEN AC
So's the situation on the ground, *Mister President*. We need State to issue evac orders *immediately*, across the board--
American lives are in serious risk, even in allied territory, and I can't be everywhere. You *know* what my budget is these days.
What about here, *Nick?* Any ideas on these riots? Things are way out of hand out there.
Well, normally I'd say this was a *Captain America* moment, but that's not an option now. I recommend you think *very* hard about deploying the National Guard, sir.
No--The last thing we can risk right now are stories of National Guardsmen firing on protesters.
Couldn't agree more, Mister President. As you yourself said so eloquently--
Violence is *not* a solution.

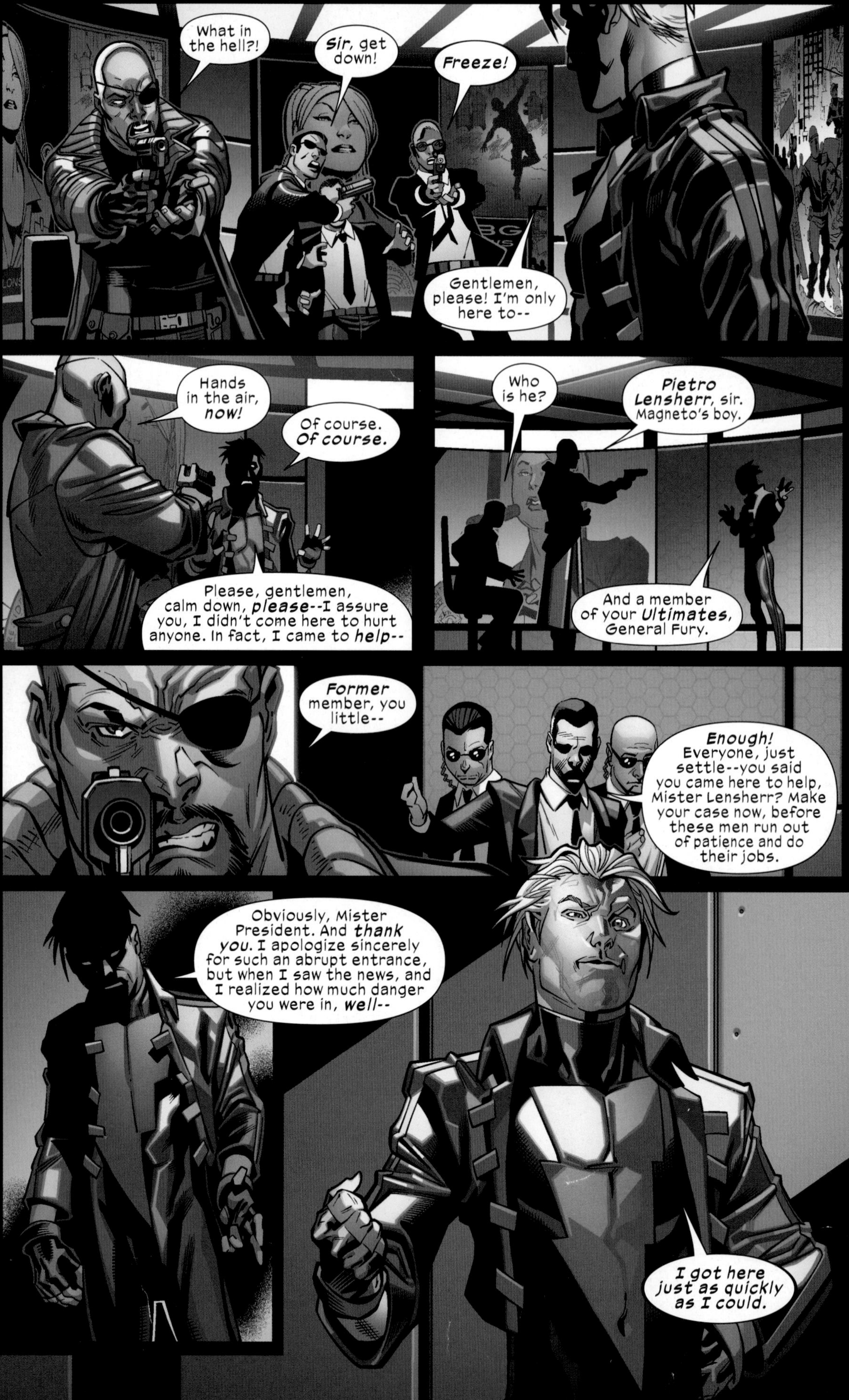
What in the hell?!
Sir, get down!
Freeze!
Gentlemen, please! I'm only here to--
Hands in the air, now!
Of course. Of course.
Please, gentlemen, calm down, please--I assure you, I didn't come here to hurt anyone. In fact, I came to help--
Who is he?
Pietro Lensherr, sir. Magneto's boy.
And a member of your Ultimates, General Fury.
Former member, you little--
Enough! Everyone, just settle--you said you came here to help, Mister Lensherr? Make your case now, before these men run out of patience and do their jobs.
Obviously, Mister President. And thank you. I apologize sincerely for such an abrupt entrance, but when I saw the news, and I realized how much danger you were in, well--
I got here just as quickly as I could.

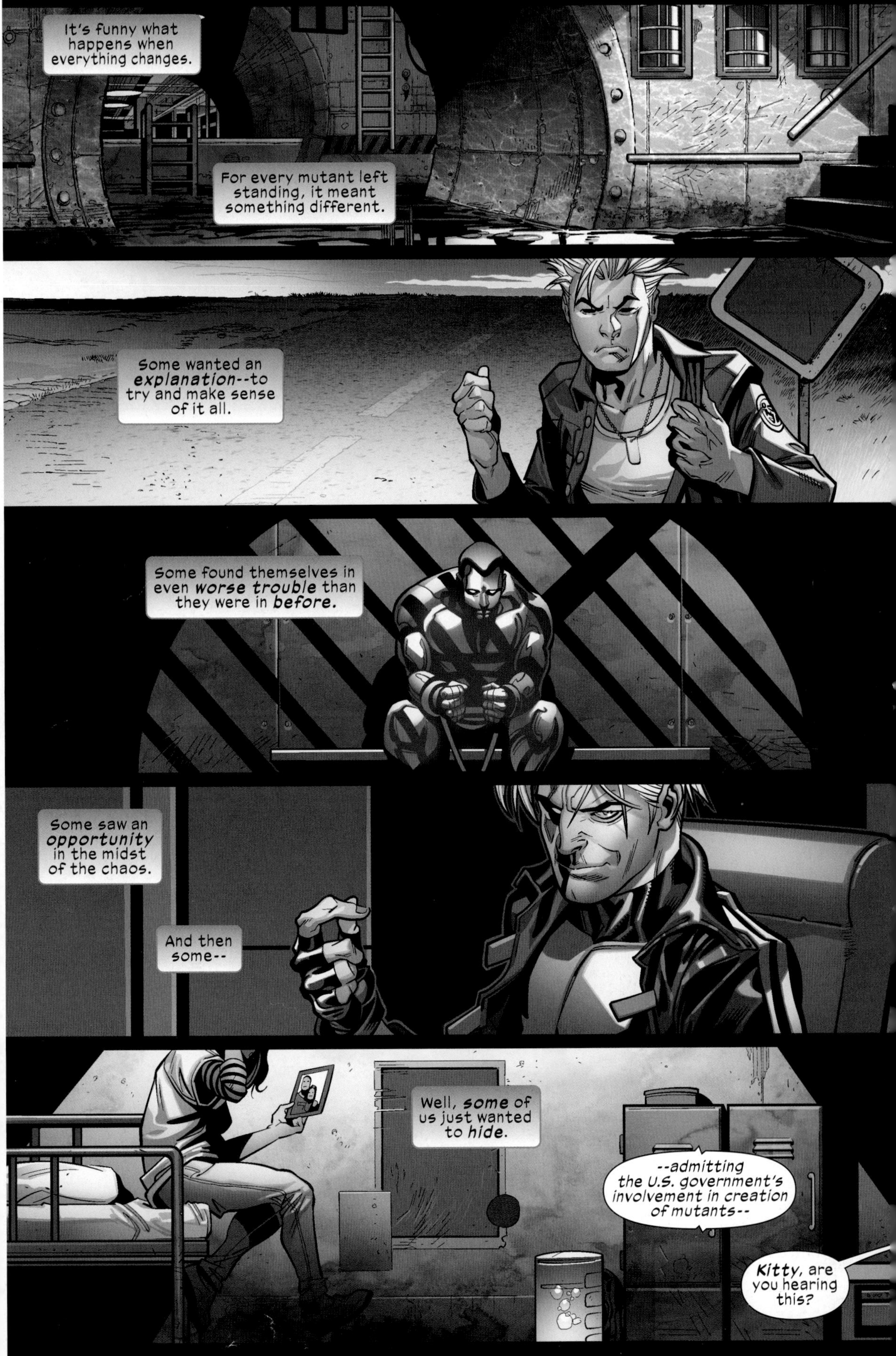
It's funny what happens when everything changes.
For every mutant left standing, it meant something different.
Some wanted an explanation--to try and make sense of it all.
Some found themselves in even worse trouble than they were in before.
Some saw an opportunity in the midst of the chaos.
And then some--
Well, some of us just wanted to hide.
--admitting the U.S. government's involvement in creation of mutants--
Kitty, are you hearing this?

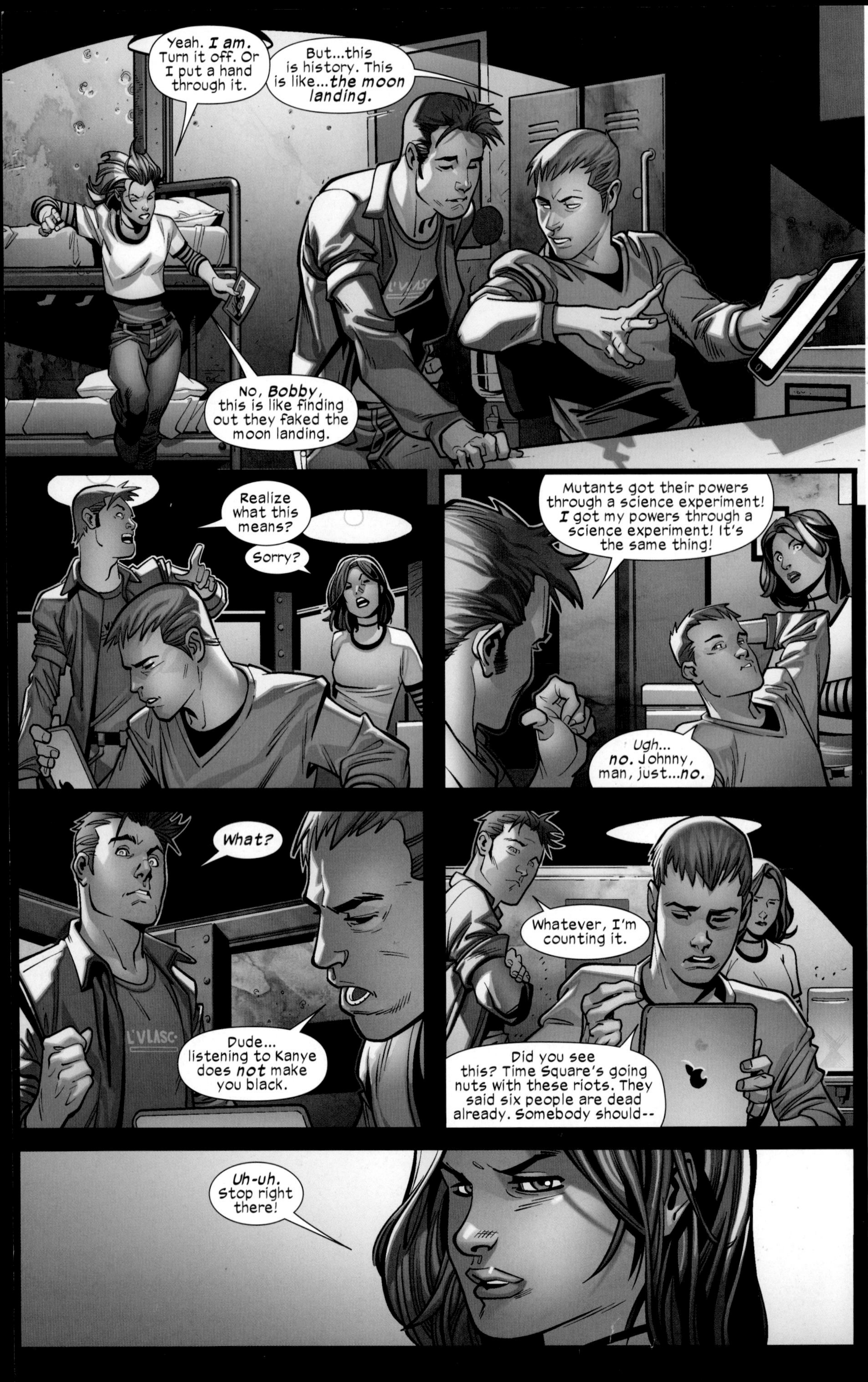

Yeah. I am. Turn it off. Or I put a hand through it.
But...this is history. This is like...the moon landing.
No, Bobby, this is like finding out they faked the moon landing.
Realize what this means?
Sorry?
Mutants got their powers through a science experiment! I got my powers through a science experiment! It's the same thing!
Ugh... no. Johnny, man, just...no.
What?
Dude... listening to Kanye does not make you black.
Whatever, I'm counting it.
Did you see this? Time Square's going nuts with these riots. They said six people are dead already. Somebody should--
Uh-uh. Stop right there!

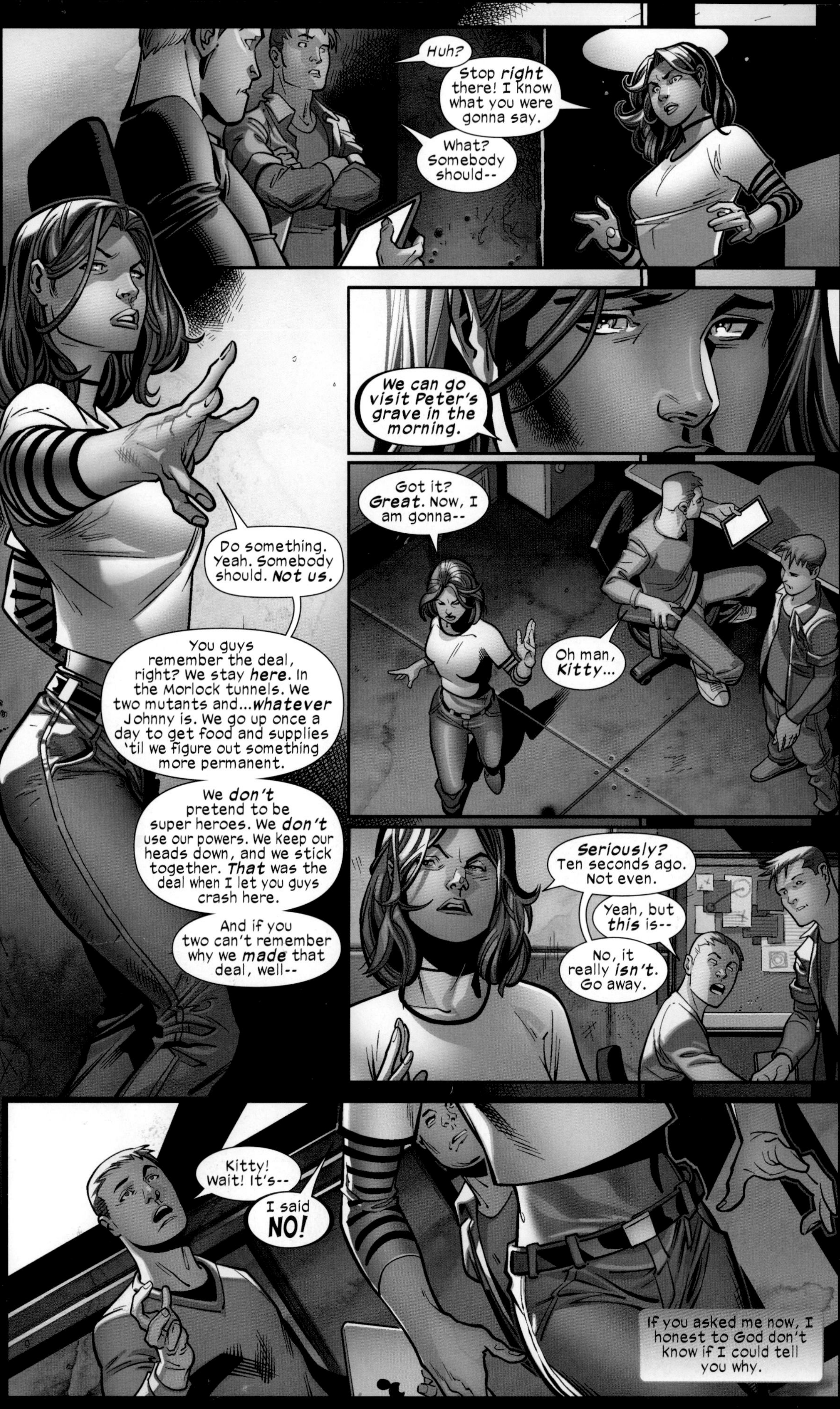
Huh?
Stop right there! I know what you were gonna say.
What? Somebody should--
Do something. Yeah. Somebody should. Not us.
You guys remember the deal, right? We stay here. In the Morlock tunnels. We two mutants and...whatever Johnny is. We go up once a day to get food and supplies 'til we figure out something more permanent.
We don't pretend to be super heroes. We don't use our powers. We keep our heads down, and we stick together. That was the deal when I let you guys crash here.
And if you two can't remember why we made that deal, well--
We can go visit Peter's grave in the morning.
Got it? Great. Now, I am gonna--
Oh man, Kitty...
Seriously? Ten seconds ago. Not even.
Yeah, but this is--
No, it really isn't. Go away.
Kitty! Wait! It's--
I said NO!
If you asked me now, I honest to God don't know if I could tell you why.

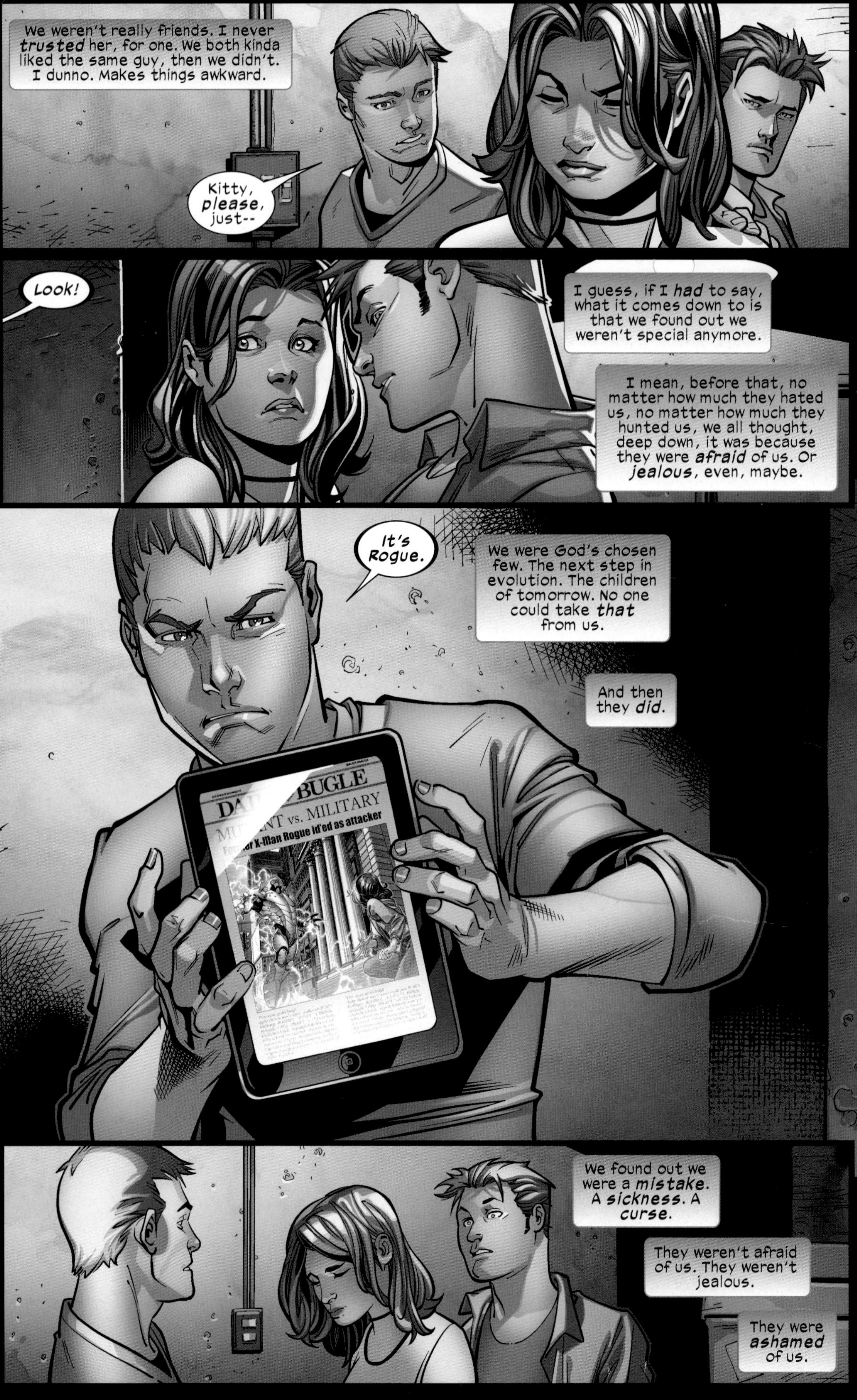
We weren't really friends. I never *trusted* her, for one. We both kinda liked the same guy, then we didn't. I dunno. Makes things awkward.
Kitty, *please*, just--
Look!
I guess, if I *had* to say, what it comes down to is that we found out we weren't special anymore.
I mean, before that, no matter how much they hated us, no matter how much they hunted us, we all thought, deep down, it was because they were *afraid* of us. Or *jealous*, even, maybe.
It's Rogue.
We were God's chosen few. The next step in evolution. The children of tomorrow. No one could take *that* from us.
And then they *did*.
BUGLE
vs. MILITARY
X-Man Rogue id'ed as attacker
We found out we were a *mistake*. A *sickness*. A *curse*.
They weren't afraid of us. They weren't jealous.
They were *ashamed* of us.

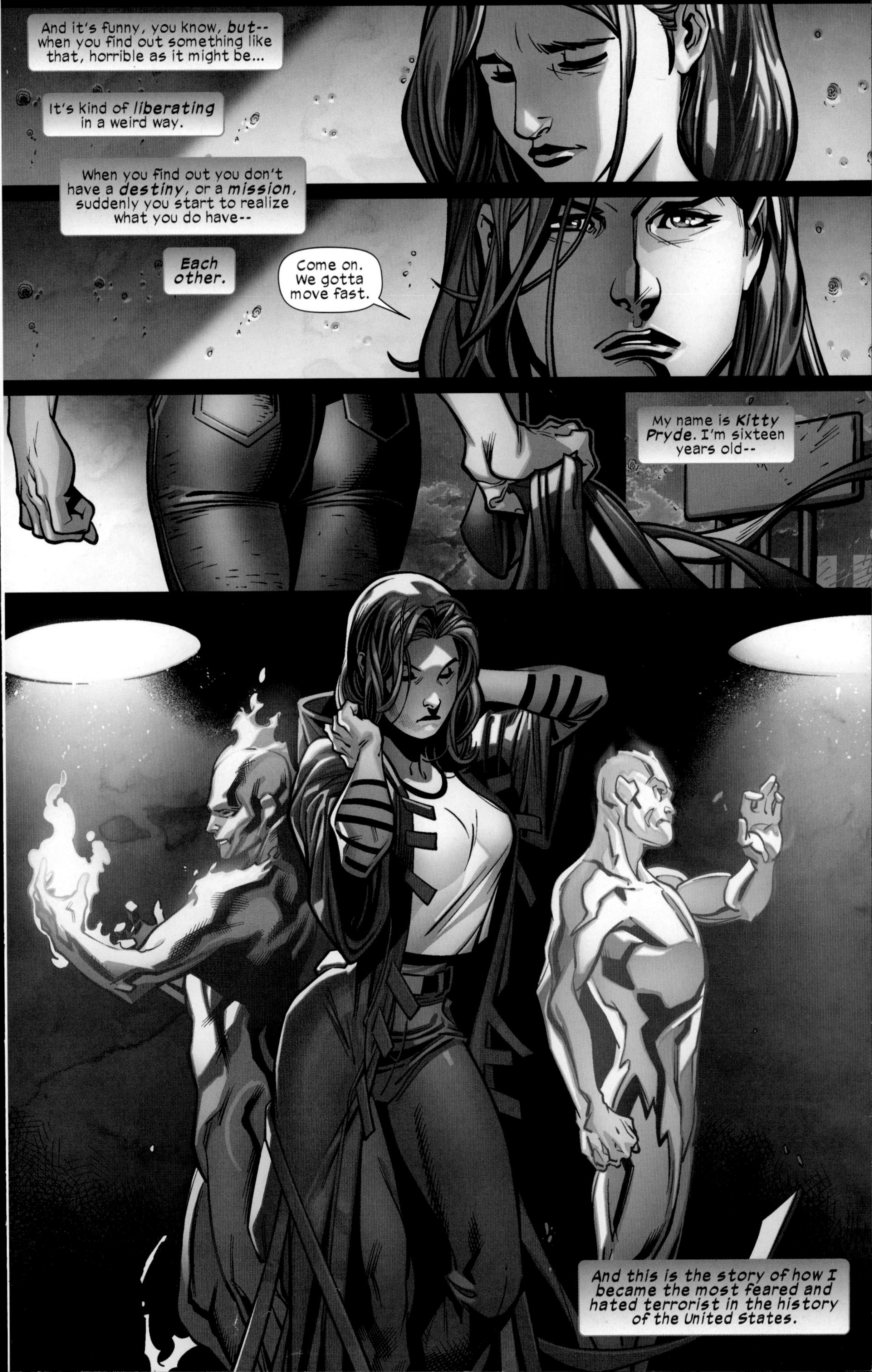
And it's funny, you know, *but*-- when you find out something like that, horrible as it might be...
It's kind of *liberating* in a weird way.
When you find out you don't have a *destiny*, or a *mission*, suddenly you start to realize what you do have--
Each other.
Come on. We gotta move fast.
My name is *Kitty Pryde*. I'm sixteen years old--
And this is the story of how I became the most feared and hated terrorist in the history of the United States.

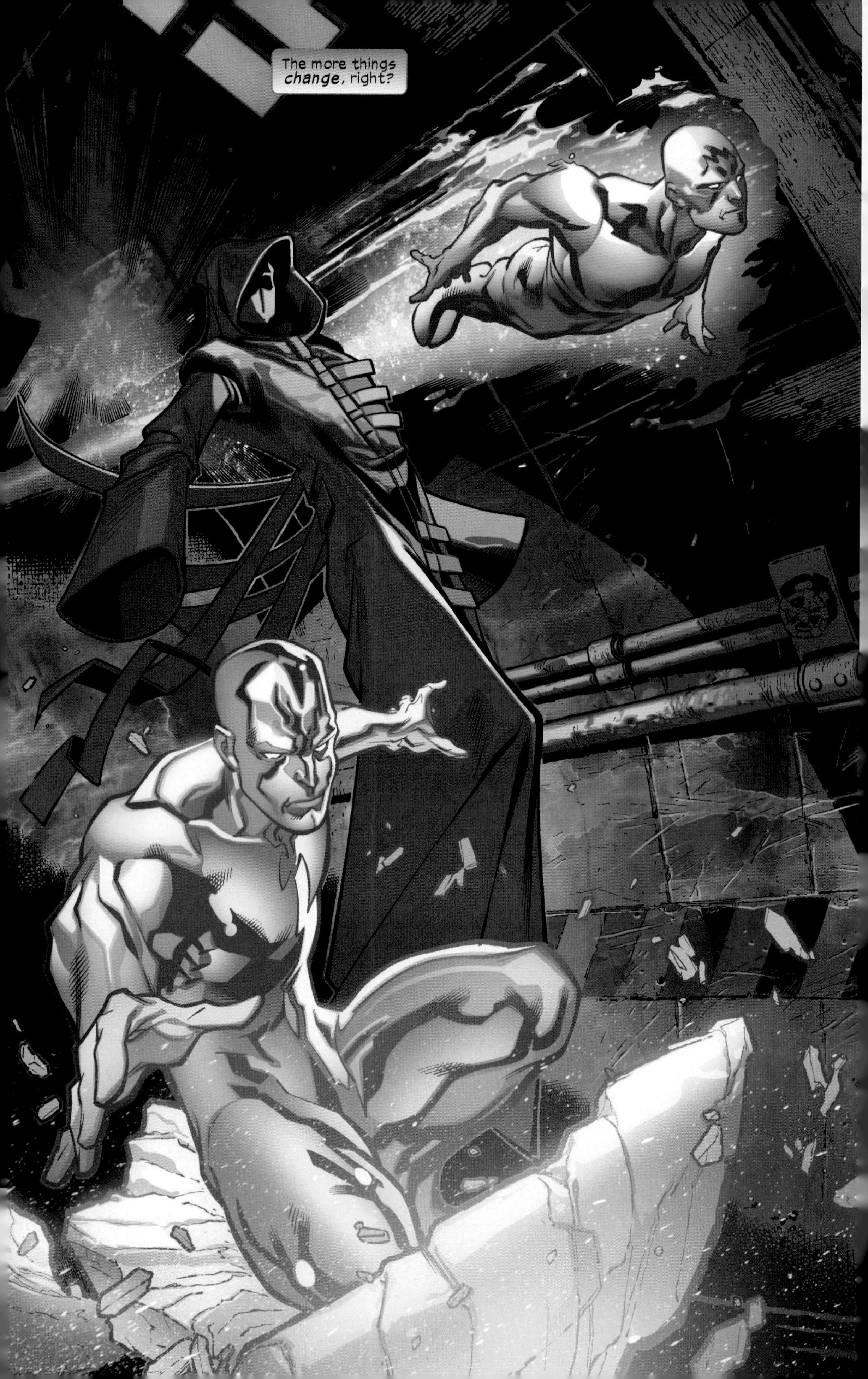
The more things *change*, right?

2

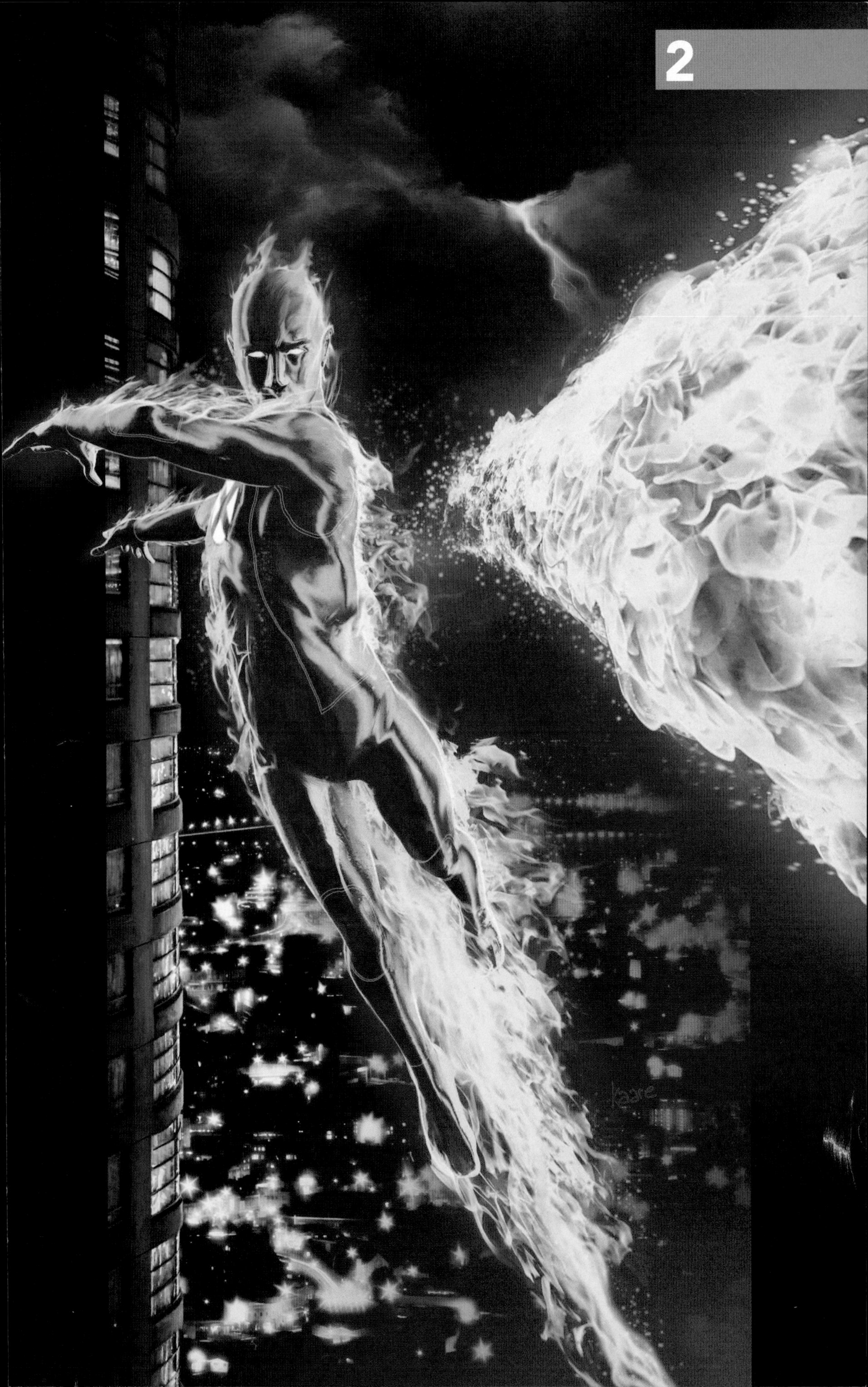

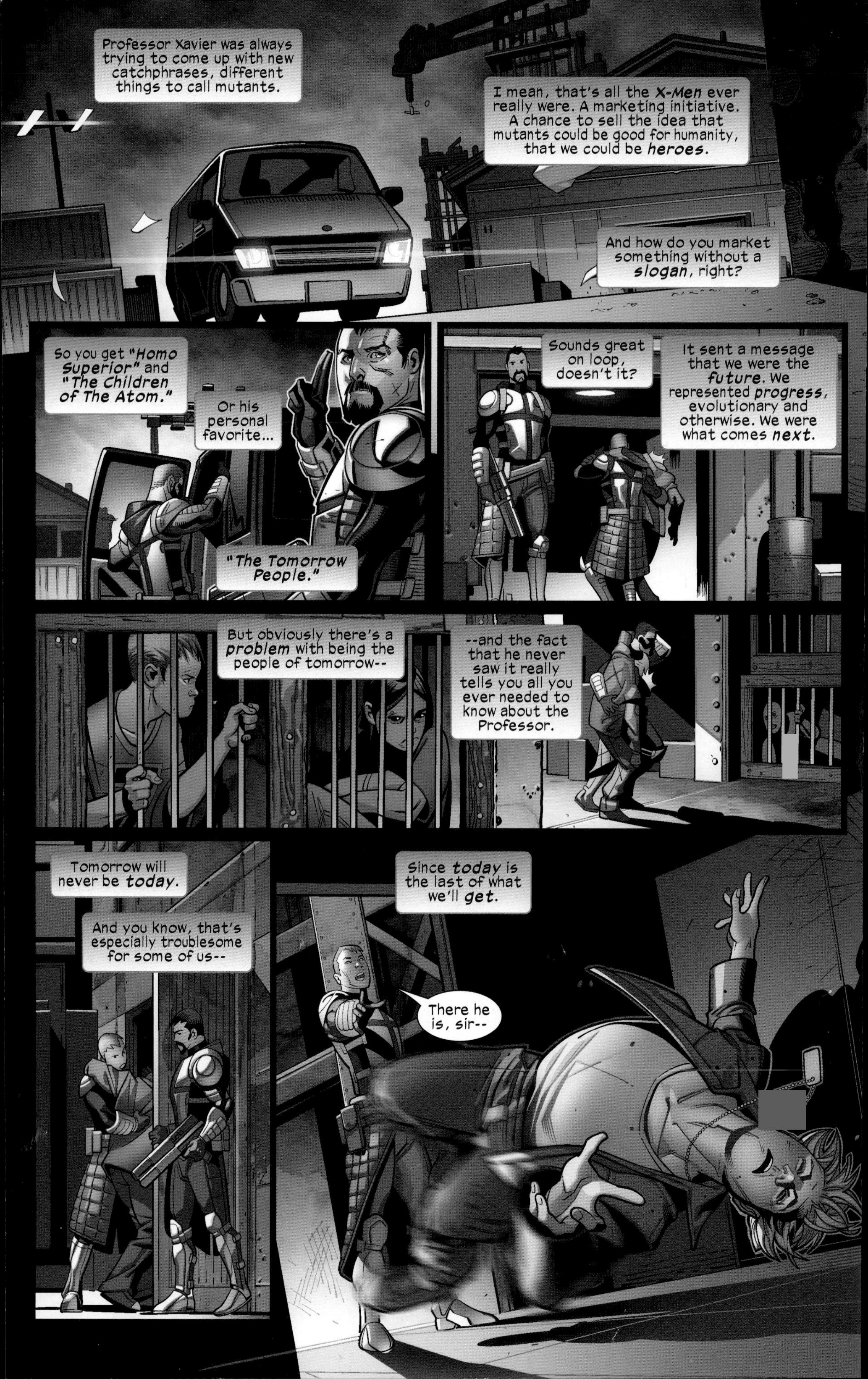

Professor Xavier was always trying to come up with new catchphrases, different things to call mutants.
I mean, that's all the X-Men ever really were. A marketing initiative. A chance to sell the idea that mutants could be good for humanity, that we could be heroes.
And how do you market something without a slogan, right?
So you get "Homo Superior" and "The Children of The Atom."
Or his personal favorite...
"The Tomorrow People."
Sounds great on loop, doesn't it?
It sent a message that we were the future. We represented progress, evolutionary and otherwise. We were what comes next.
But obviously there's a problem with being the people of tomorrow--
--and the fact that he never saw it really tells you all you ever needed to know about the Professor.
Tomorrow will never be today.
And you know, that's especially troublesome for some of us--
Since today is the last of what we'll get.
There he is, sir--

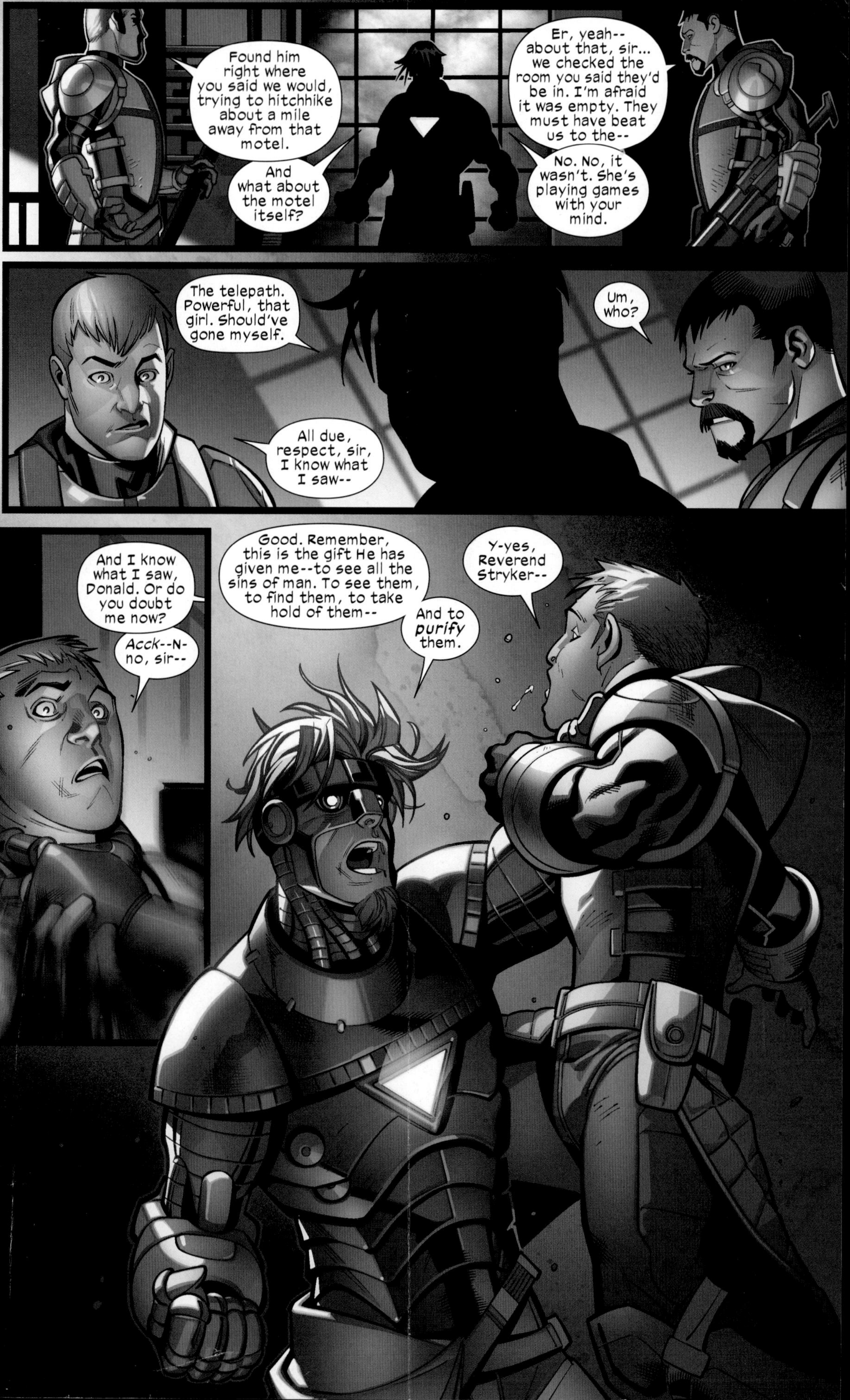
Found him right where you said we would, trying to hitchhike about a mile away from that motel.
And what about the motel itself?
Er, yeah-- about that, sir... we checked the room you said they'd be in. I'm afraid it was empty. They must have beat us to the--
No. No, it wasn't. She's playing games with your mind.
The telepath. Powerful, that girl. Should've gone myself.
Um, who?
All due, respect, sir, I know what I saw--
And I know what I saw, Donald. Or do you doubt me now?
Acck--N-no, sir--
Good. Remember, this is the gift He has given me--to see all the sins of man. To see them, to find them, to take hold of them--
And to *purify* them.
Y-yes, Reverend Stryker--

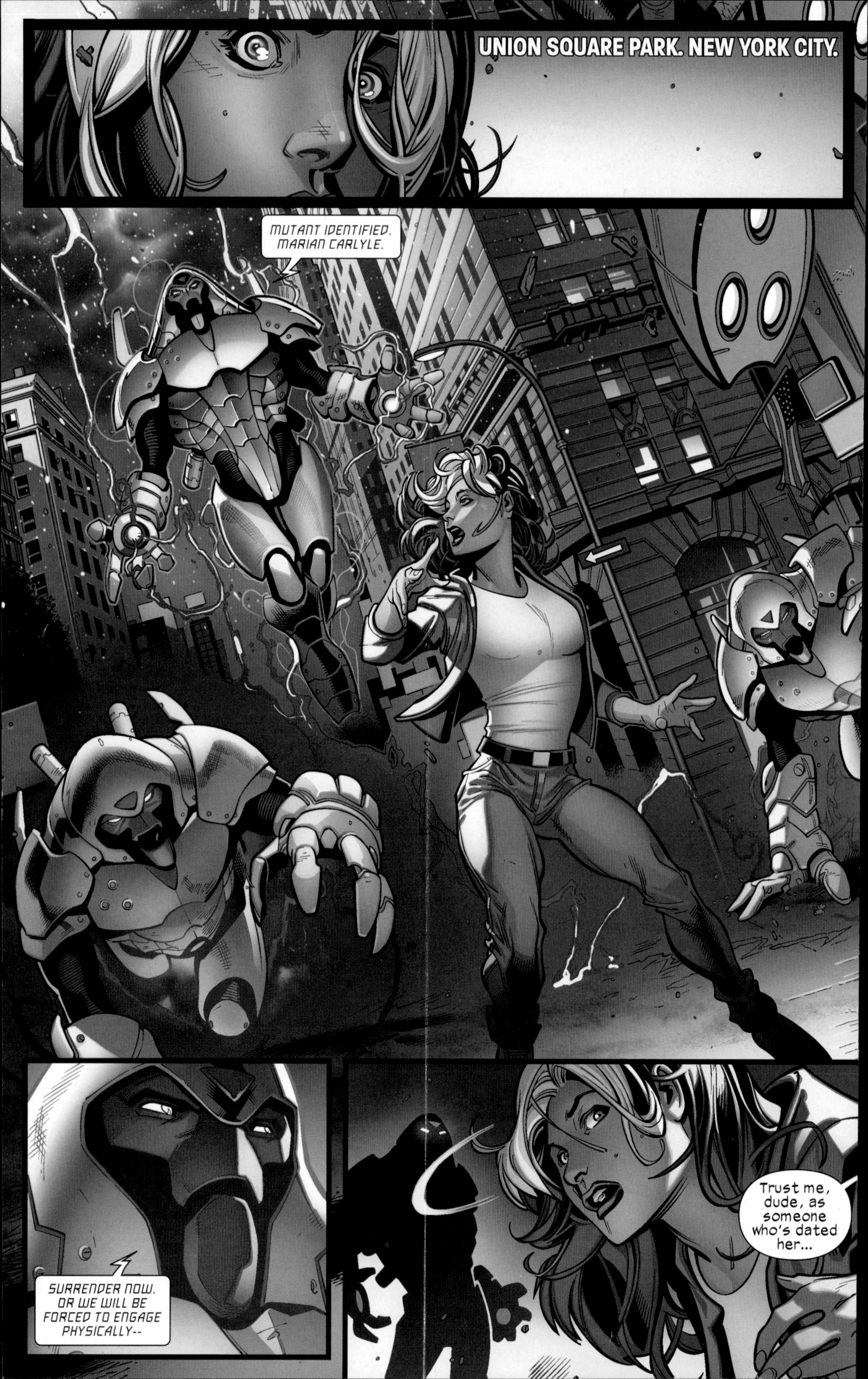
UNION SQUARE PARK. NEW YORK CITY.
MUTANT IDENTIFIED. MARIAN CARLYLE.
SURRENDER NOW. OR WE WILL BE FORCED TO ENGAGE PHYSICALLY--
Trust me, dude, as someone who's dated her...

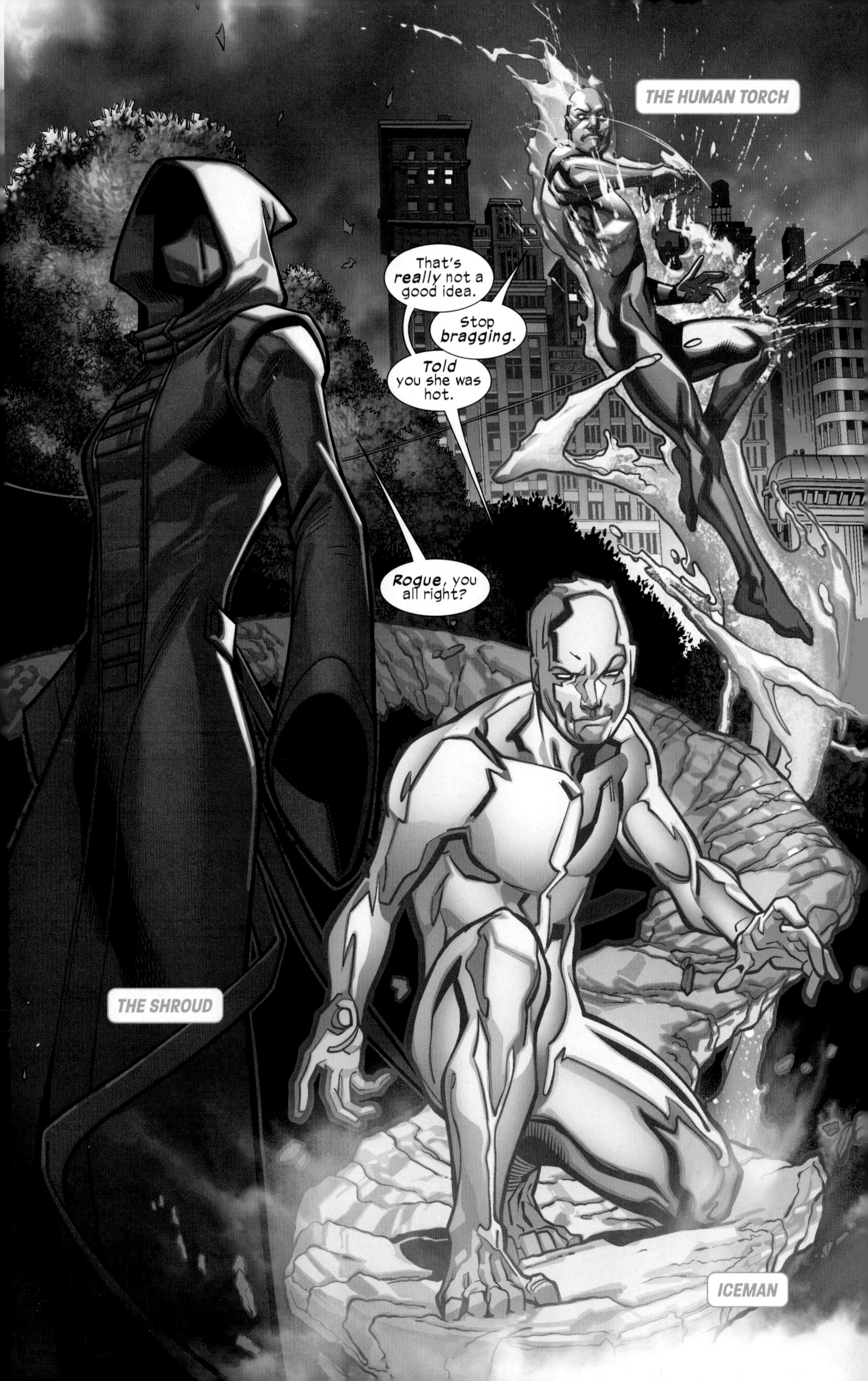
THE HUMAN TORCH
That's really not a good idea.
Stop bragging.
Told you she was hot.
Rogue, you all right?
THE SHROUD
ICEMAN

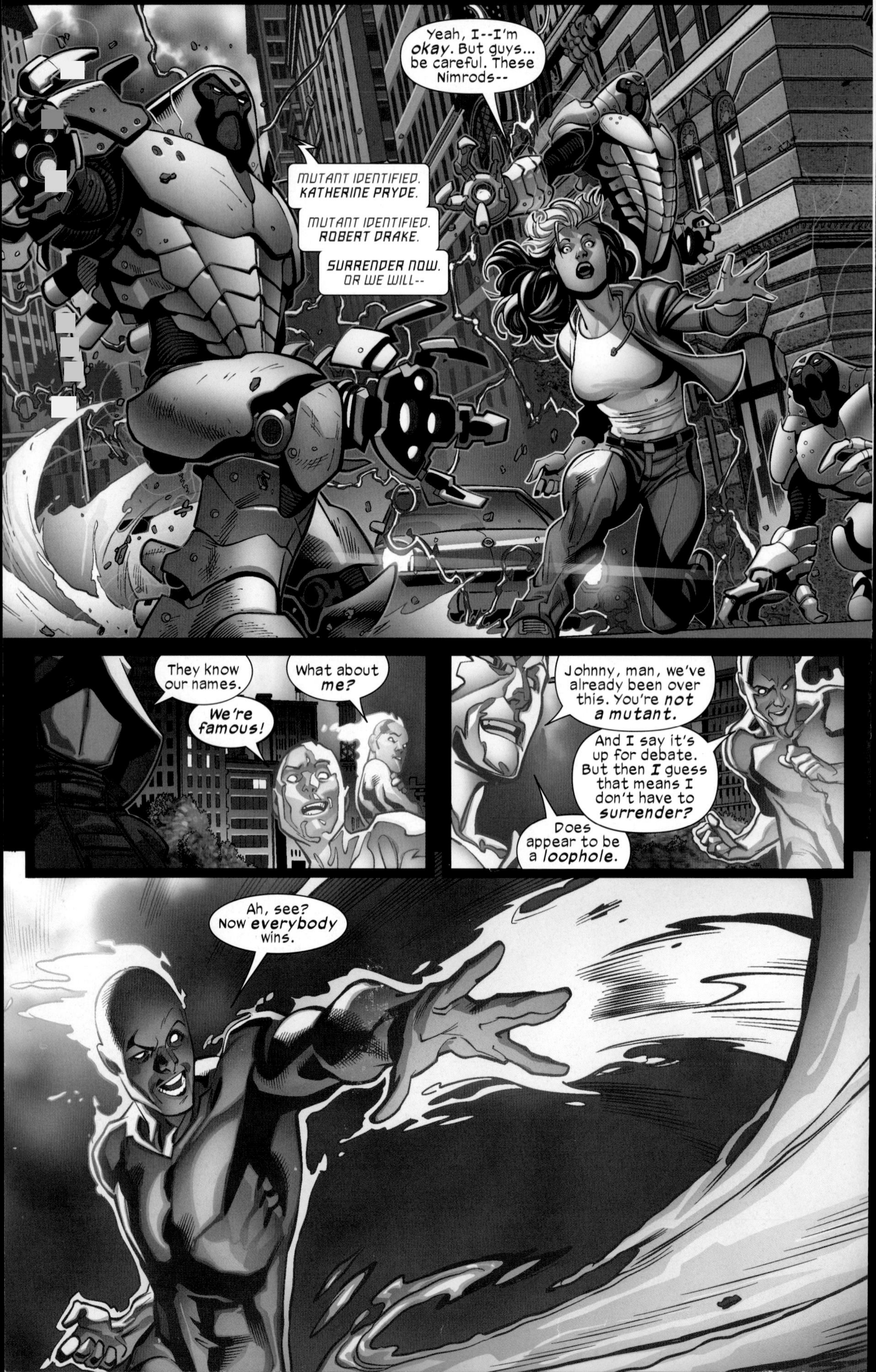
Yeah, I--I'm okay. But guys... be careful. These Nimrods--
MUTANT IDENTIFIED. KATHERINE PRYDE.
MUTANT IDENTIFIED. ROBERT DRAKE.
SURRENDER NOW. OR WE WILL--
They know our names.
We're famous!
What about me?
Johnny, man, we've already been over this. You're not a mutant.
And I say it's up for debate. But then I guess that means I don't have to surrender?
Does appear to be a loophole.
Ah, see? Now everybody wins.

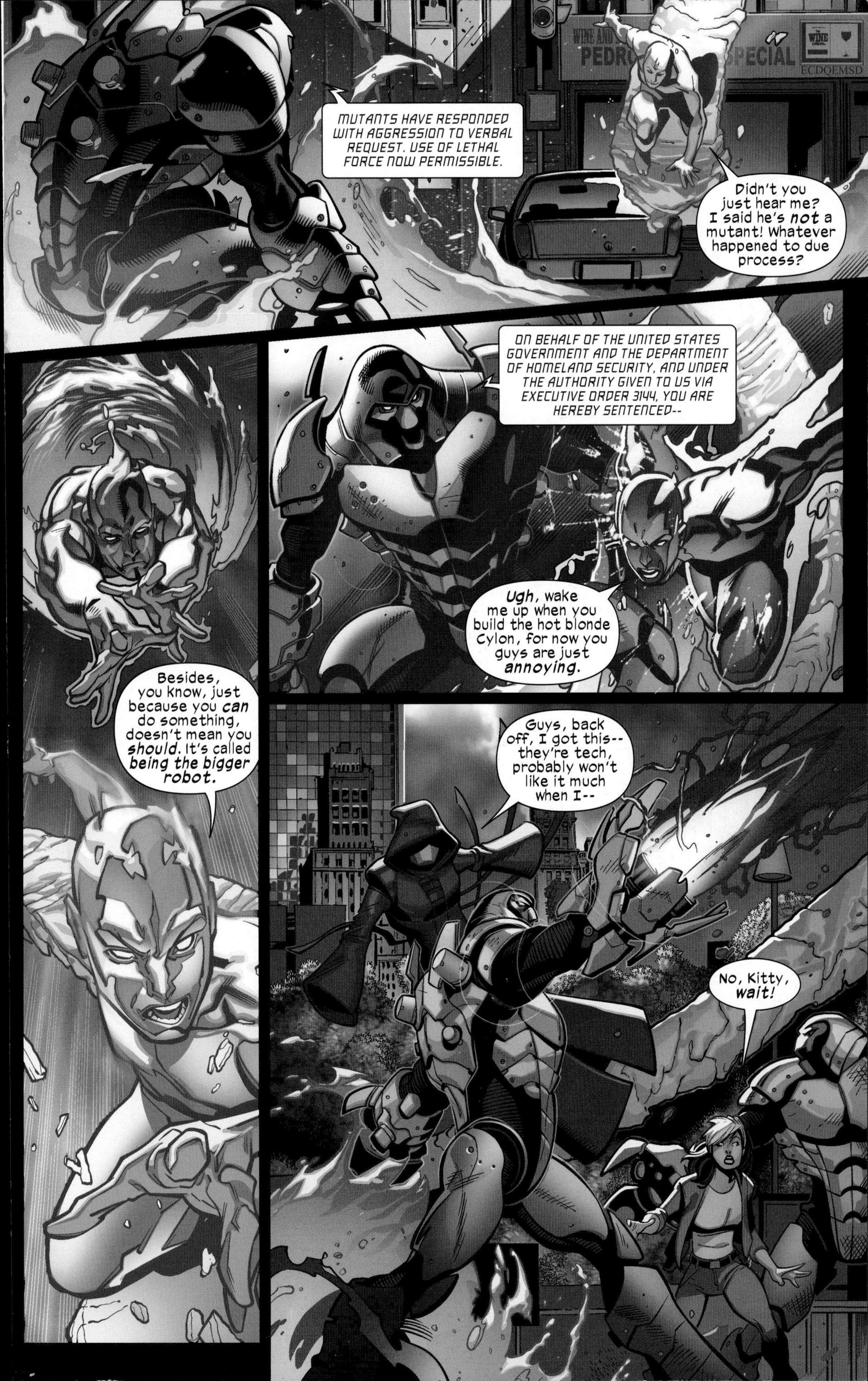
MUTANTS HAVE RESPONDED WITH AGGRESSION TO VERBAL REQUEST. USE OF LETHAL FORCE NOW PERMISSIBLE.
Didn't you just hear me? I said he's not a mutant! Whatever happened to due process?
ON BEHALF OF THE UNITED STATES GOVERNMENT AND THE DEPARTMENT OF HOMELAND SECURITY, AND UNDER THE AUTHORITY GIVEN TO US VIA EXECUTIVE ORDER 3144, YOU ARE HEREBY SENTENCED--
Ugh, wake me up when you build the hot blonde Cylon, for now you guys are just annoying.
Besides, you know, just because you can do something, doesn't mean you should. It's called being the bigger robot.
Guys, back off, I got this-- they're tech, probably won't like it much when I--
No, Kitty, wait!

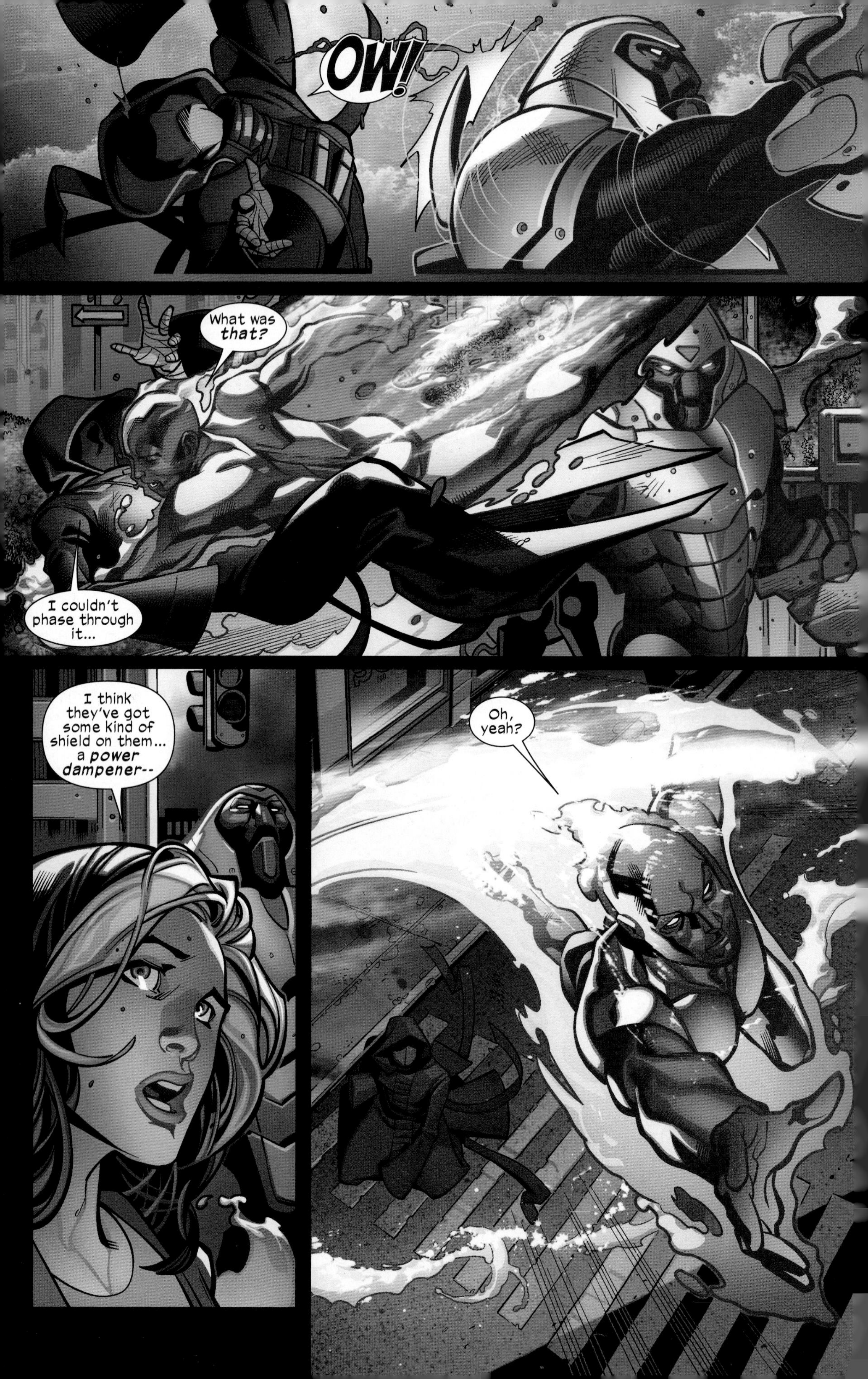
OW!
What was that?
I couldn't phase through it...
I think they've got some kind of shield on them... a power dampener--
Oh, yeah?

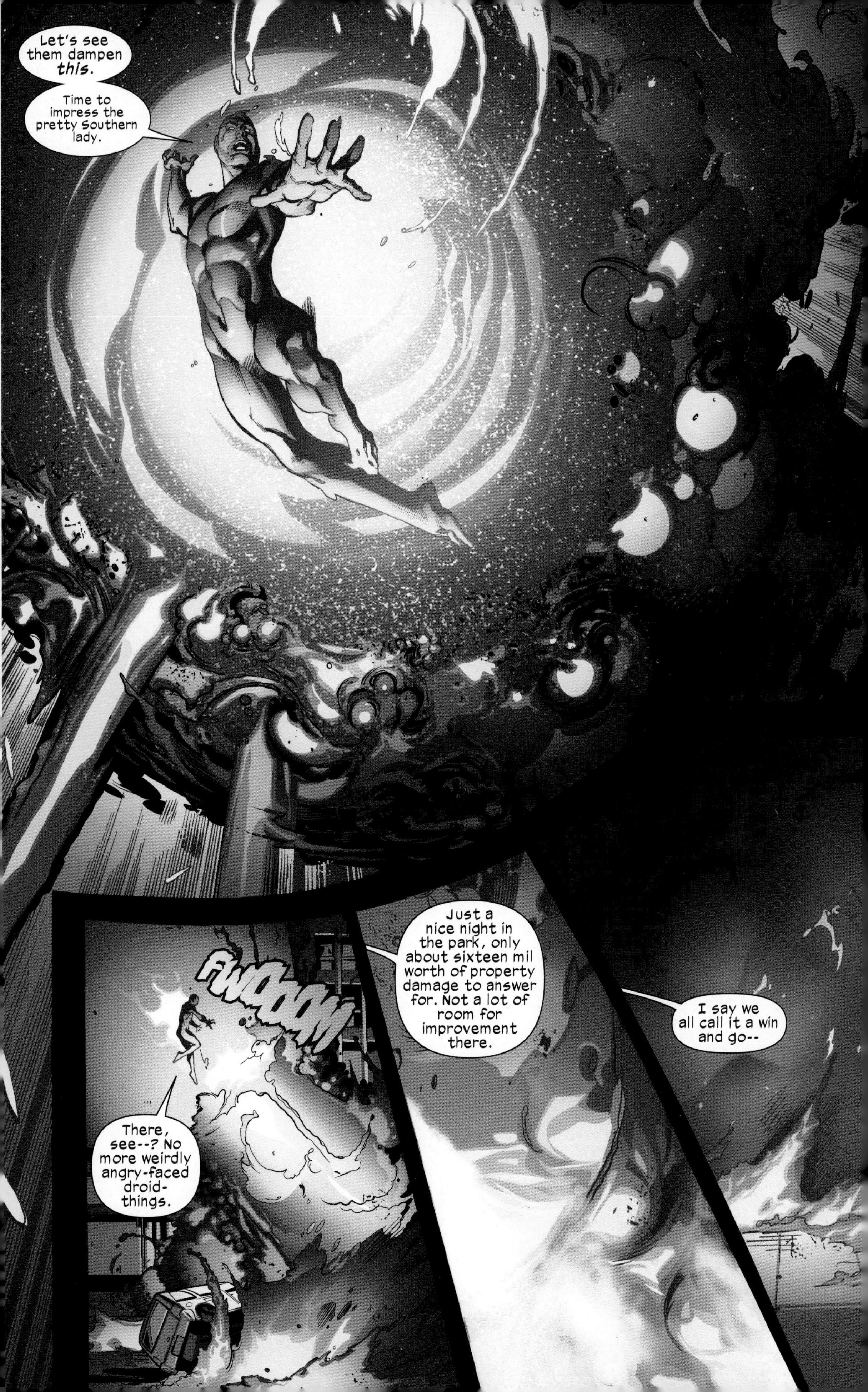
Let's see them dampen *this*.
Time to impress the pretty Southern lady.
FWOOOM
There, see--? No more weirdly angry-faced droid-things.
Just a nice night in the park, only about sixteen mil worth of property damage to answer for. Not a lot of room for improvement there.
I say we all call it a win and go--

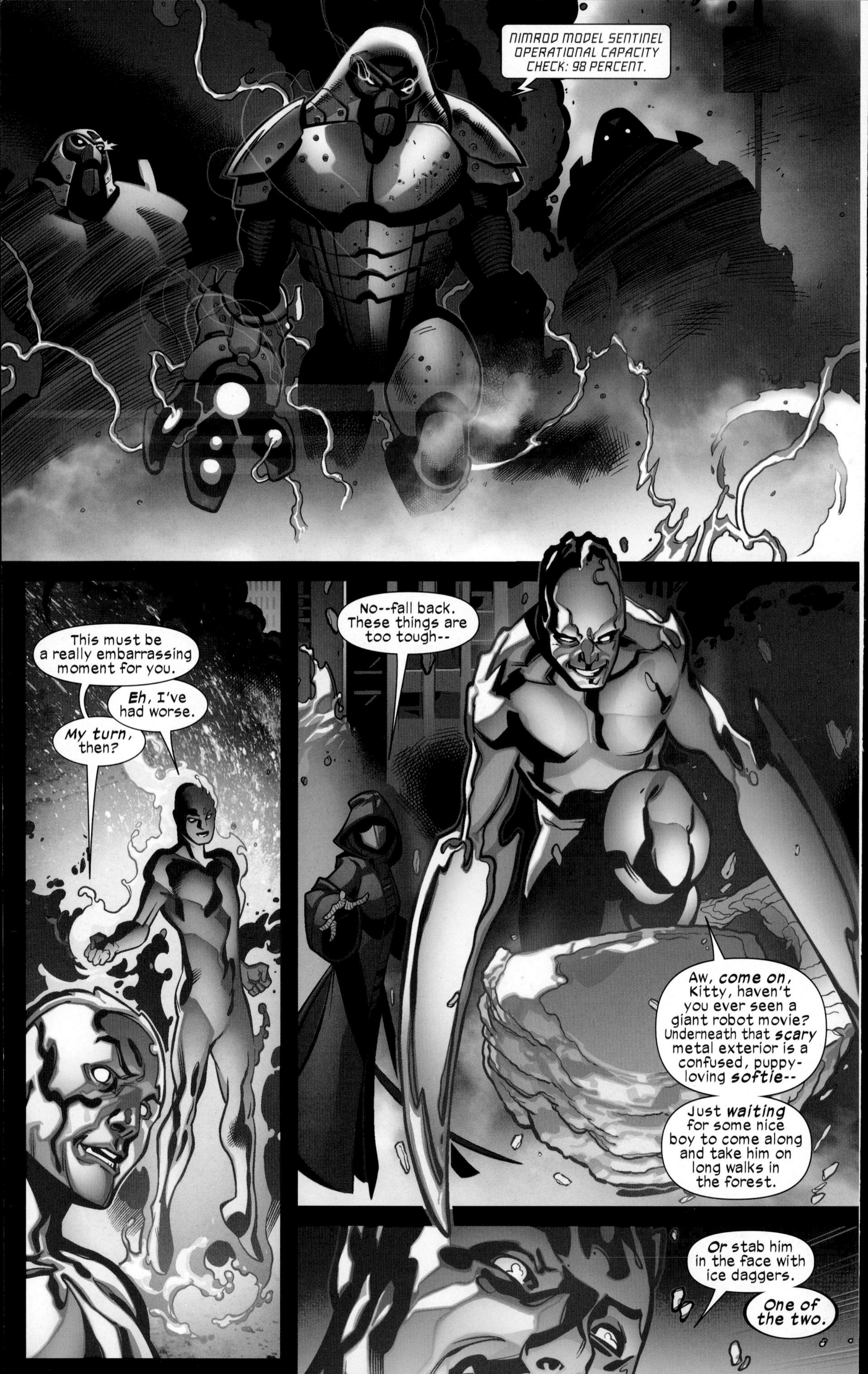
NIMROD MODEL SENTINEL OPERATIONAL CAPACITY CHECK: 98 PERCENT.
This must be a really embarrassing moment for you.
Eh, I've had worse.
My turn, then?
No--fall back. These things are too tough--
Aw, come on, Kitty, haven't you ever seen a giant robot movie? Underneath that scary metal exterior is a confused, puppy-loving softie--
Just waiting for some nice boy to come along and take him on long walks in the forest.
Or stab him in the face with ice daggers.
One of the two.

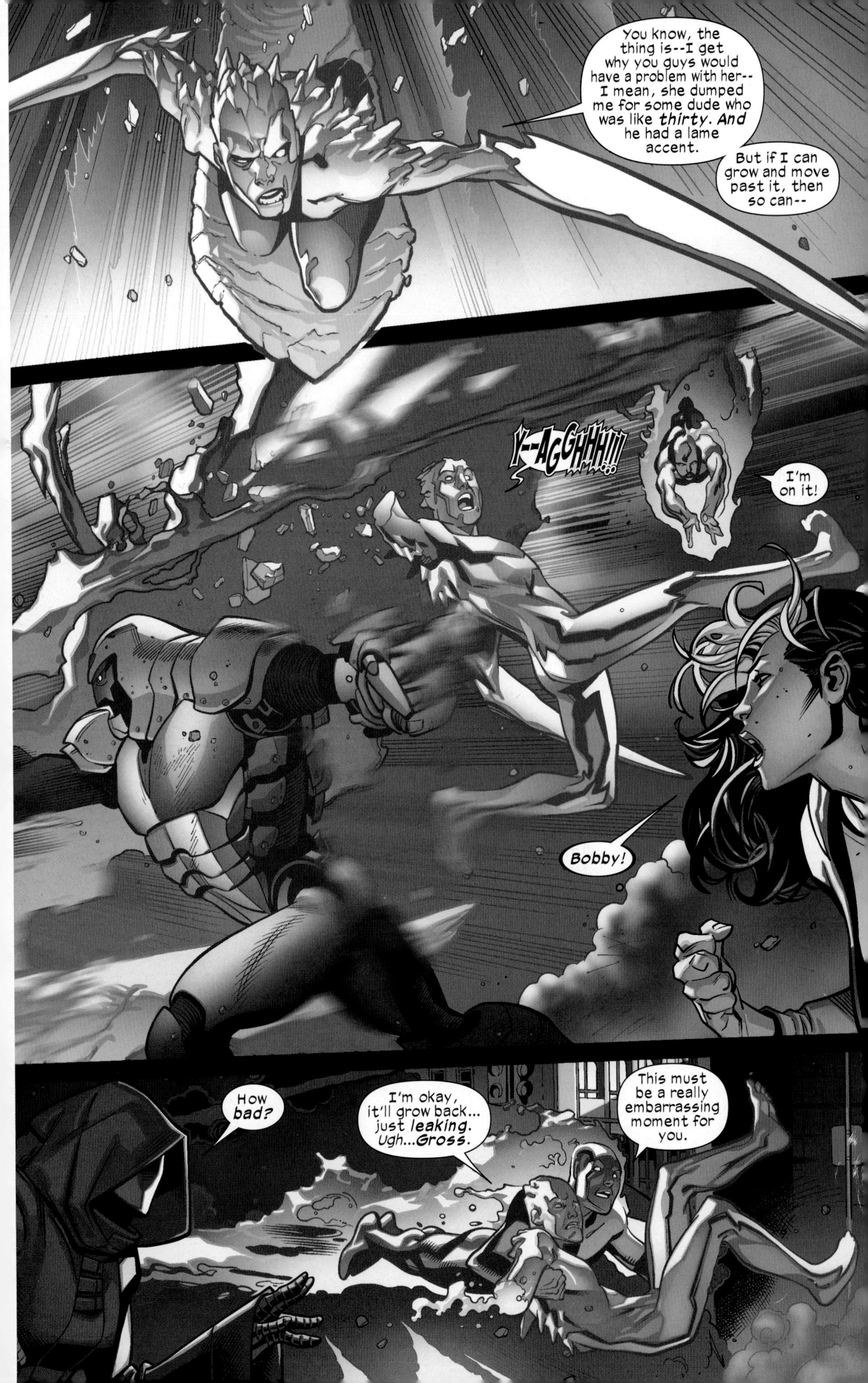

You know, the thing is--I get why you guys would have a problem with her--I mean, she dumped me for some dude who was like *thirty*. *And* he had a lame accent.
But if I can grow and move past it, then so can--
Y--AGGHHH!!!
I'm on it!
Bobby!
How *bad?*
I'm okay, it'll grow back... just *leaking*. Ugh...*Gross*.
This must be a really embarrassing moment for you.

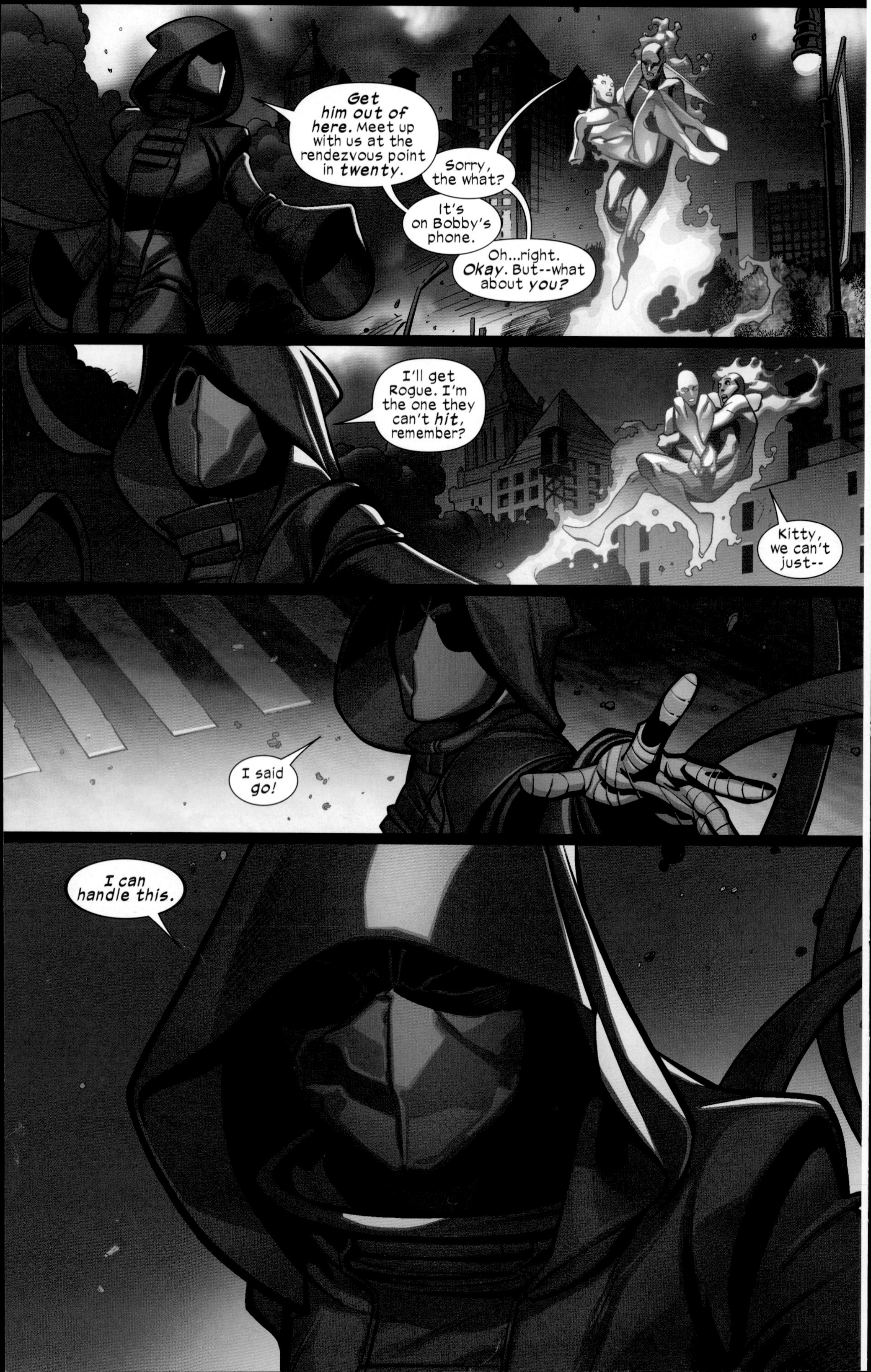
Get him out of here. Meet up with us at the rendezvous point in twenty.
Sorry, the what?
It's on Bobby's phone.
Oh...right. Okay. But--what about you?
I'll get Rogue. I'm the one they can't hit, remember?
Kitty, we can't just--
I said go!
I can handle this.

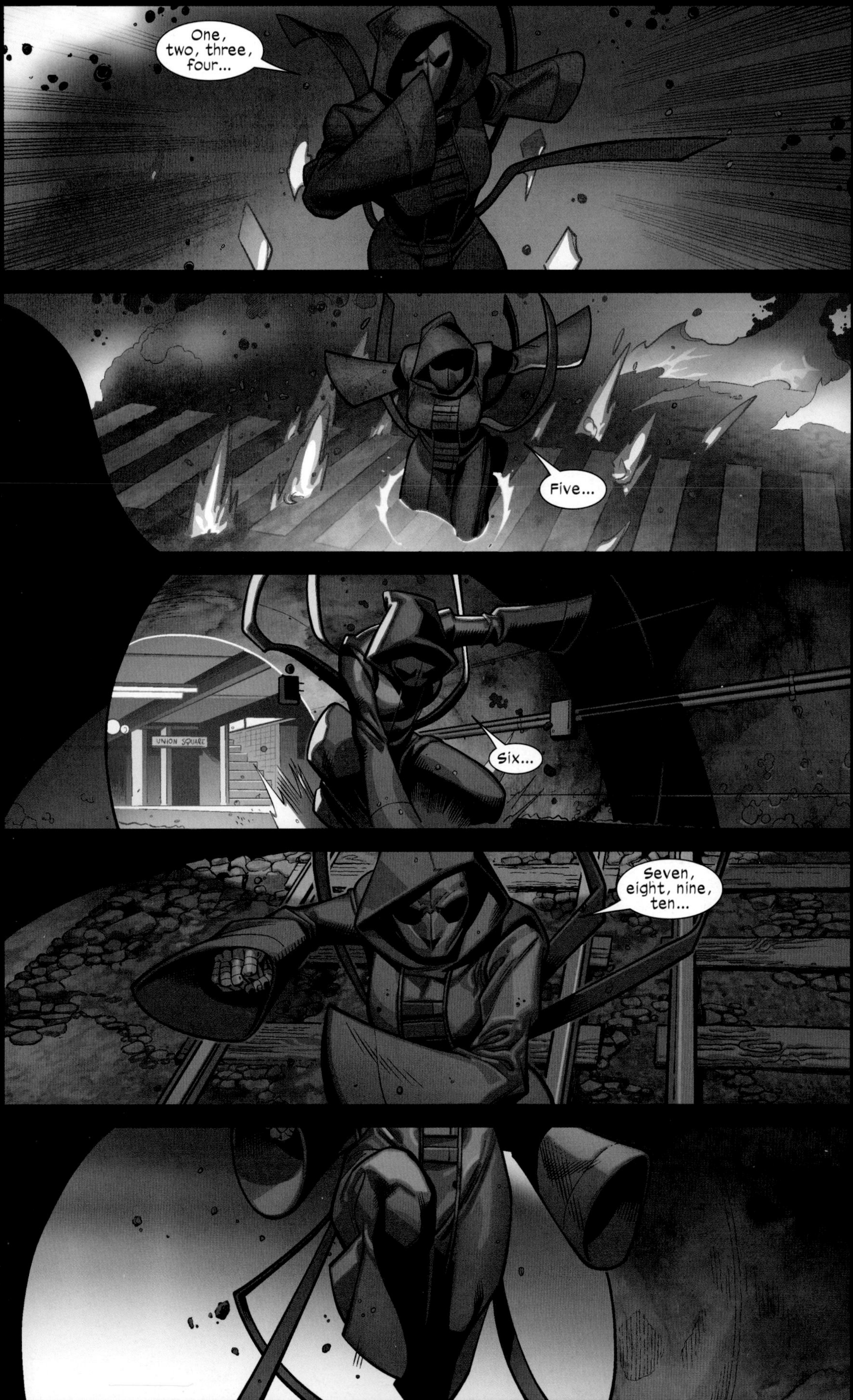
One, two, three, four...
Five...
UNION SQUARE
Six...
Seven, eight, nine, ten...

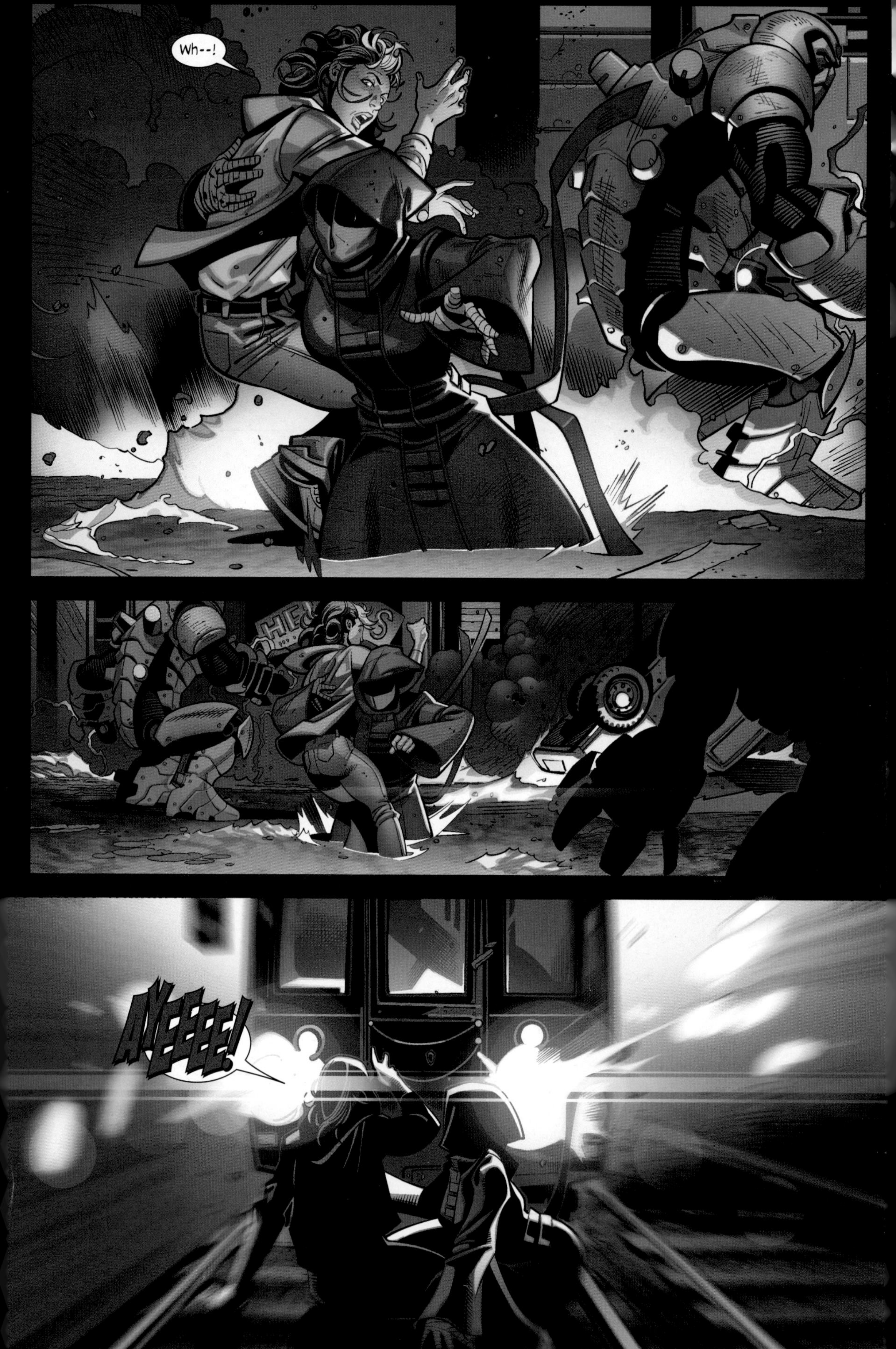

Wh--!
AYEEEE!

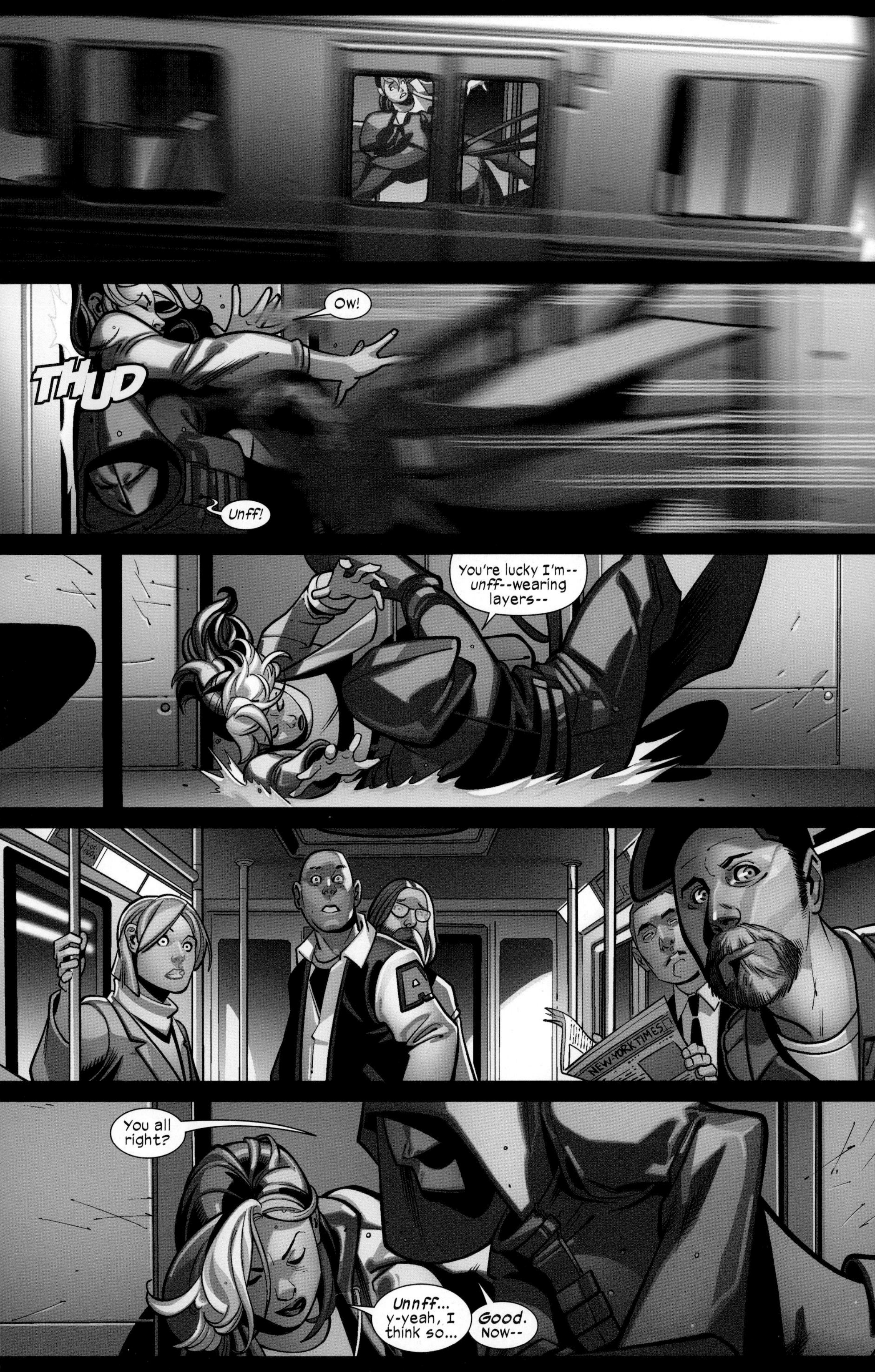

Ow!
THUD
Unff!
You're lucky I'm--
unff--wearing
layers--
NEW-YORK TIMES
You all right?
Unnff...
y-yeah, I think so...
Good. Now--

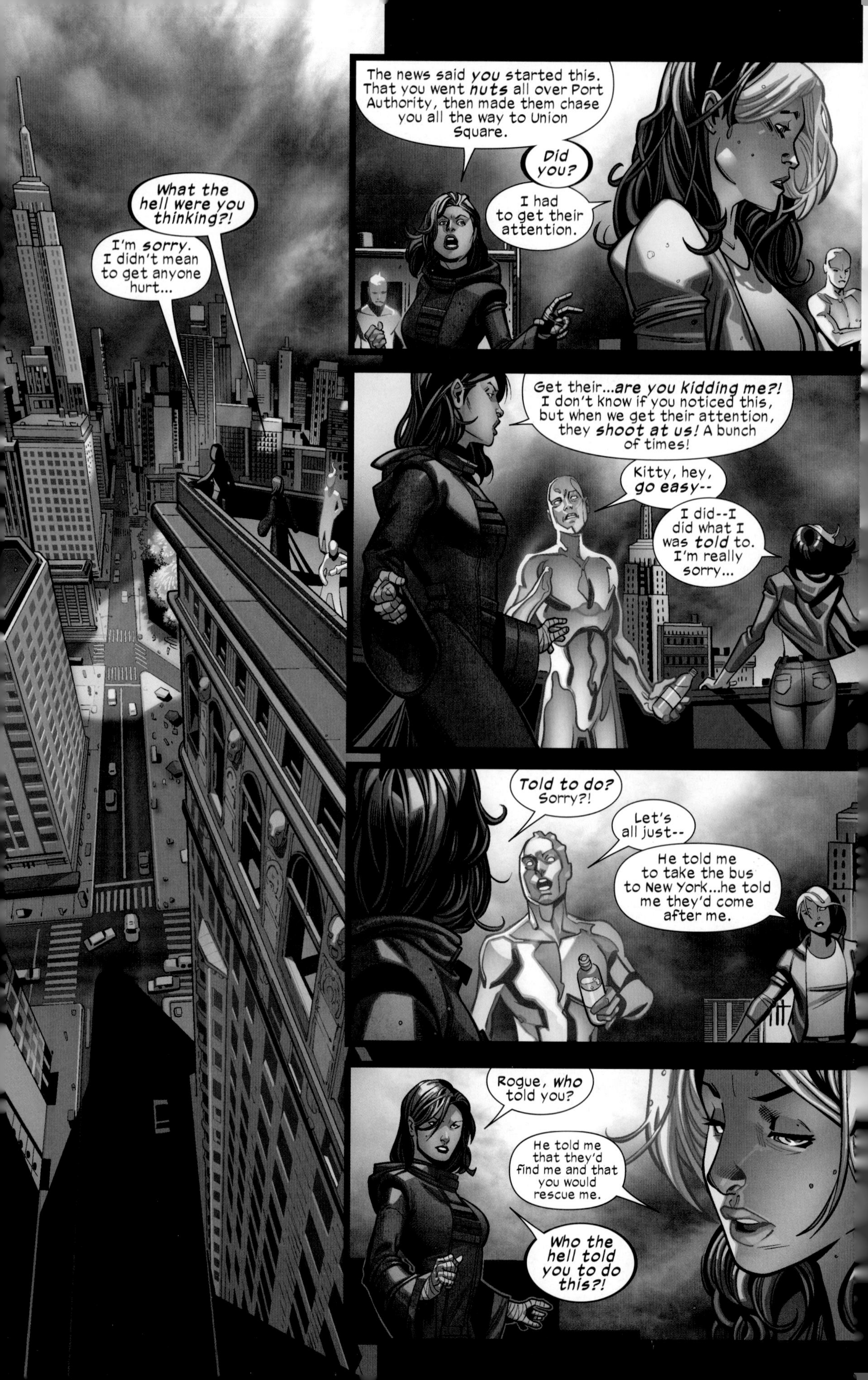
What the hell were you thinking?!
I'm sorry. I didn't mean to get anyone hurt...
The news said you started this. That you went nuts all over Port Authority, then made them chase you all the way to Union Square.
Did you?
I had to get their attention.
Get their...are you kidding me?! I don't know if you noticed this, but when we get their attention, they shoot at us! A bunch of times!
Kitty, hey, go easy--
I did--I did what I was told to. I'm really sorry...
Told to do? Sorry?!
Let's all just--
He told me to take the bus to New York...he told me they'd come after me.
Rogue, who told you?
He told me that they'd find me and that you would rescue me.
Who the hell told you to do this?!

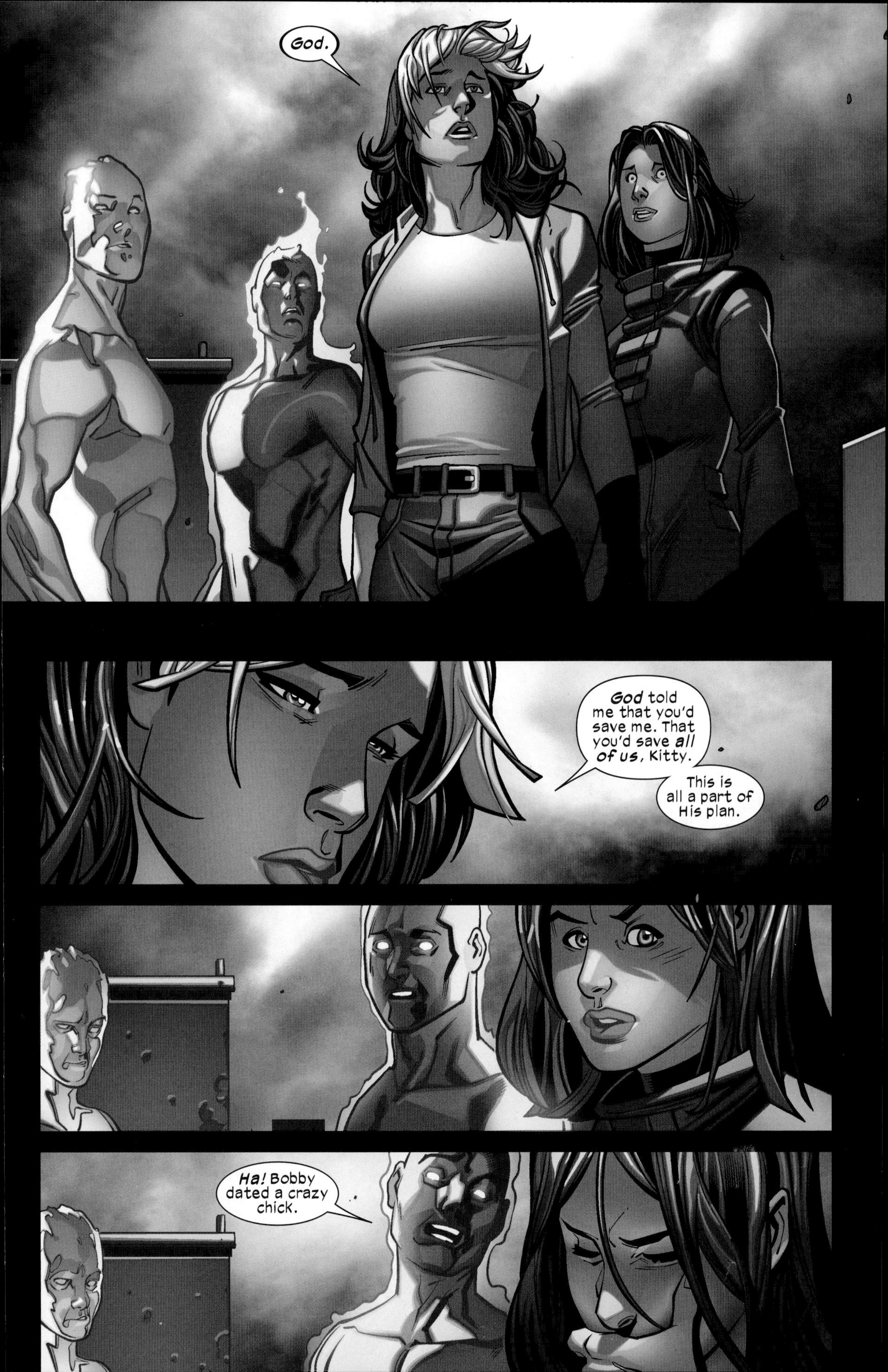
God.
God told me that you'd save me. That you'd save all of us, Kitty.
This is all a part of His plan.
Ha! Bobby dated a crazy chick.

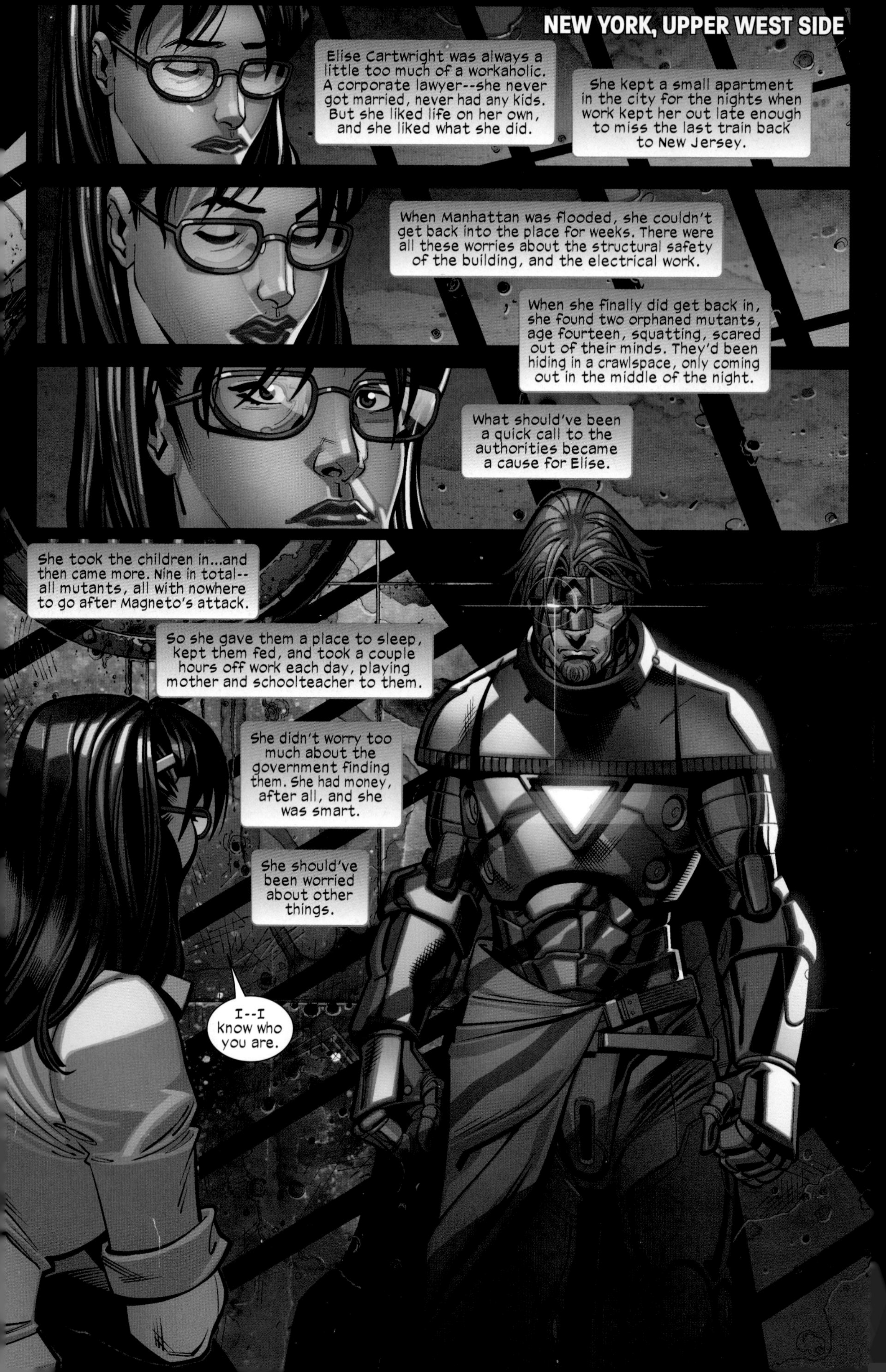
NEW YORK, UPPER WEST SIDE
Elise Cartwright was always a little too much of a workaholic. A corporate lawyer--she never got married, never had any kids. But she liked life on her own, and she liked what she did.
She kept a small apartment in the city for the nights when work kept her out late enough to miss the last train back to New Jersey.
When Manhattan was flooded, she couldn't get back into the place for weeks. There were all these worries about the structural safety of the building, and the electrical work.
When she finally did get back in, she found two orphaned mutants, age fourteen, squatting, scared out of their minds. They'd been hiding in a crawlspace, only coming out in the middle of the night.
What should've been a quick call to the authorities became a cause for Elise.
She took the children in...and then came more. Nine in total--all mutants, all with nowhere to go after Magneto's attack.
So she gave them a place to sleep, kept them fed, and took a couple hours off work each day, playing mother and schoolteacher to them.
She didn't worry too much about the government finding them. She had money, after all, and she was smart.
She should've been worried about other things.
I--I know who you are.

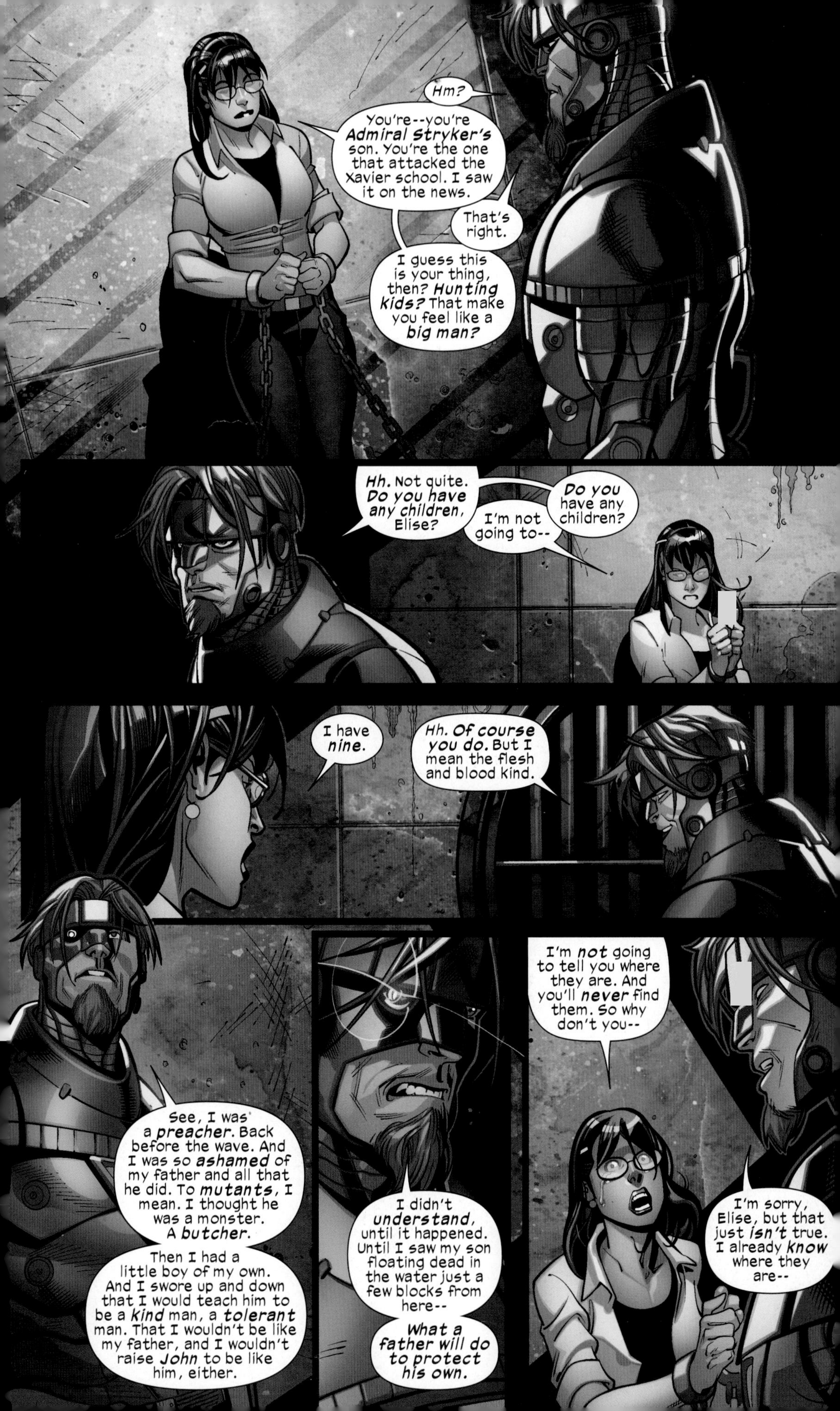

Hm?
You're--you're Admiral Stryker's son. You're the one that attacked the Xavier school. I saw it on the news.
That's right.
I guess this is your thing, then? Hunting kids? That make you feel like a big man?
Hh. Not quite. Do you have any children, Elise?
I'm not going to--
Do you have any children?
I have nine.
Hh. Of course you do. But I mean the flesh and blood kind.
See, I was a preacher. Back before the wave. And I was so ashamed of my father and all that he did. To mutants, I mean. I thought he was a monster. A butcher.
Then I had a little boy of my own. And I swore up and down that I would teach him to be a kind man, a tolerant man. That I wouldn't be like my father, and I wouldn't raise John to be like him, either.
I didn't understand, until it happened. Until I saw my son floating dead in the water just a few blocks from here--
What a father will do to protect his own.
I'm not going to tell you where they are. And you'll never find them. So why don't you--
I'm sorry, Elise, but that just isn't true. I already know where they are--

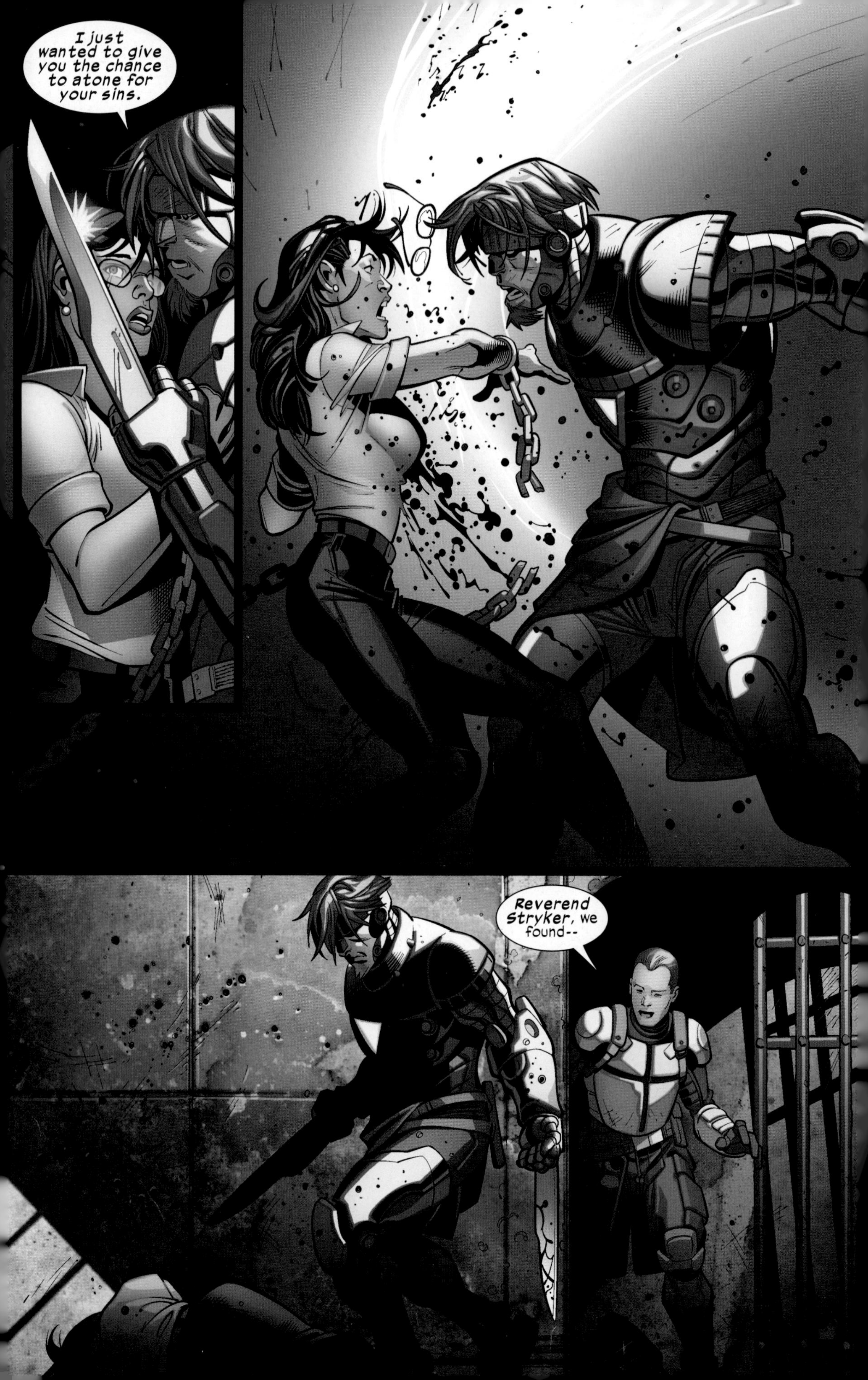
I just wanted to give you the chance to atone for your sins.
Reverend Stryker, we found--

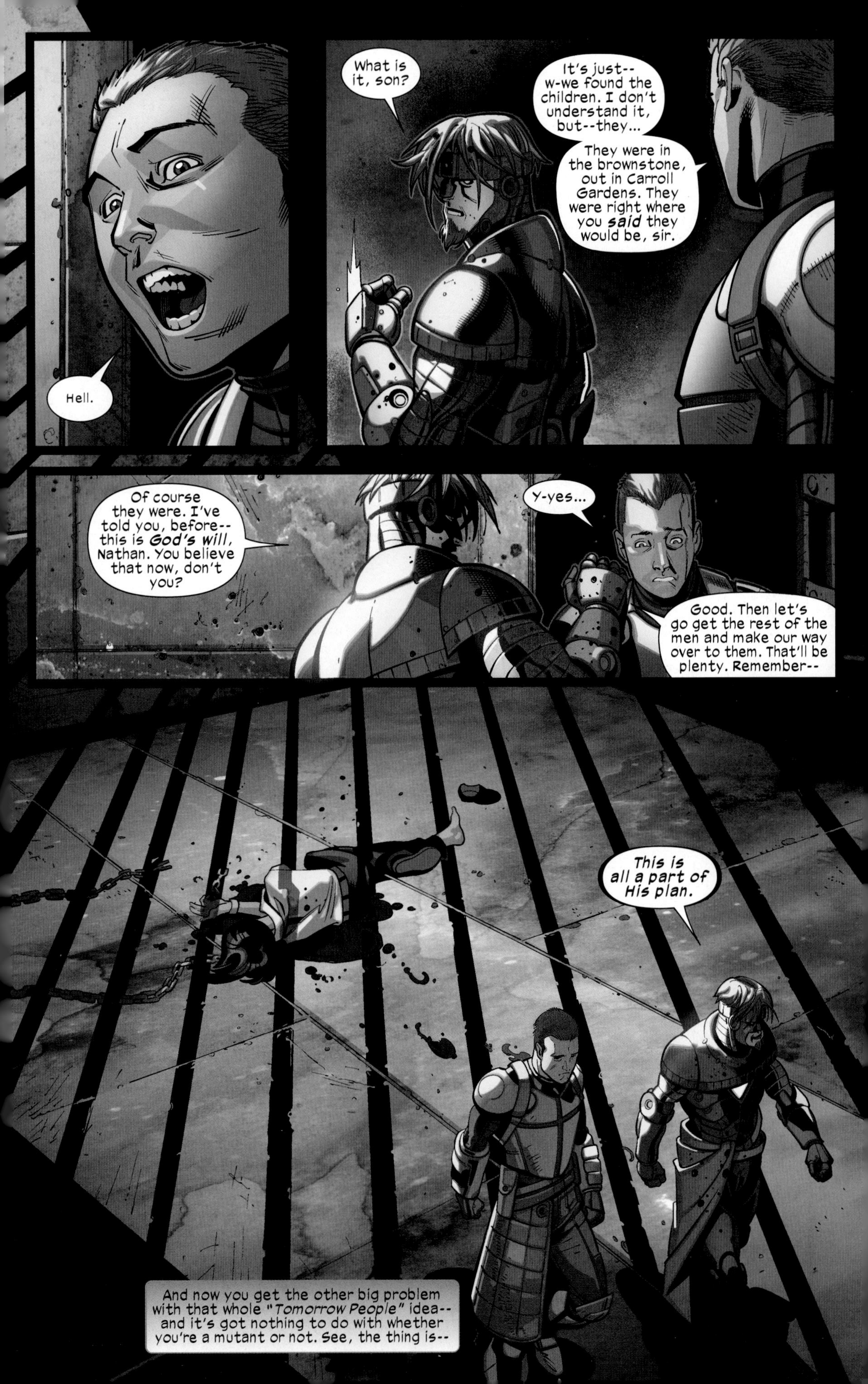
Hell.
What is it, son?
It's just-- w-we found the children. I don't understand it, but--they...
They were in the brownstone, out in Carroll Gardens. They were right where you *said* they would be, sir.
Of course they were. I've told you, before-- this is *God's will*, Nathan. You believe that now, don't you?
Y-yes...
Good. Then let's go get the rest of the men and make our way over to them. That'll be plenty. Remember--
This is all a part of His plan.
And now you get the other big problem with that whole "*Tomorrow People*" idea-- and it's got nothing to do with whether you're a mutant or not. See, the thing is--

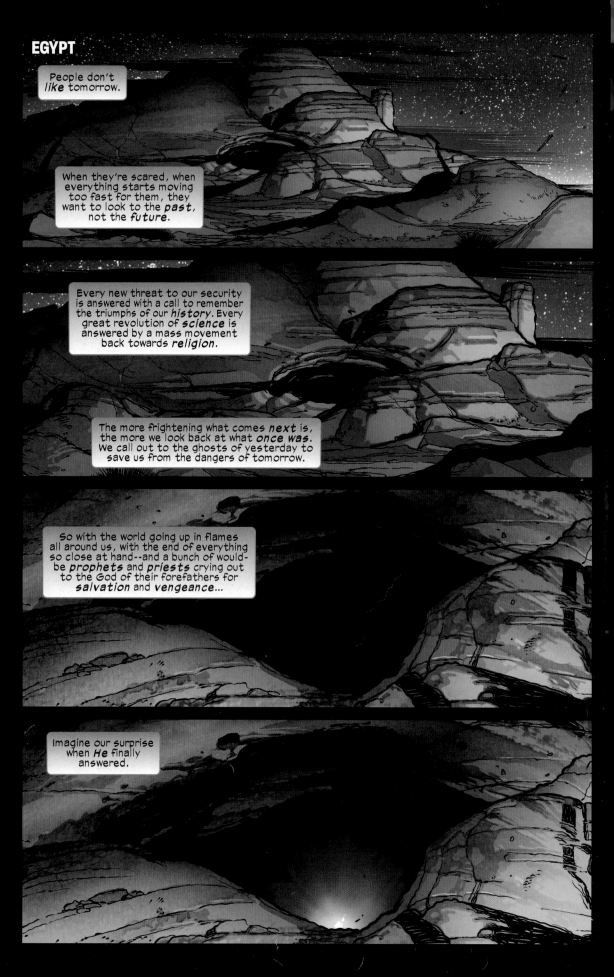

EGYPT

People don't *like* tomorrow.

When they're scared, when everything starts moving too fast for them, they want to look to the *past*, not the *future*.

Every new threat to our security is answered with a call to remember the triumphs of our *history*. Every great revolution of *science* is answered by a mass movement back towards *religion*.

The more frightening what comes *next* is, the more we look back at what *once was*. We call out to the ghosts of yesterday to save us from the dangers of tomorrow.

So with the world going up in flames all around us, with the end of everything so close at hand--and a bunch of would-be *prophets* and *priests* crying out to the God of their forefathers for *salvation* and *vengeance*...

Imagine our surprise when *He* finally answered.

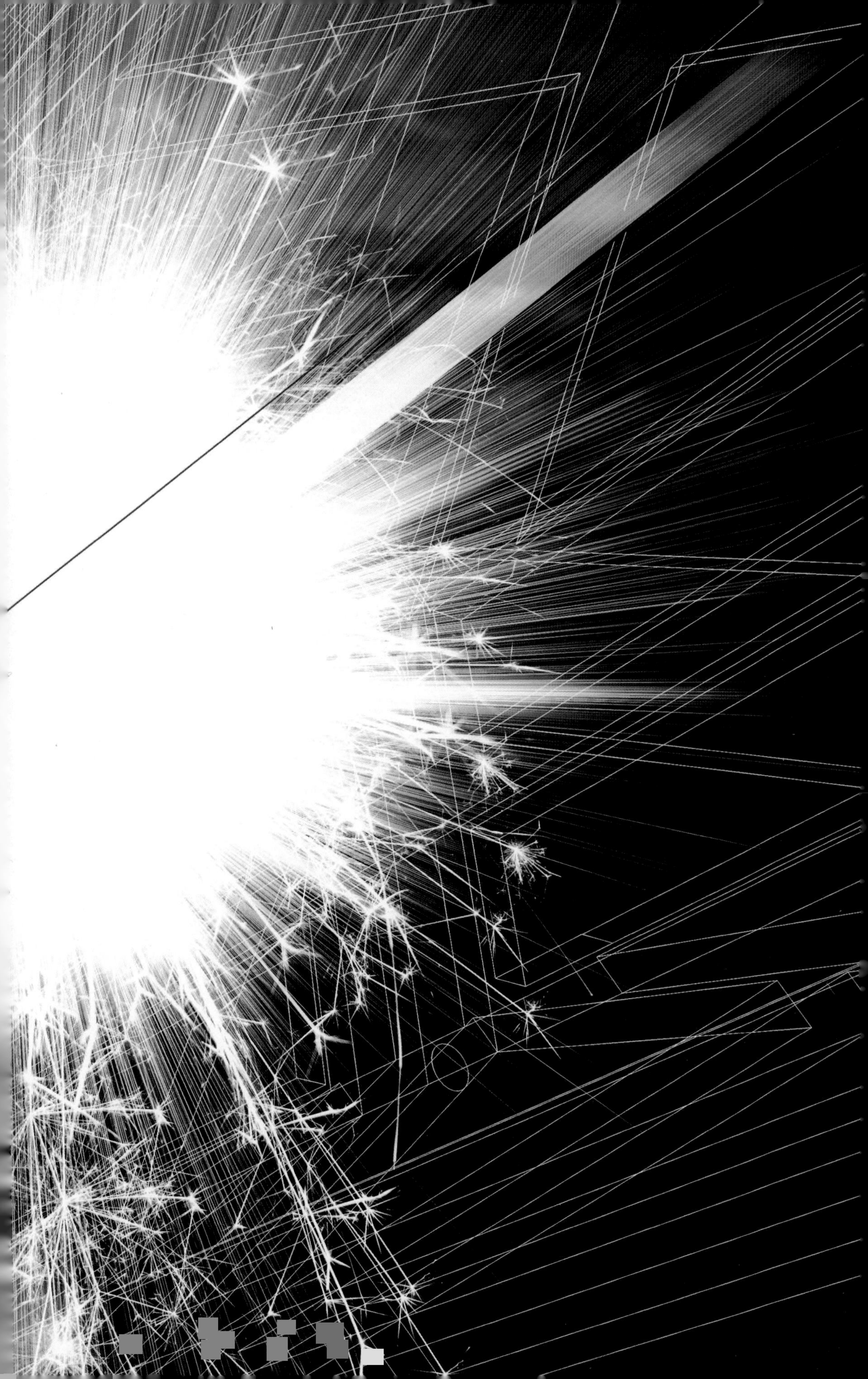

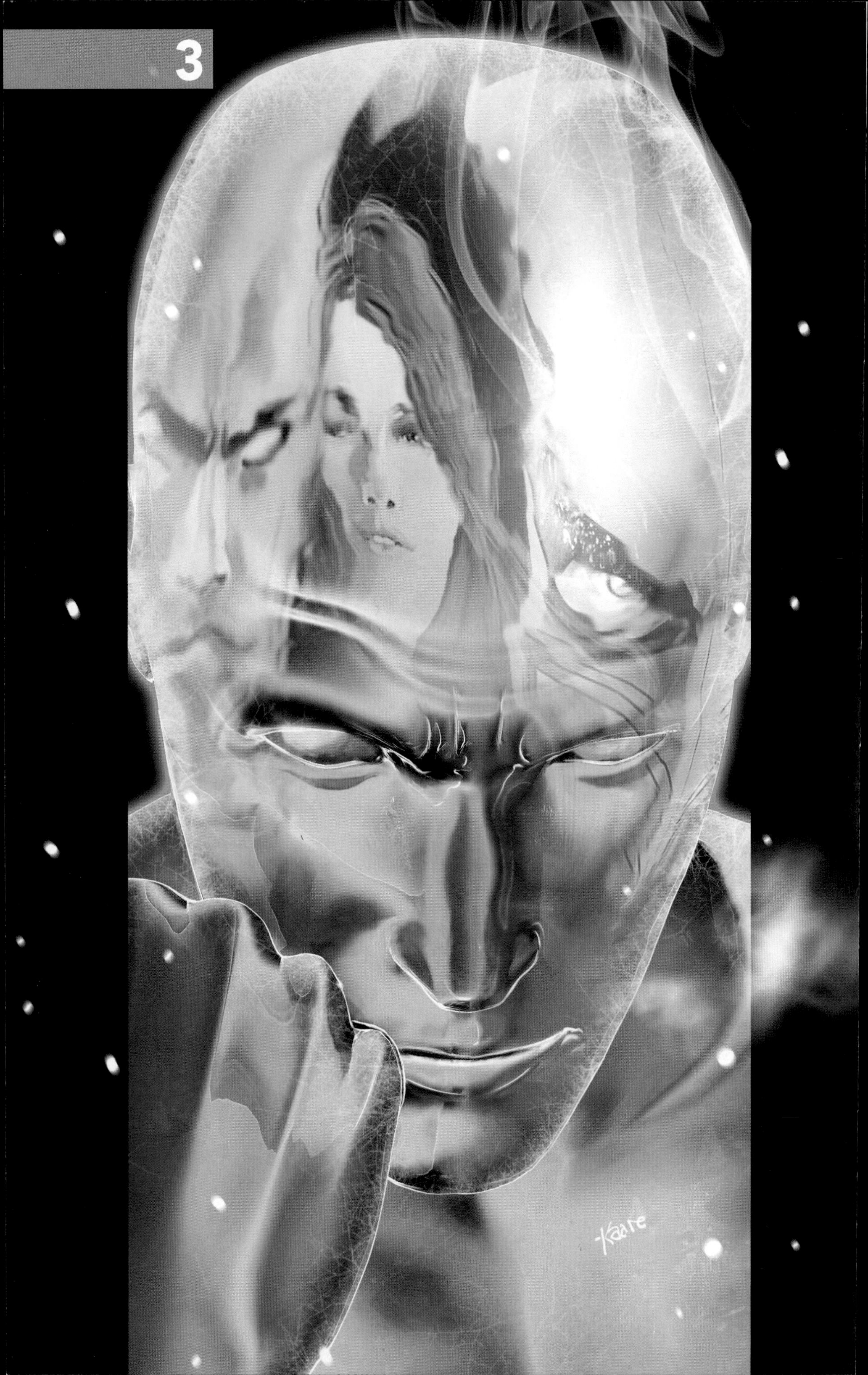
3
Kaare

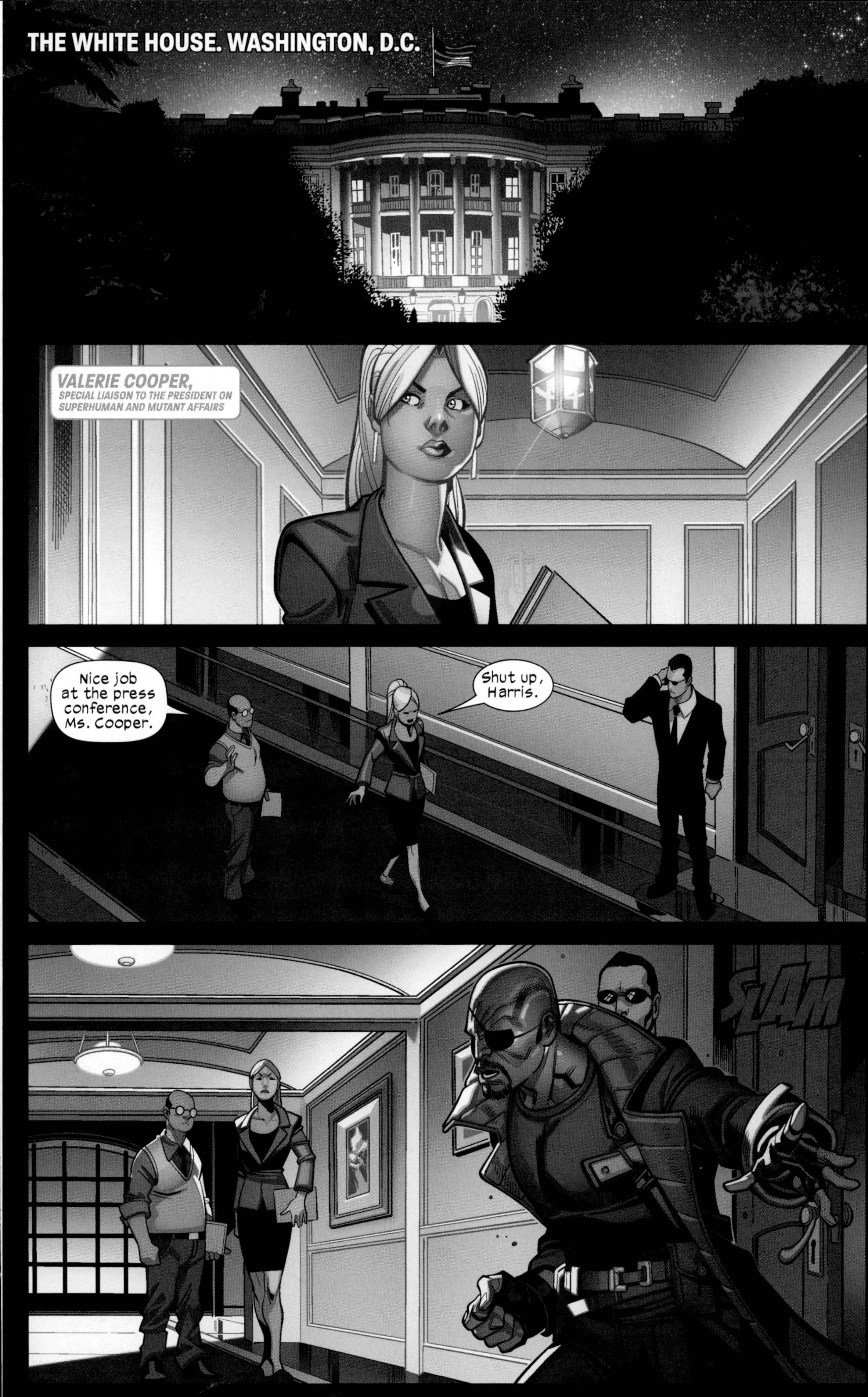
THE WHITE HOUSE. WASHINGTON, D.C.
VALERIE COOPER, SPECIAL LIAISON TO THE PRESIDENT ON SUPERHUMAN AND MUTANT AFFAIRS
Nice job at the press conference, Ms. Cooper.
Shut up, Harris.
SLAM

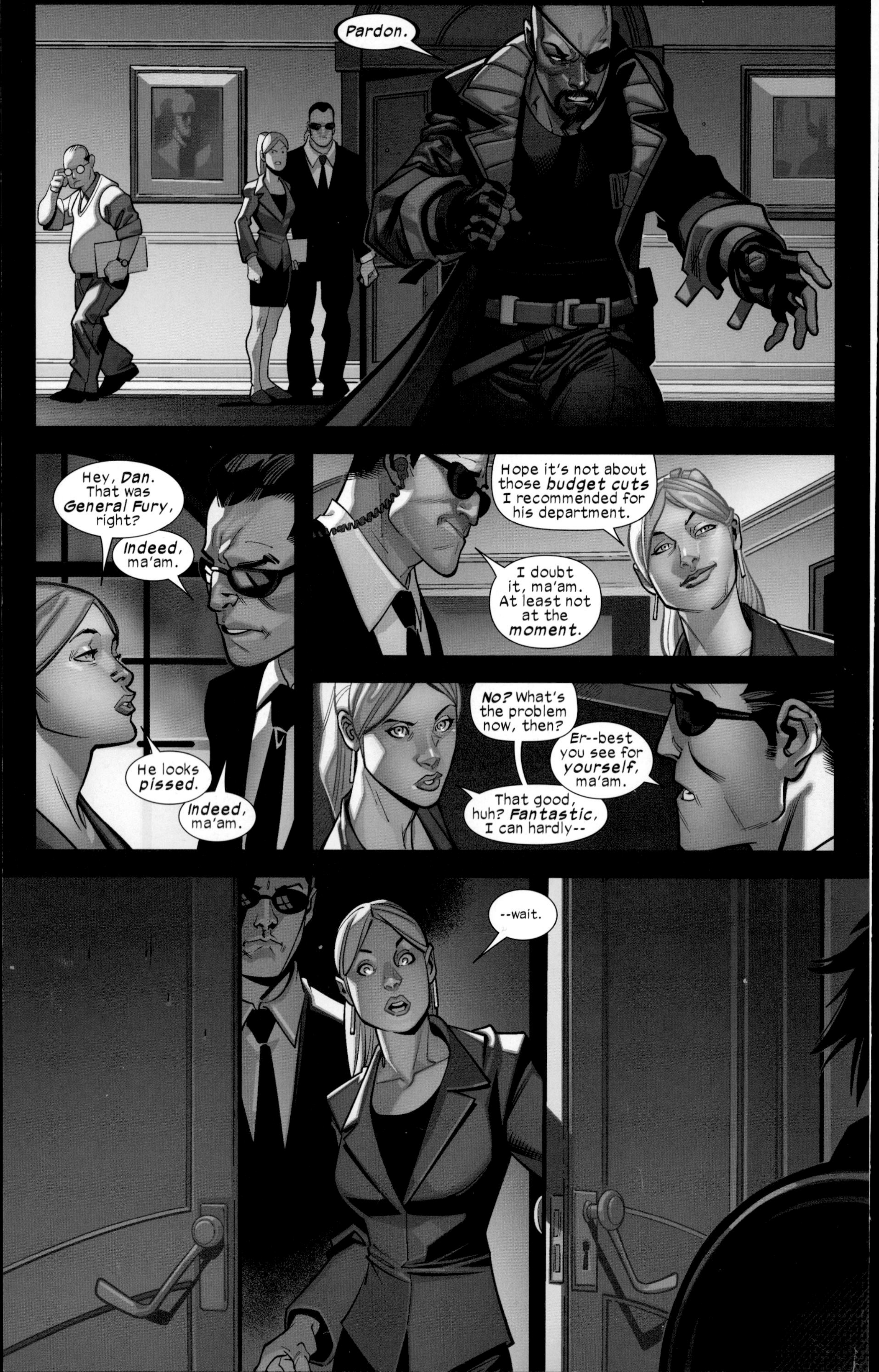
Pardon.
Hey, Dan. That was General Fury, right?
Indeed, ma'am.
He looks pissed.
Indeed, ma'am.
Hope it's not about those budget cuts I recommended for his department.
I doubt it, ma'am. At least not at the moment.
No? What's the problem now, then?
Er--best you see for yourself, ma'am.
That good, huh? Fantastic, I can hardly--
--wait.

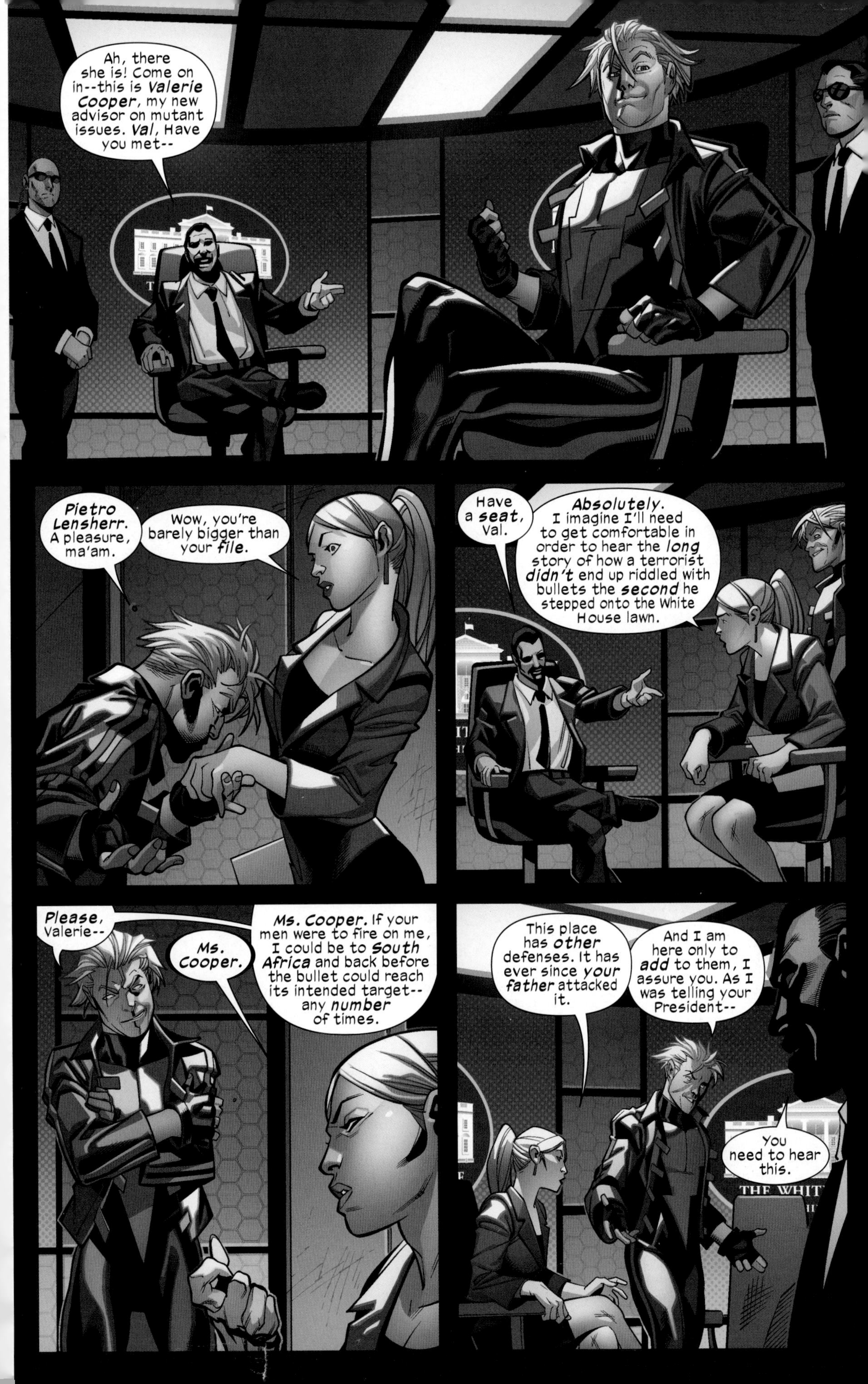
Ah, there she is! Come on in--this is Valerie Cooper, my new advisor on mutant issues. Val, Have you met--
Pietro Lensherr. A pleasure, ma'am.
Wow, you're barely bigger than your file.
Have a seat, Val.
Absolutely. I imagine I'll need to get comfortable in order to hear the long story of how a terrorist didn't end up riddled with bullets the second he stepped onto the White House lawn.
Please, Valerie--
Ms. Cooper.
Ms. Cooper. If your men were to fire on me, I could be to South Africa and back before the bullet could reach its intended target--any number of times.
This place has other defenses. It has ever since your father attacked it.
And I am here only to add to them, I assure you. As I was telling your President--
You need to hear this.

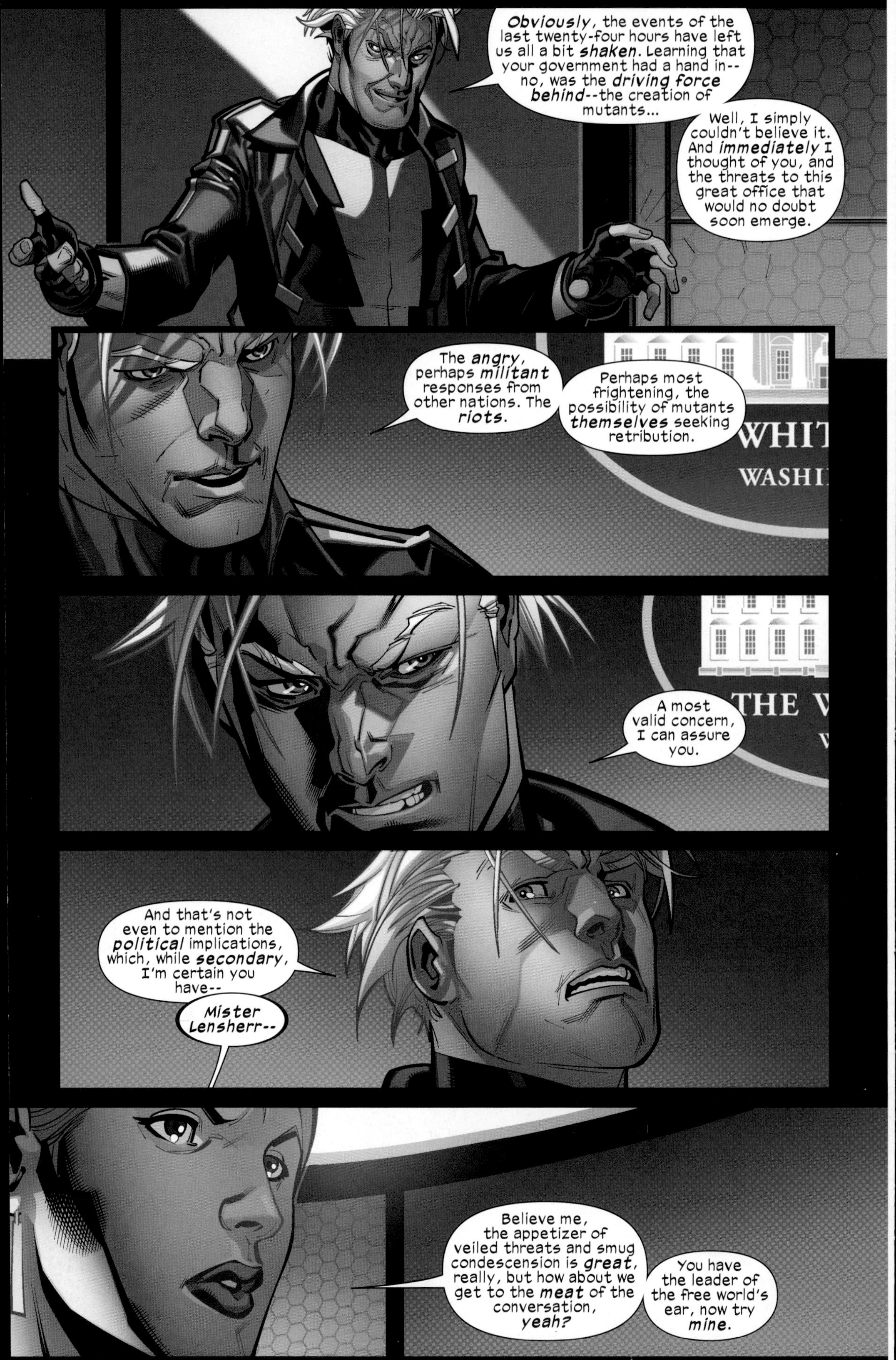
Obviously, the events of the last twenty-four hours have left us all a bit shaken. Learning that your government had a hand in--no, was the driving force behind--the creation of mutants...
Well, I simply couldn't believe it. And immediately I thought of you, and the threats to this great office that would no doubt soon emerge.
The angry, perhaps militant responses from other nations. The riots.
Perhaps most frightening, the possibility of mutants themselves seeking retribution.
WHIT
WASHI
A most valid concern, I can assure you.
THE W
And that's not even to mention the political implications, which, while secondary, I'm certain you have--
Mister Lensherr--
Believe me, the appetizer of veiled threats and smug condescension is great, really, but how about we get to the meat of the conversation, yeah?
You have the leader of the free world's ear, now try mine.

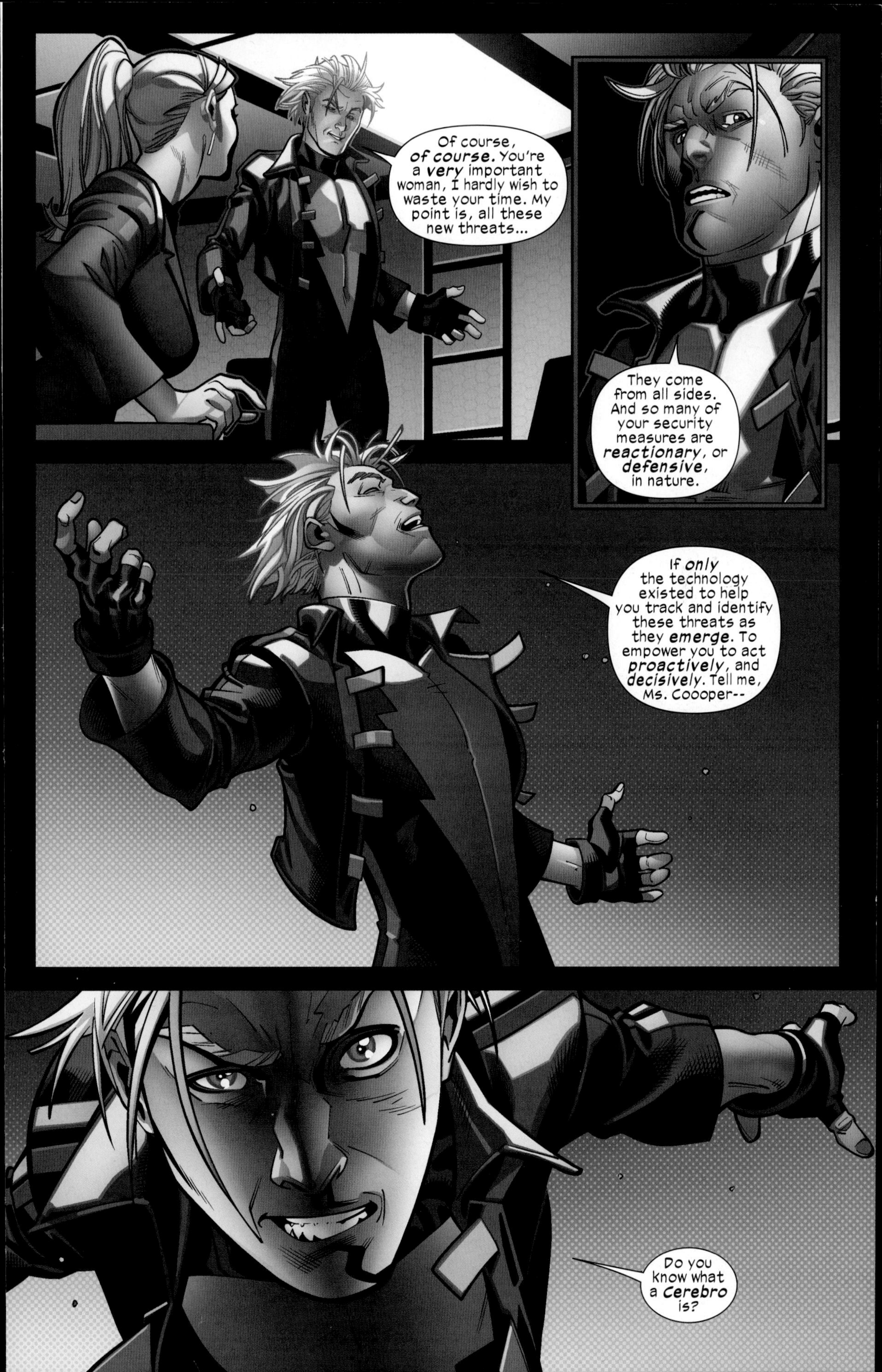
Of course, *of course*. You're a *very* important woman, I hardly wish to waste your time. My point is, all these new threats...
They come from all sides. And so many of your security measures are *reactionary*, or *defensive*, in nature.
If *only* the technology existed to help you track and identify these threats as they *emerge*. To empower you to act *proactively*, and *decisively*. Tell me, Ms. Coooper--
Do you know what a *Cerebro* is?

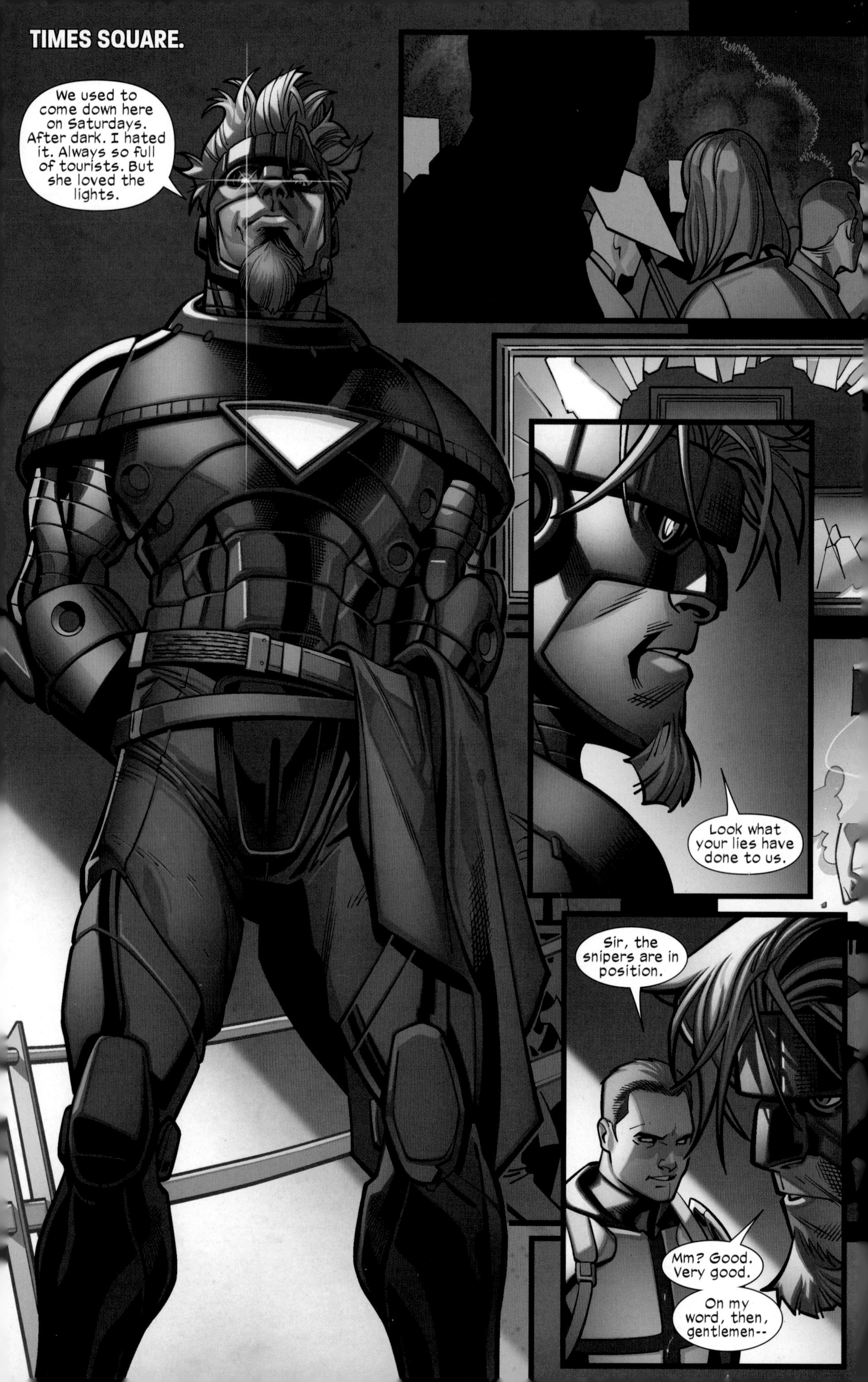
TIMES SQUARE.
We used to come down here on Saturdays. After dark. I hated it. Always so full of tourists. But she loved the lights.
Look what your lies have done to us.
Sir, the snipers are in position.
Mm? Good. Very good.
On my word, then, gentlemen--

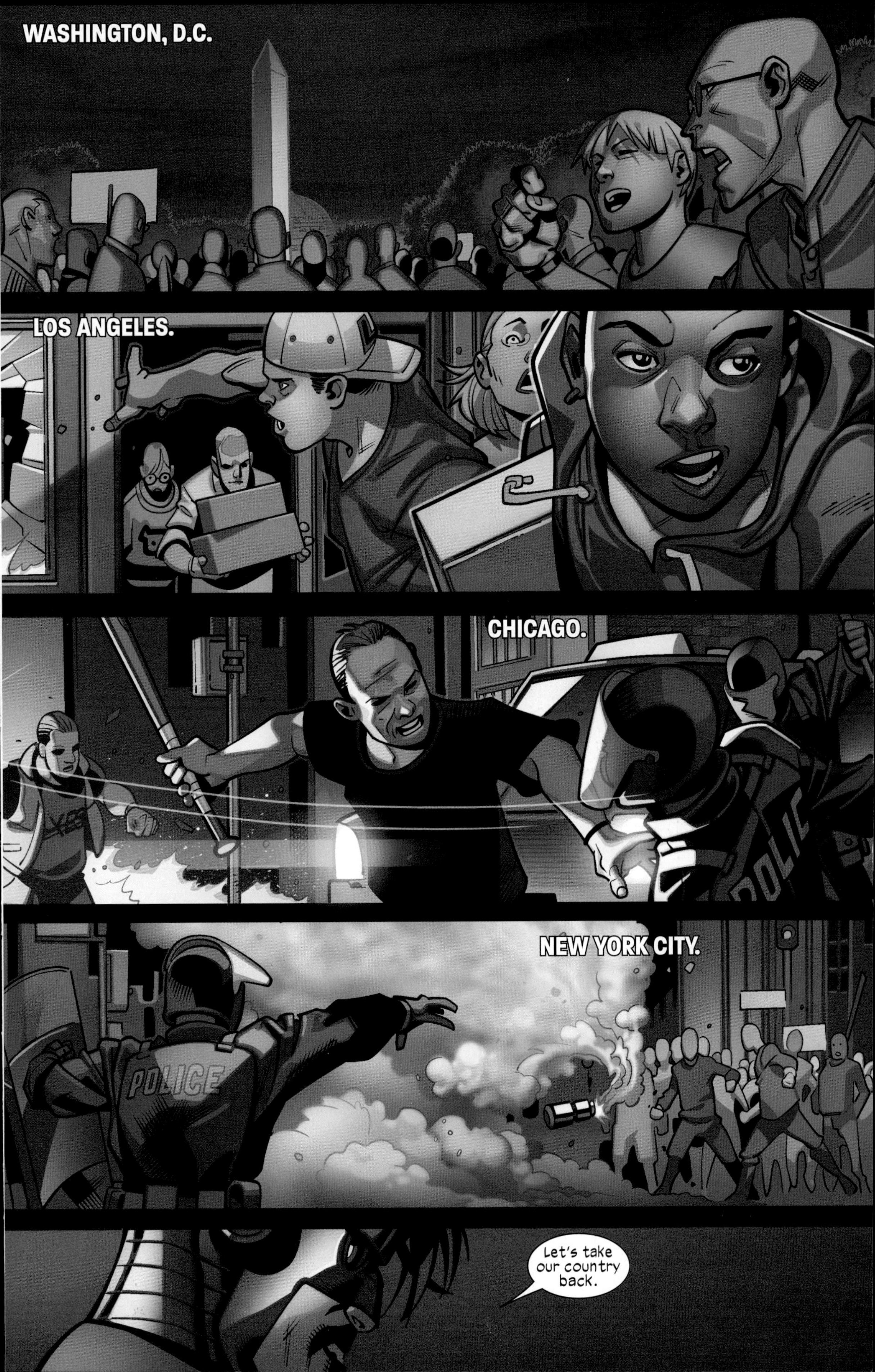
WASHINGTON, D.C.
LOS ANGELES.
CHICAGO.
POLICE
NEW YORK CITY.
POLICE
Let's take our country back.

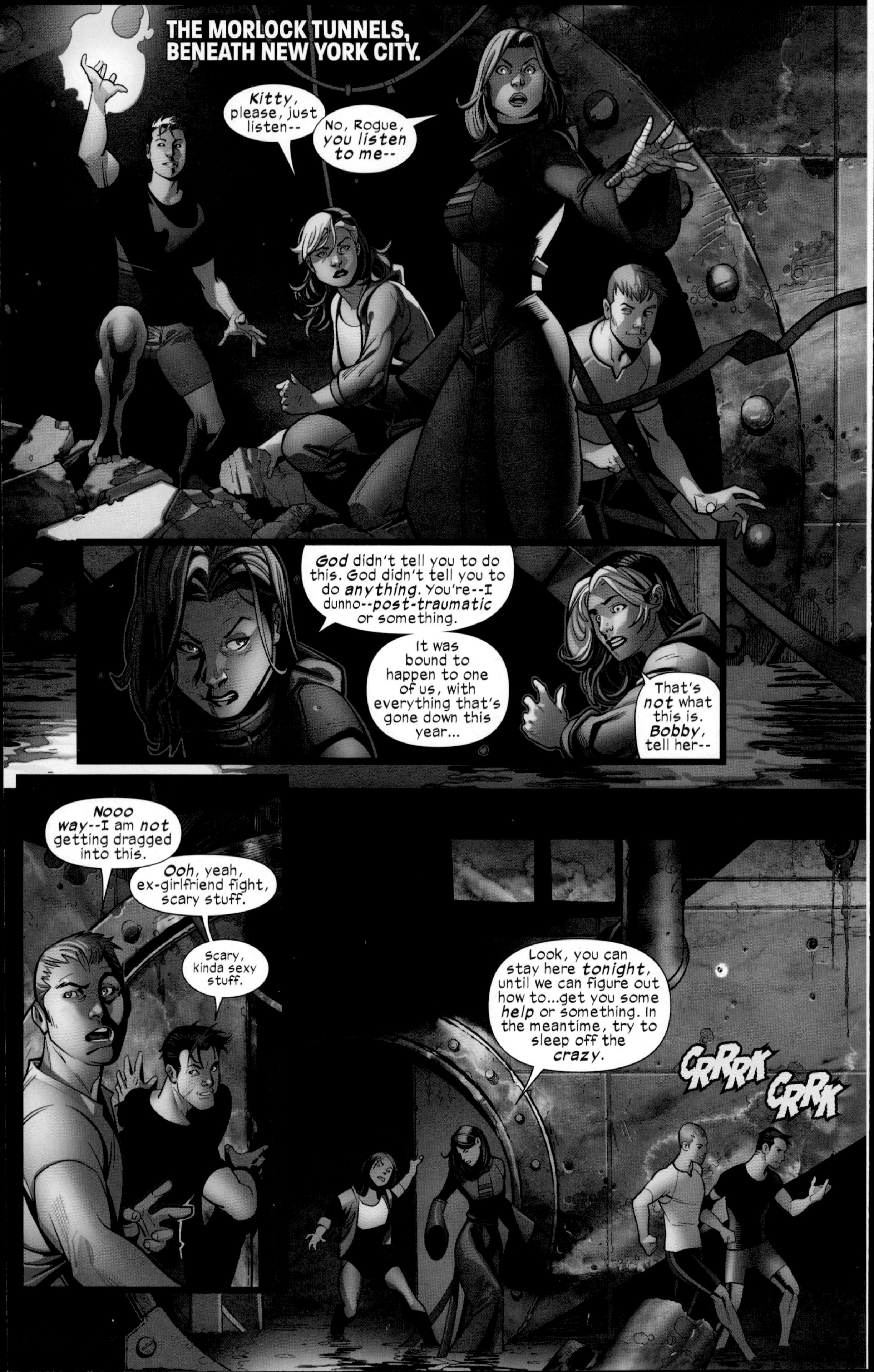
THE MORLOCK TUNNELS, BENEATH NEW YORK CITY.
Kitty, please, just listen--
No, Rogue, you listen to me--
God didn't tell you to do this. God didn't tell you to do anything. You're--I dunno--post-traumatic or something.
It was bound to happen to one of us, with everything that's gone down this year...
That's not what this is. Bobby, tell her--
Nooo way--I am not getting dragged into this.
Ooh, yeah, ex-girlfriend fight, scary stuff.
Scary, kinda sexy stuff.
Look, you can stay here tonight, until we can figure out how to...get you some help or something. In the meantime, try to sleep off the crazy.
CRRRK
CRRK

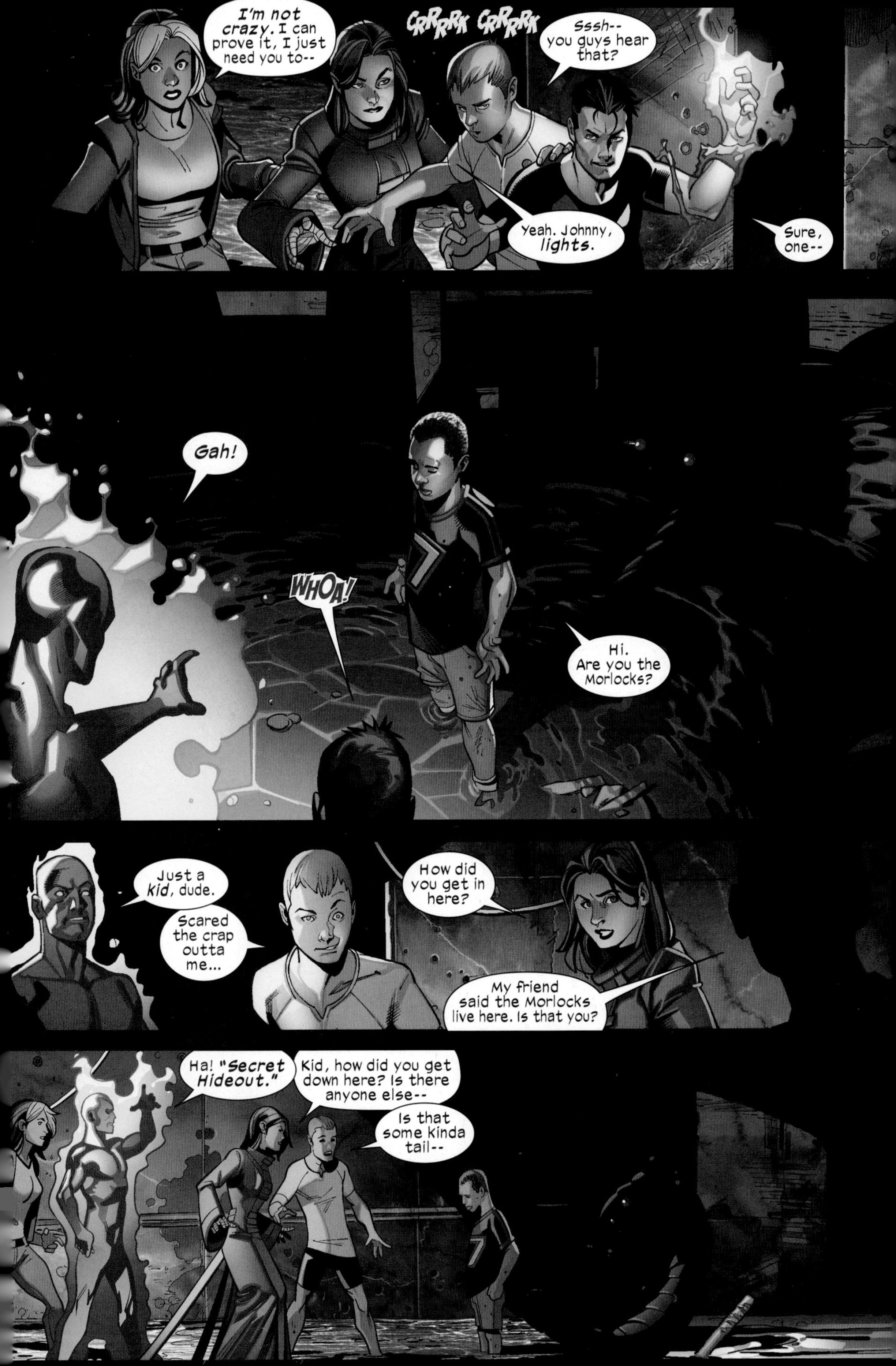
I'm not crazy. I can prove it, I just need you to--
CRRRK CRRRK
Sssh-- you guys hear that?
Yeah. Johnny, lights.
Sure, one--
Gah!
WHOA!
Hi. Are you the Morlocks?
Just a kid, dude.
Scared the crap outta me...
How did you get in here?
My friend said the Morlocks live here. Is that you?
Ha! "Secret Hideout."
Kid, how did you get down here? Is there anyone else--
Is that some kinda tail--

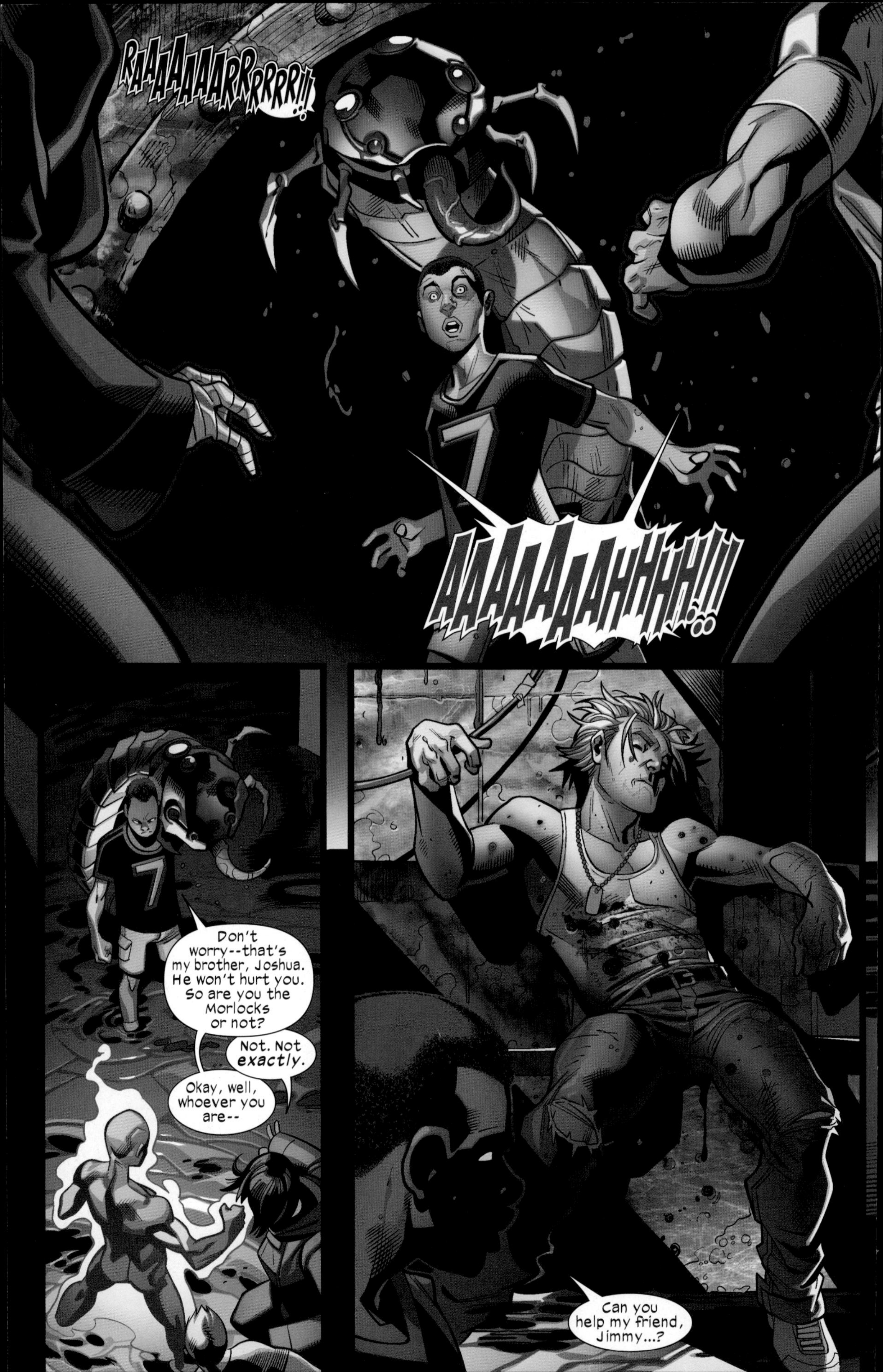
RAAAAAAARRRRR!!
AAAAAAAHHHH!!!
Don't worry--that's my brother, Joshua. He won't hurt you. So are you the Morlocks or not?
Not. Not *exactly*.
Okay, well, whoever you are--
Can you help my friend, Jimmy...?

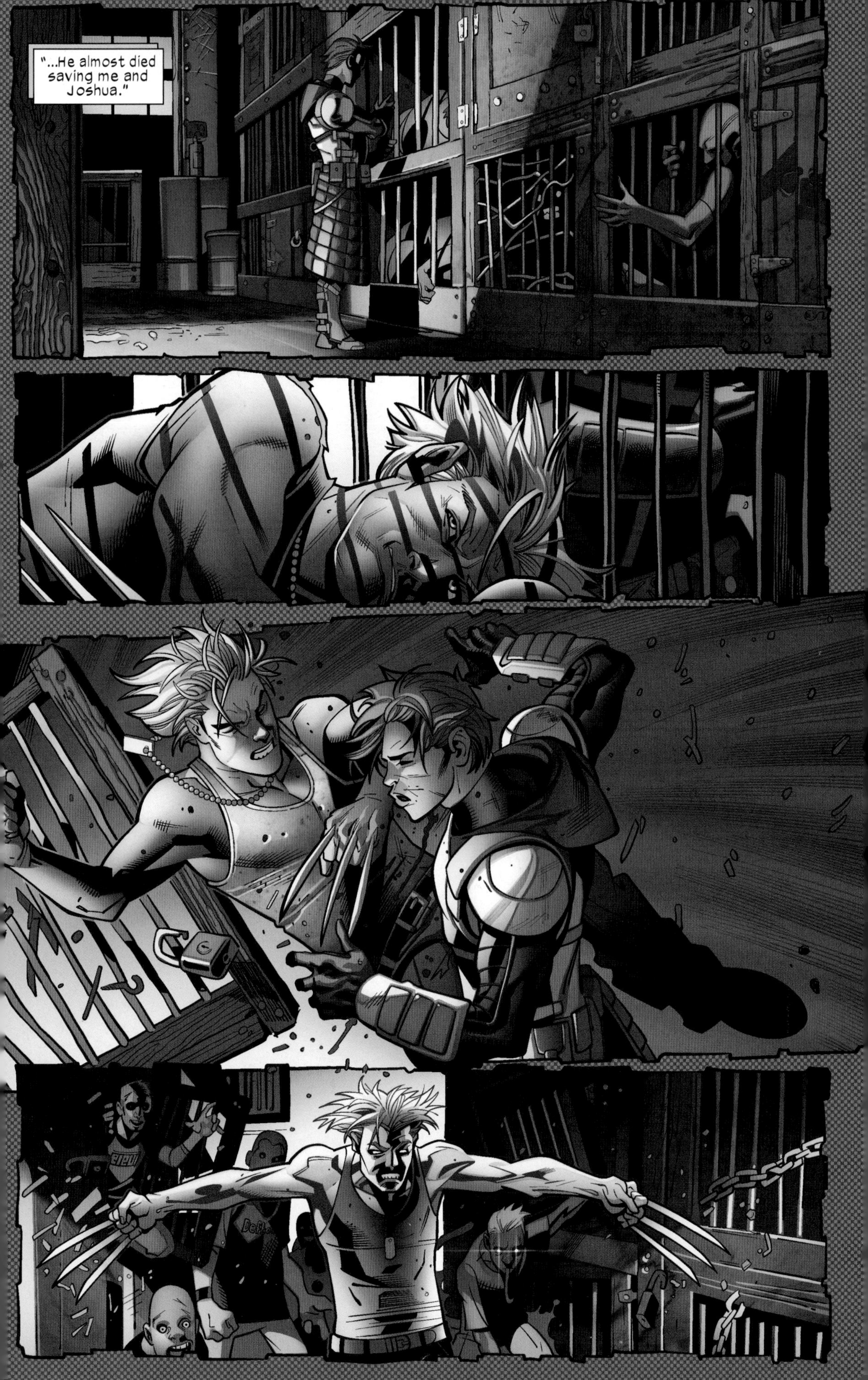
"...He almost died saving me and Joshua."

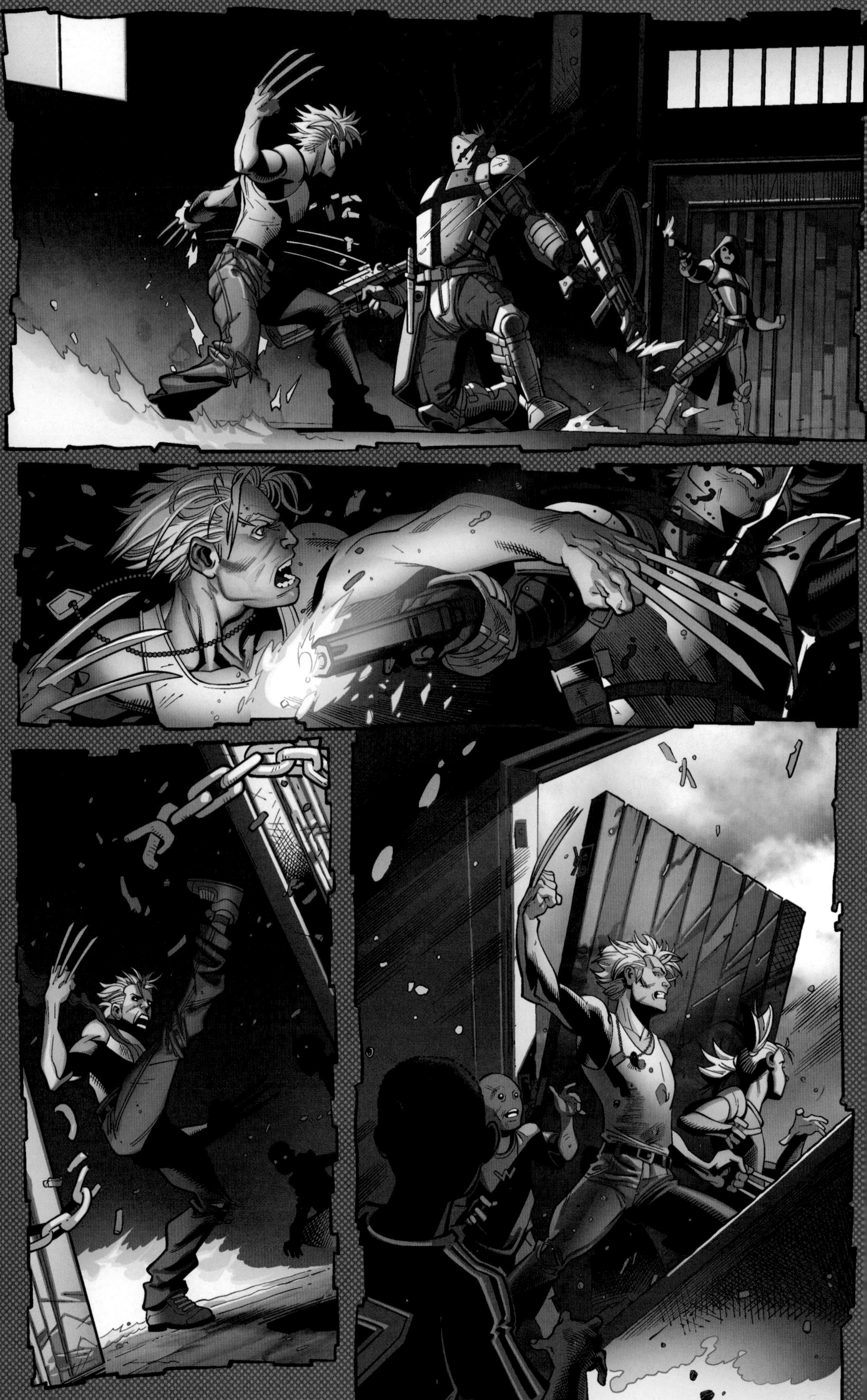

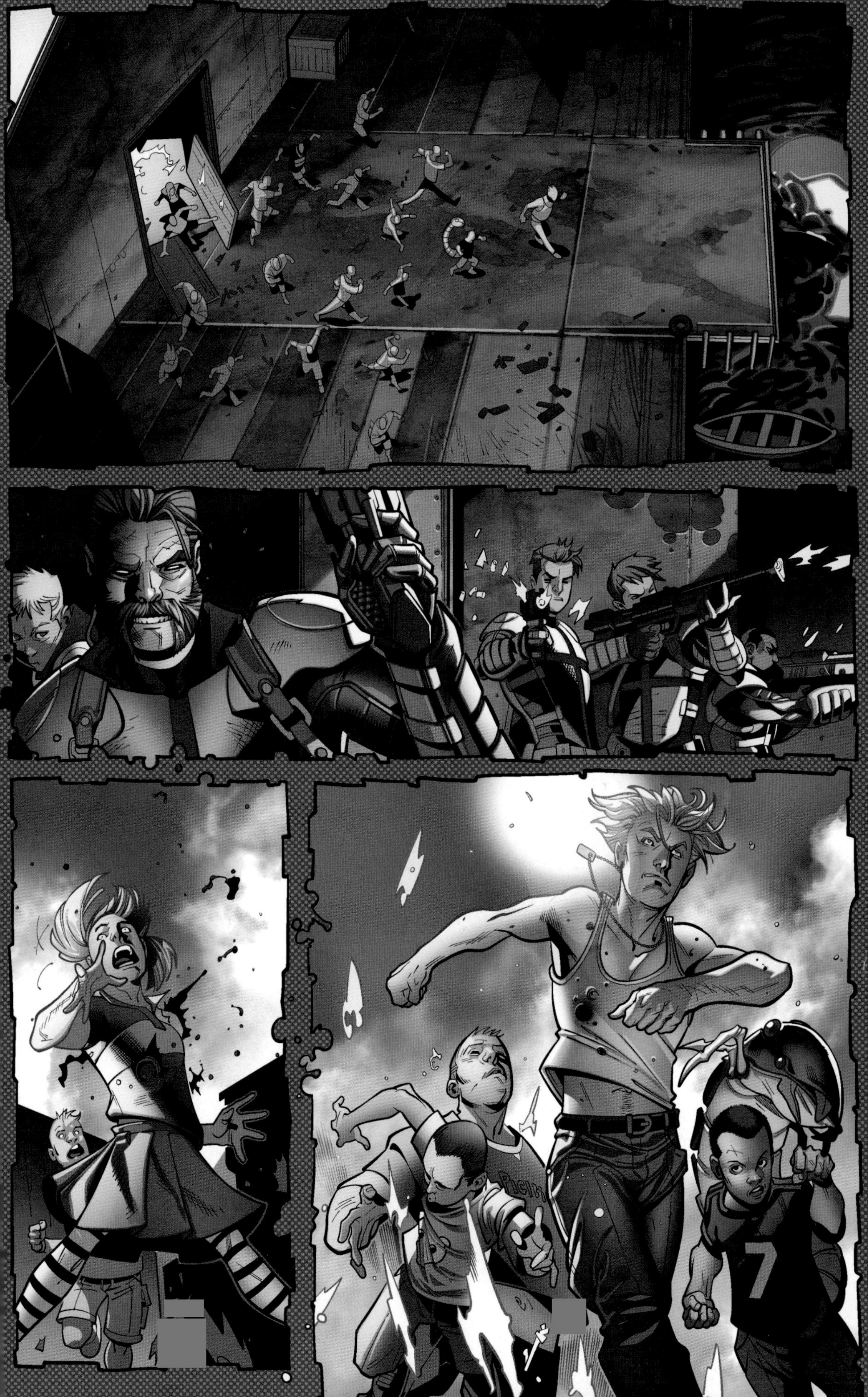

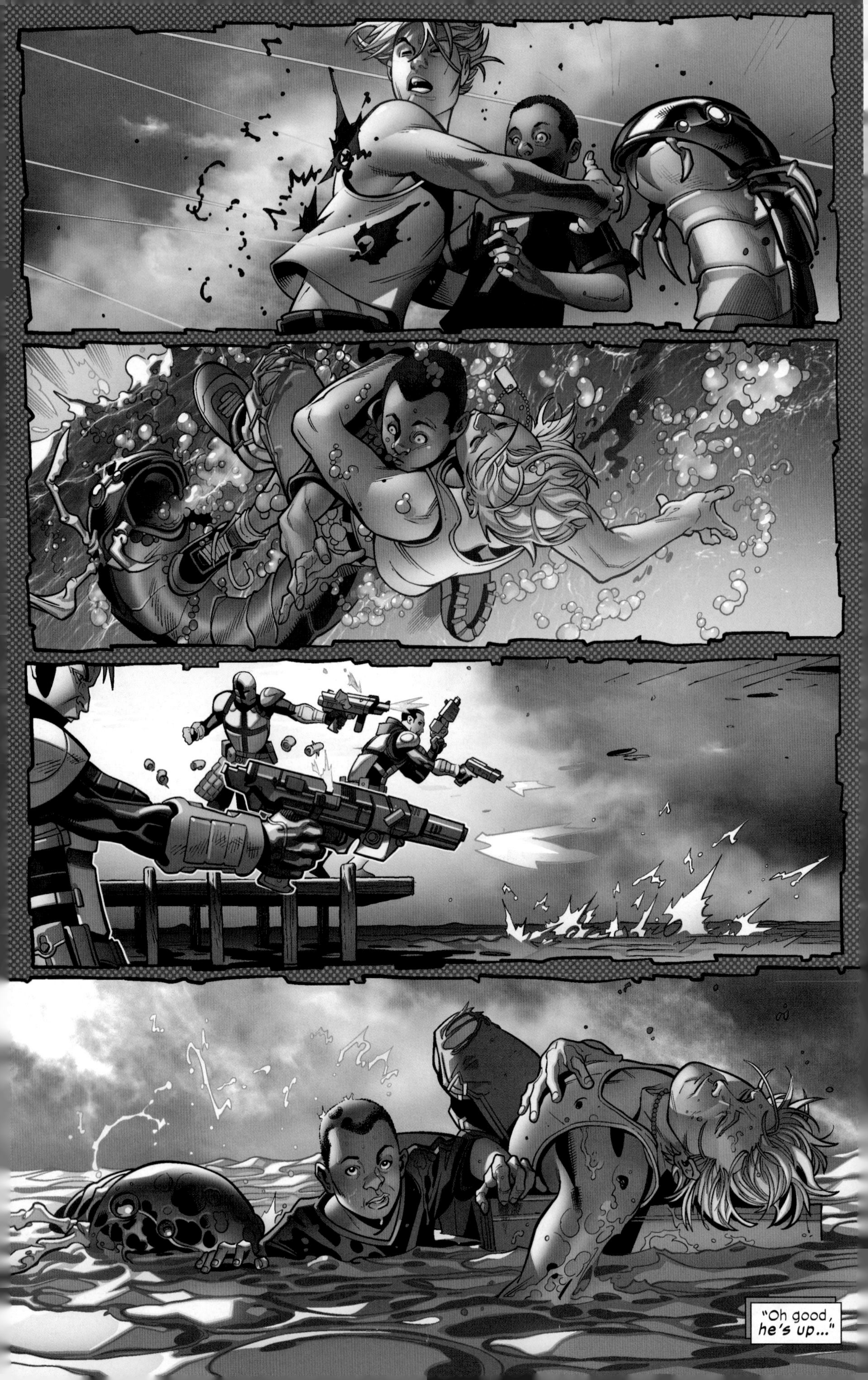
"Oh good, he's up..."

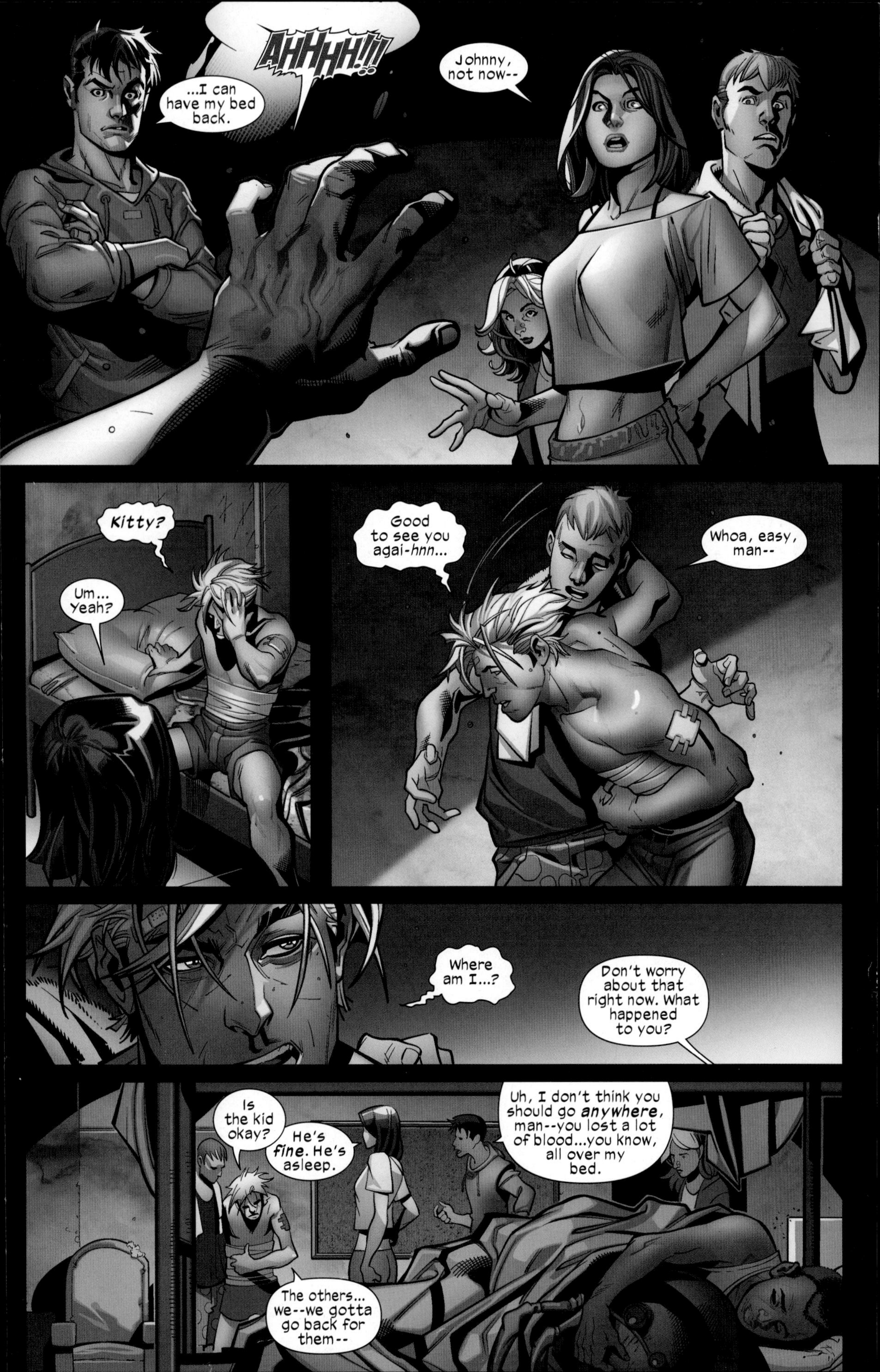
...I can have my bed back.
AHHHH!!!
Johnny, not now--
Kitty?
Um... Yeah?
Good to see you agai-hnn...
Whoa, easy, man--
Where am I...?
Don't worry about that right now. What happened to you?
Is the kid okay?
He's fine. He's asleep.
Uh, I don't think you should go anywhere, man--you lost a lot of blood...you know, all over my bed.
The others... we--we gotta go back for them--

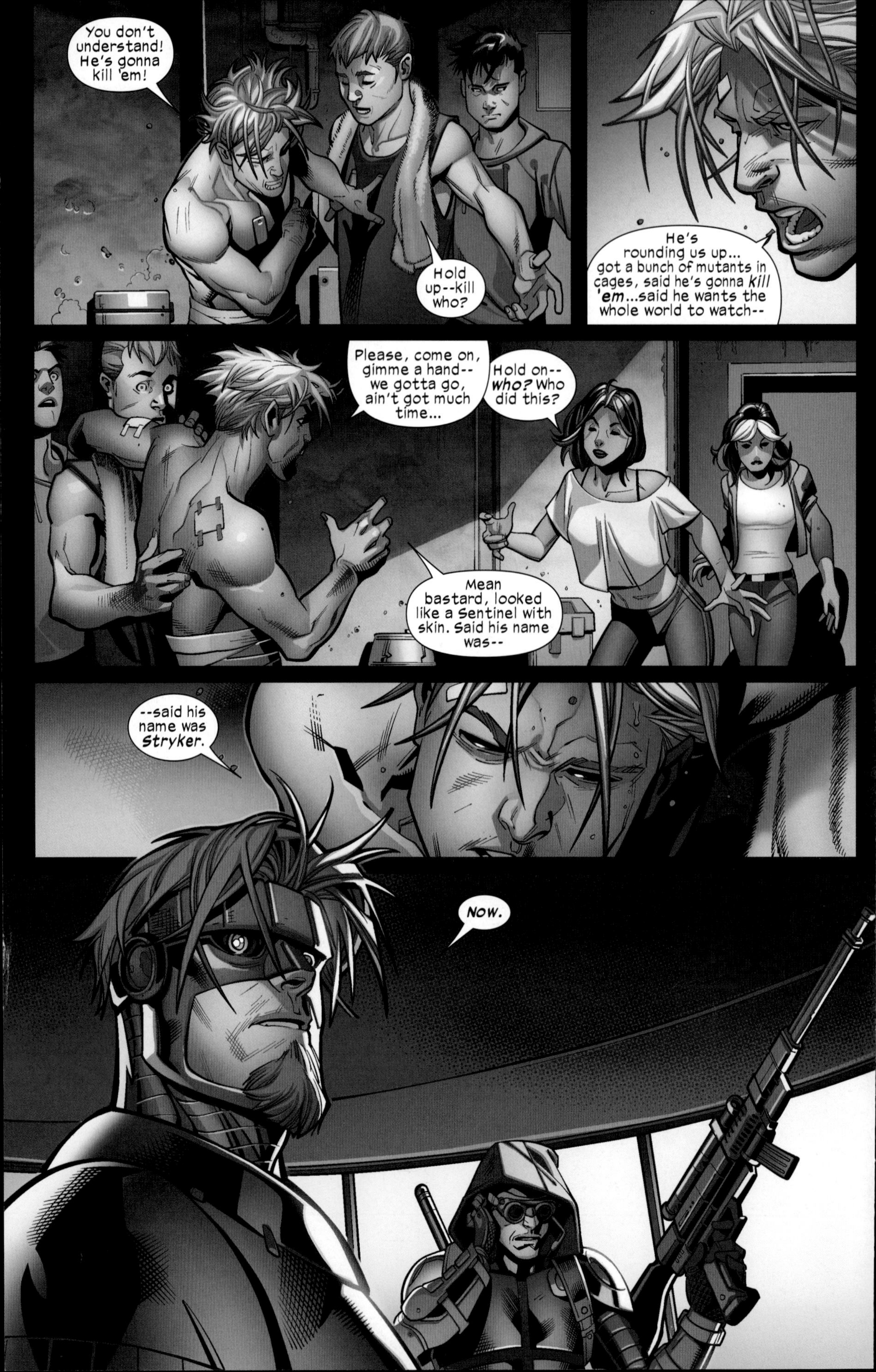
You don't understand! He's gonna kill 'em!
Hold up--kill who?
He's rounding us up... got a bunch of mutants in cages, said he's gonna kill 'em...said he wants the whole world to watch--
Please, come on, gimme a hand-- we gotta go, ain't got much time...
Hold on-- who? Who did this?
Mean bastard, looked like a Sentinel with skin. Said his name was--
--said his name was Stryker.
Now.

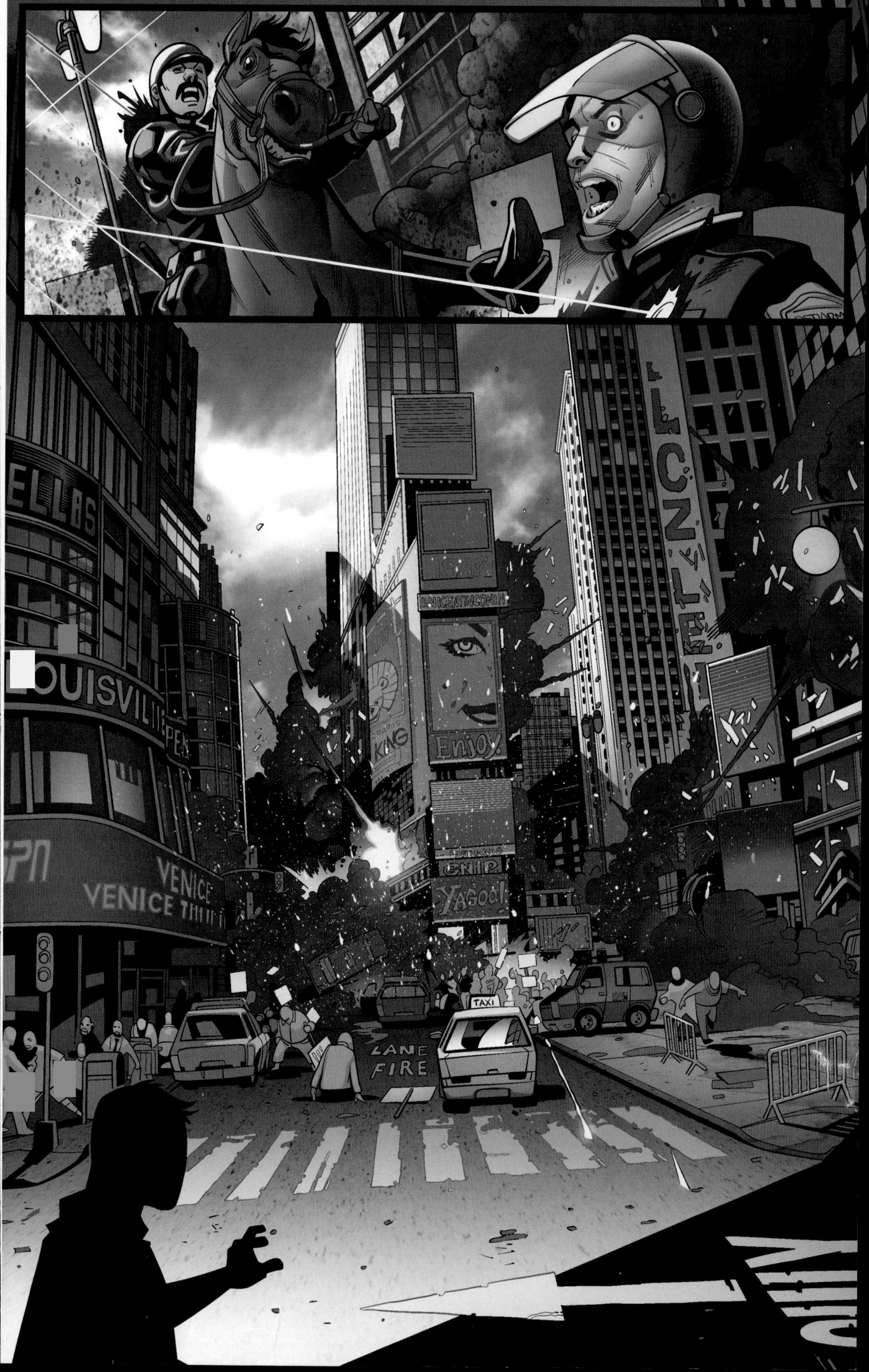
VENICE
VENICE
Enjoy.
KING
GNIP
YAGOO!
TAXI
LANE
FIRE

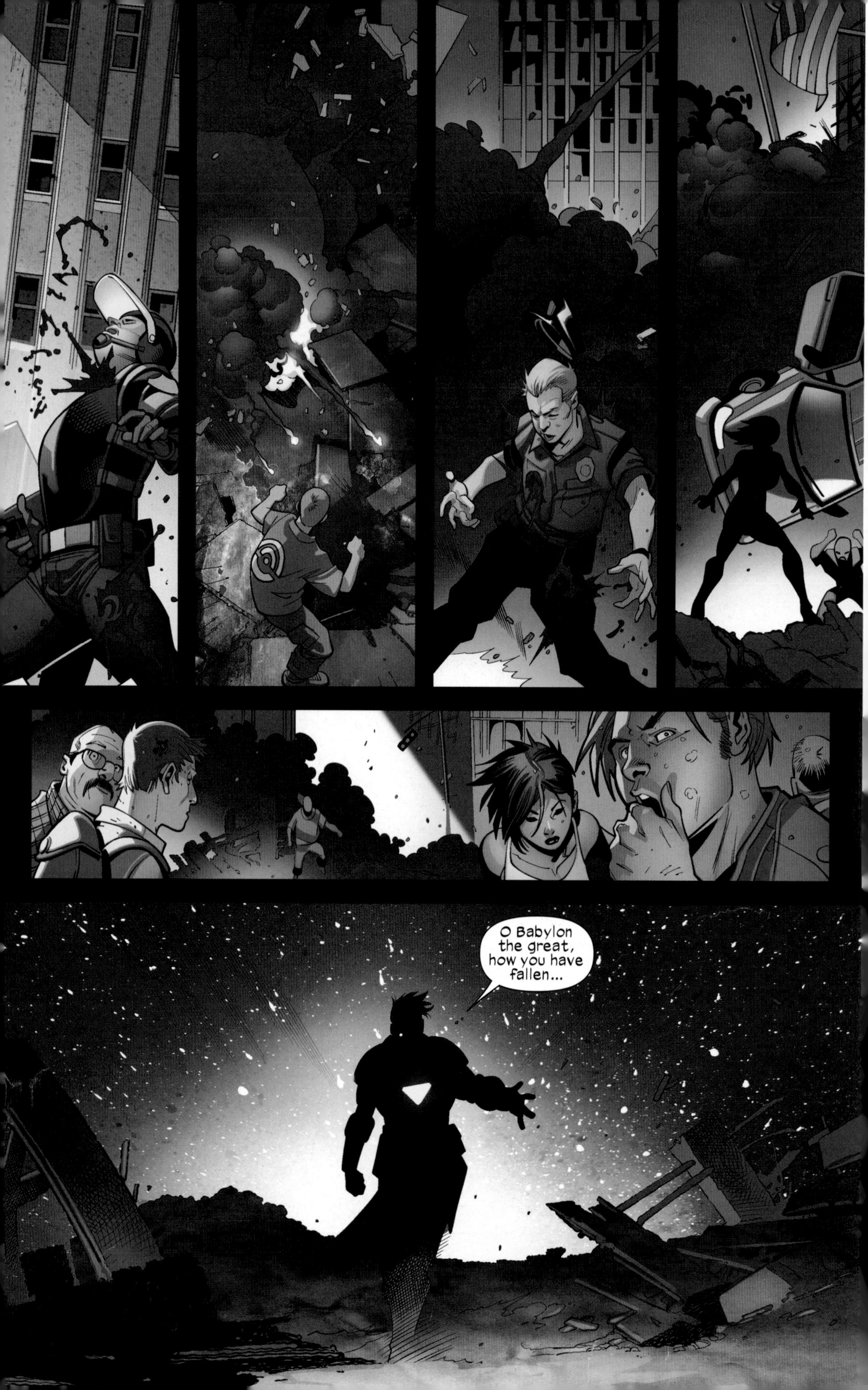
O Babylon the great, how you have fallen...

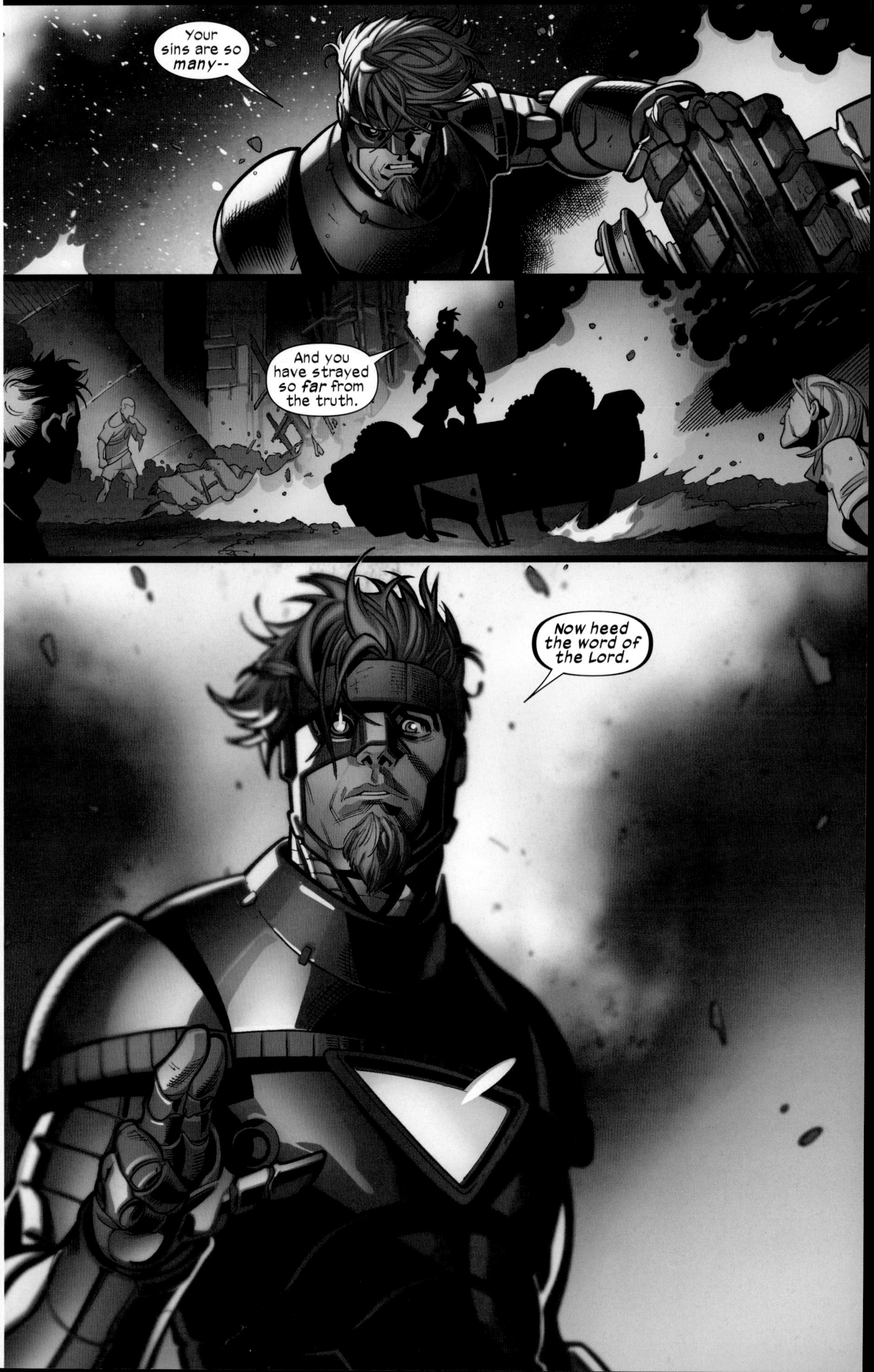
Your sins are so *many*--
And you have strayed so *far* from the truth.
Now heed the word of the Lord.

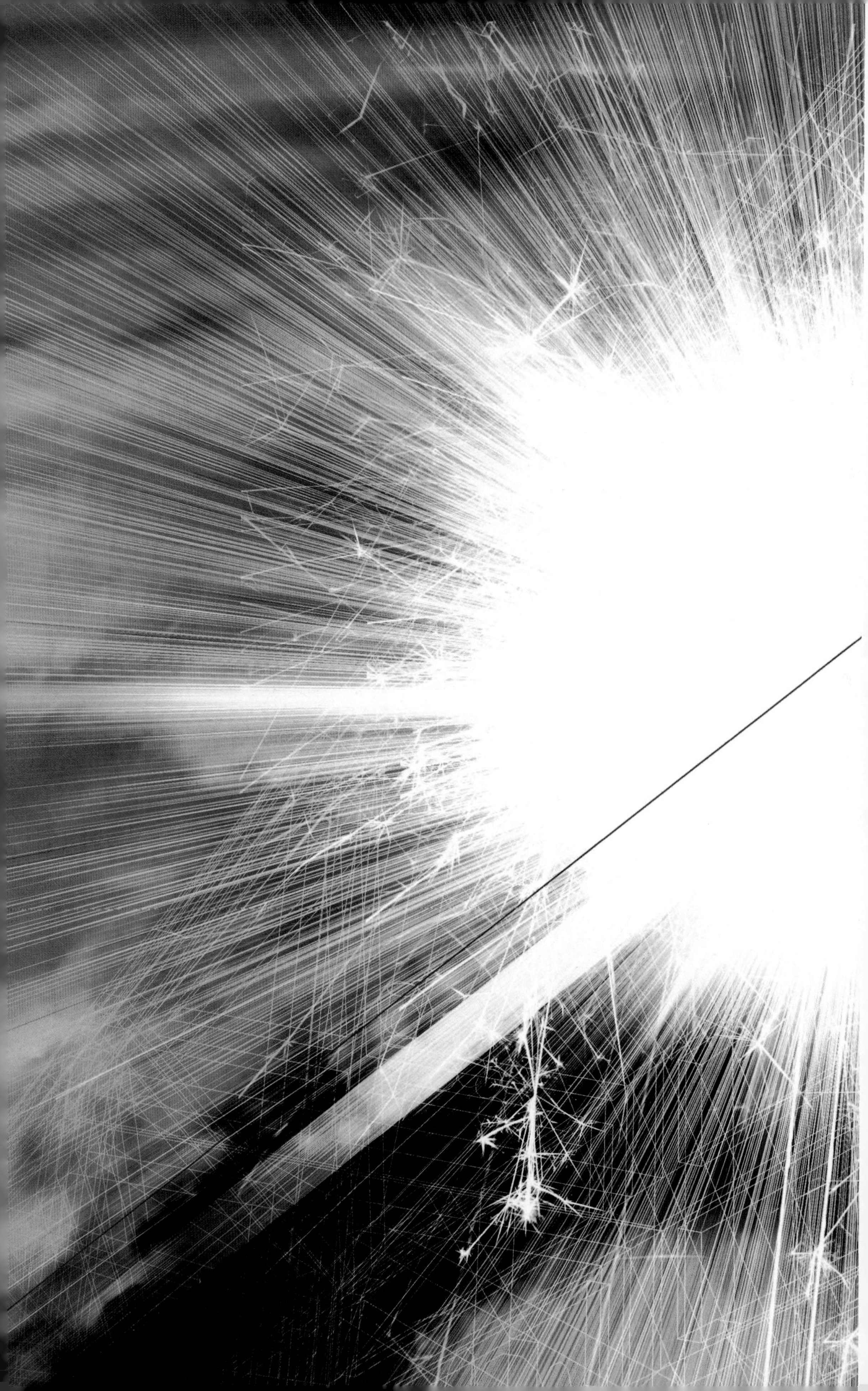

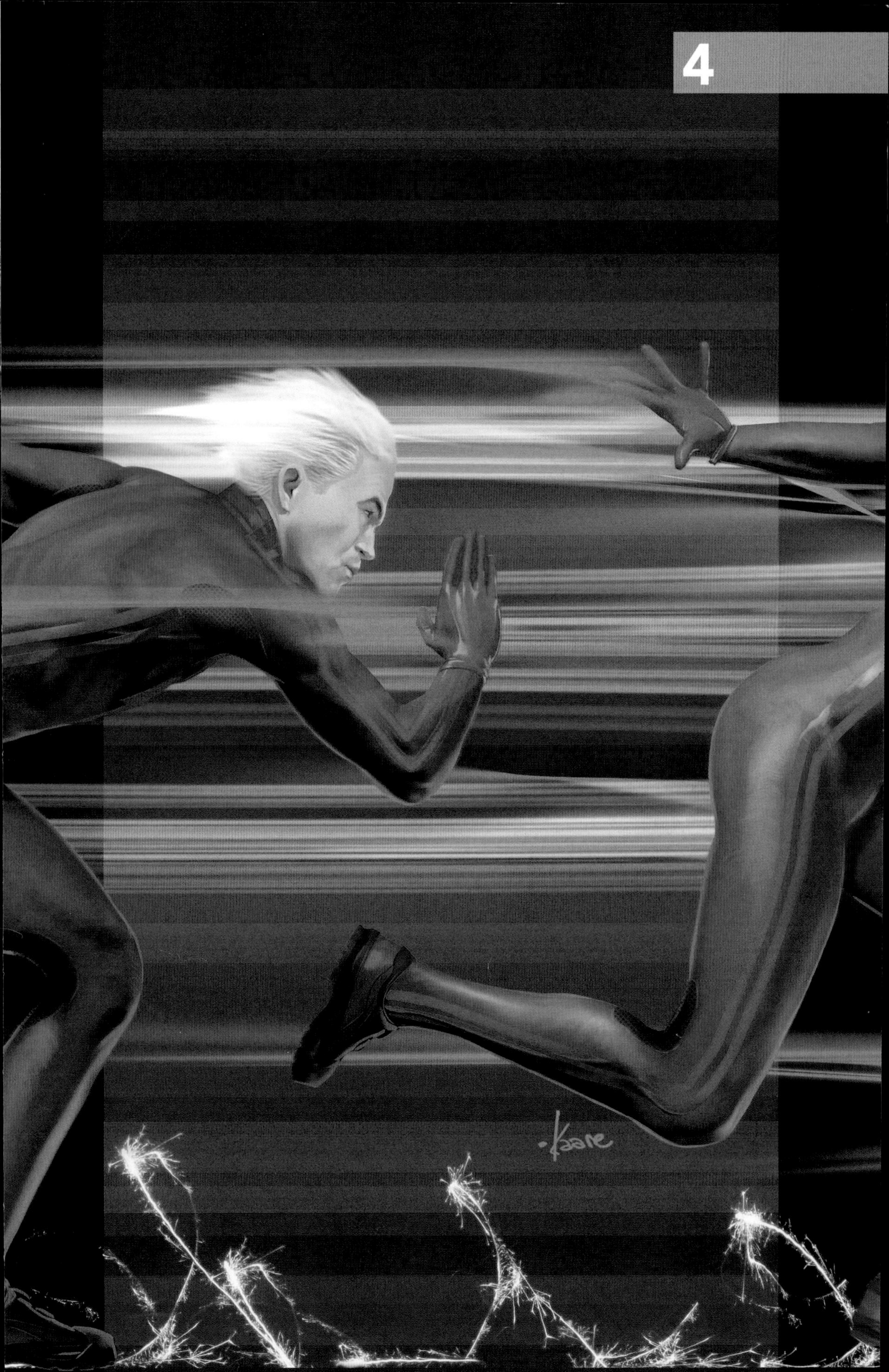
4

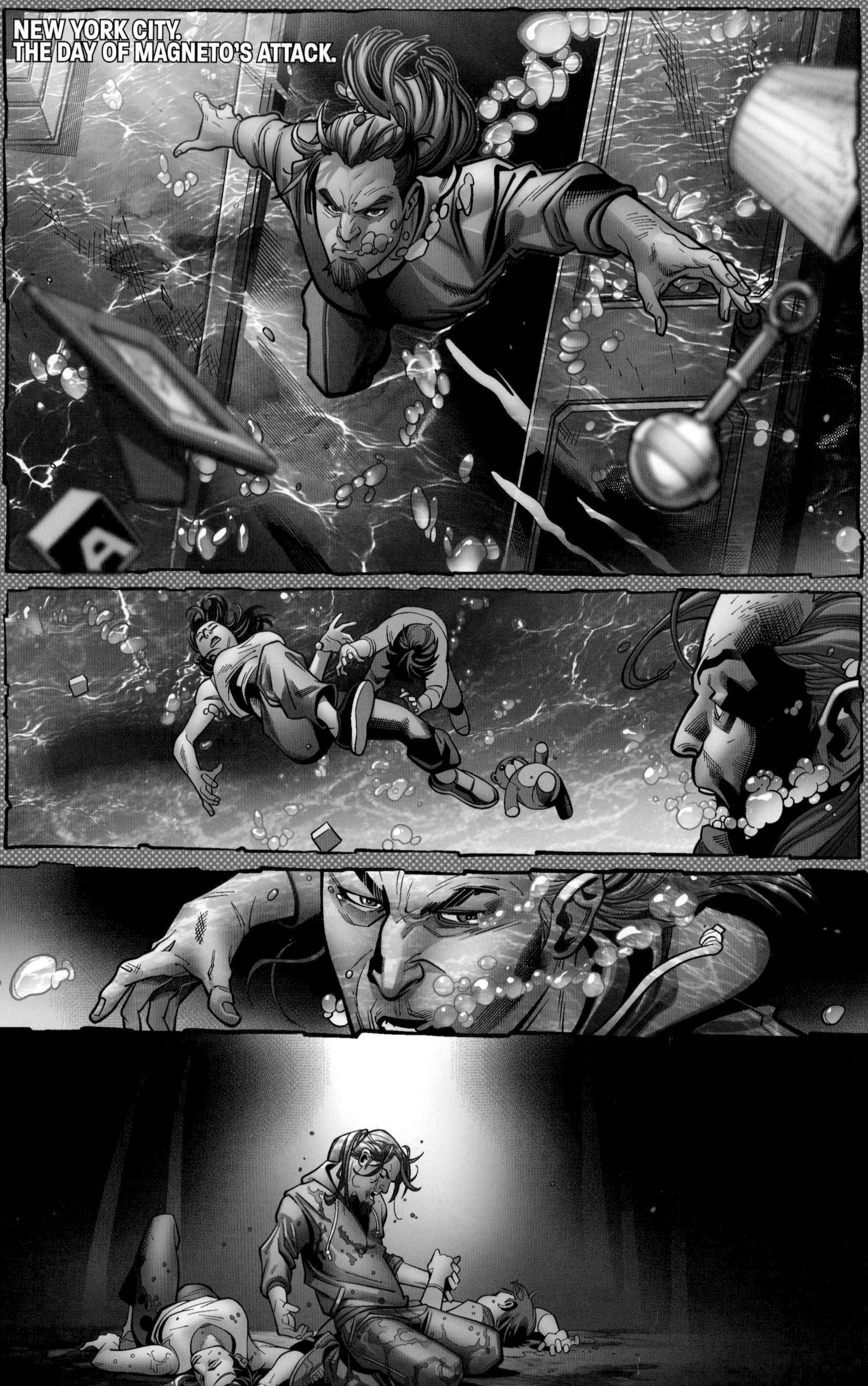
NEW YORK CITY.
THE DAY OF MAGNETO'S ATTACK.

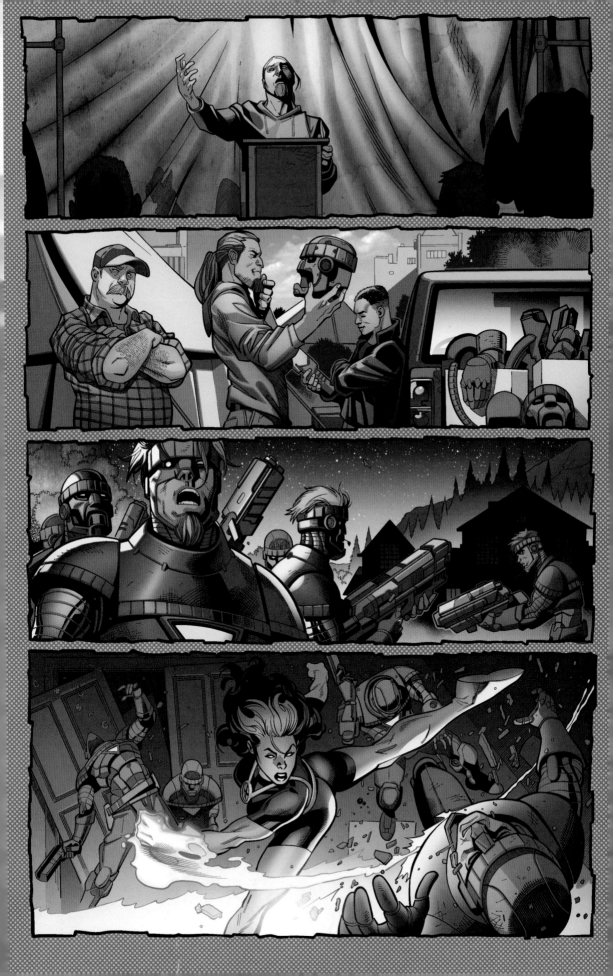

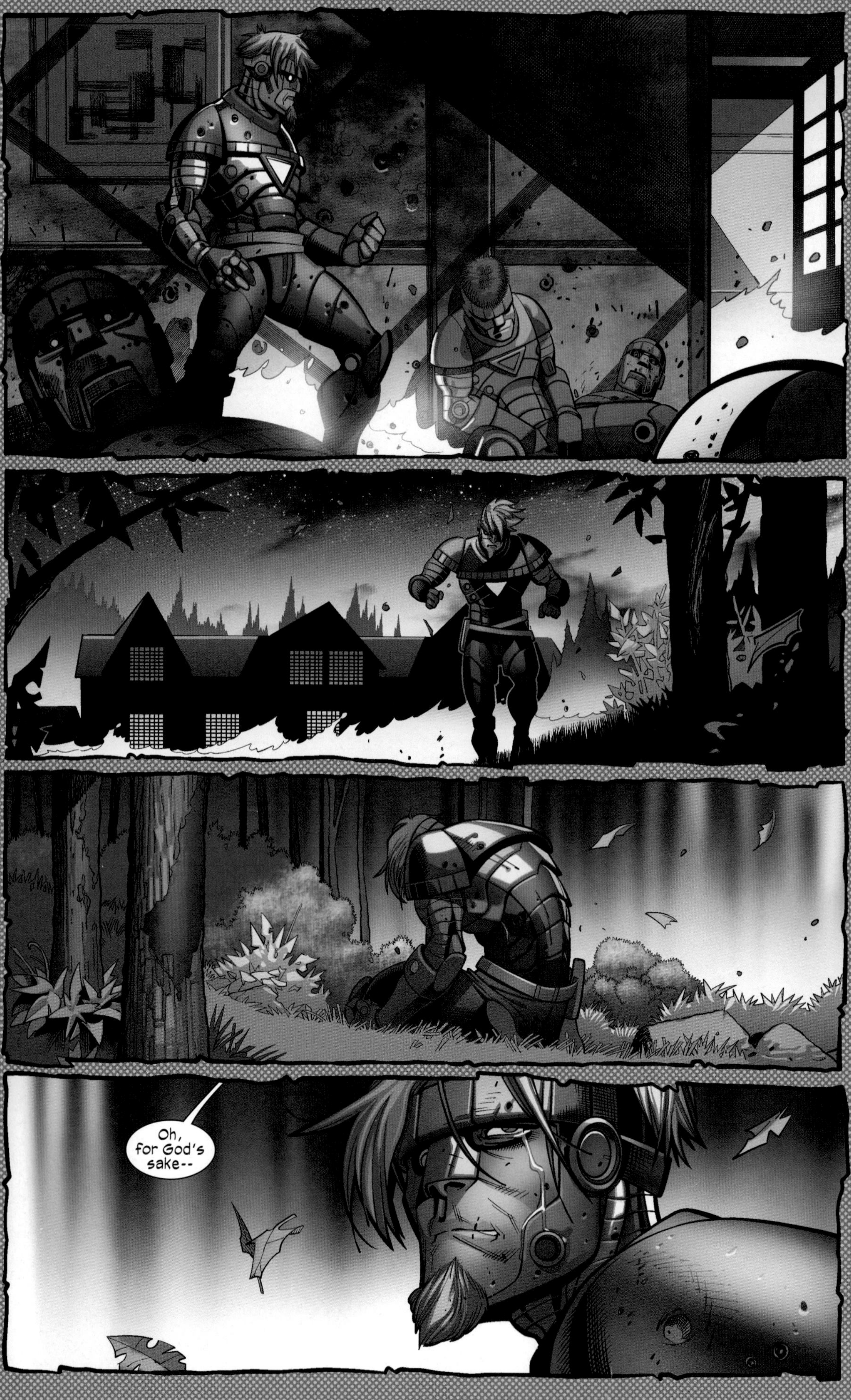
Oh, for God's sake--

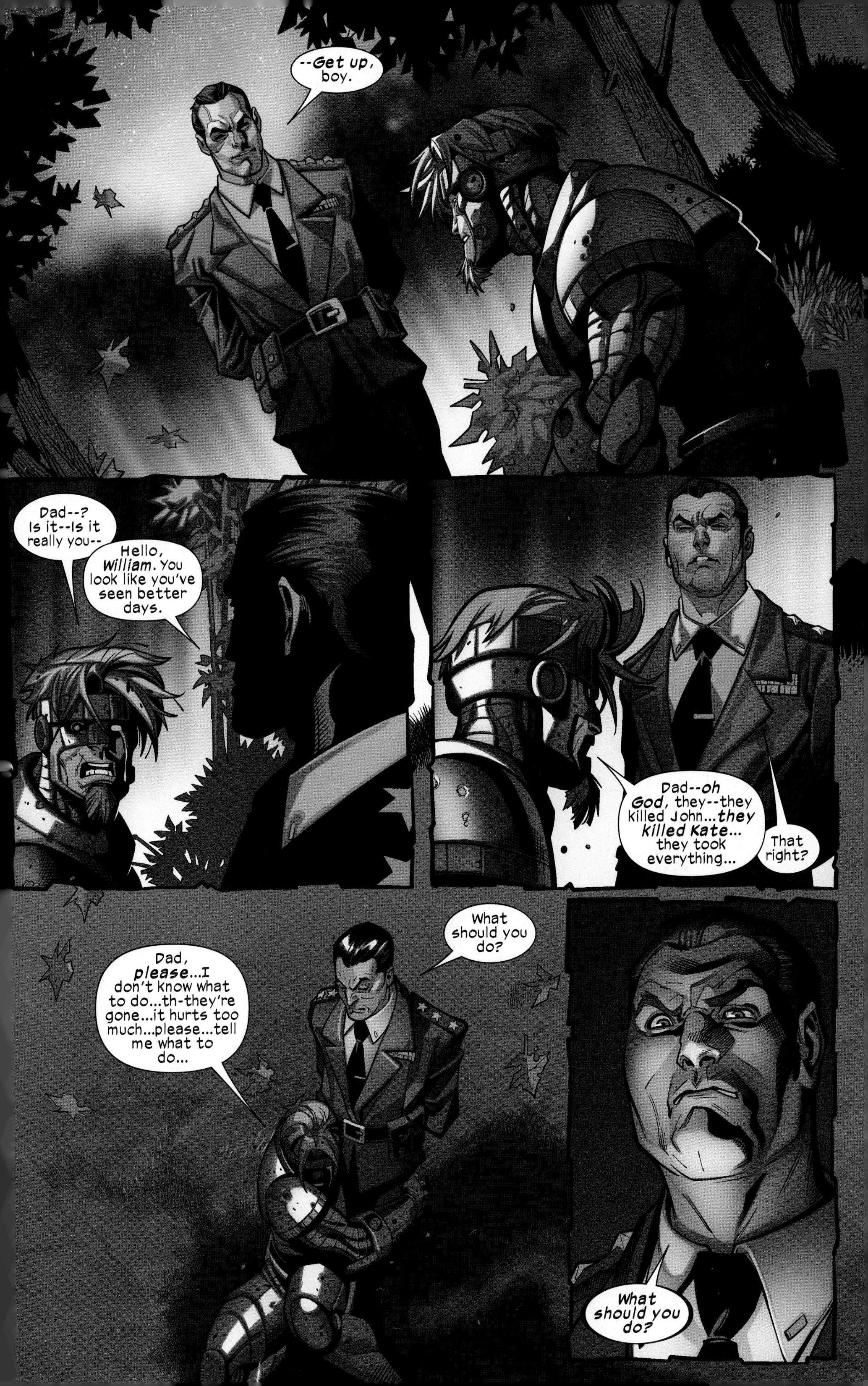
--Get up, boy.
Dad--? Is it--Is it really you--
Hello, William. You look like you've seen better days.
Dad--oh God, they--they killed John...they killed Kate... they took everything...
That right?
Dad, please...I don't know what to do...th-they're gone...it hurts too much...please...tell me what to do...
What should you do?
What should you do?

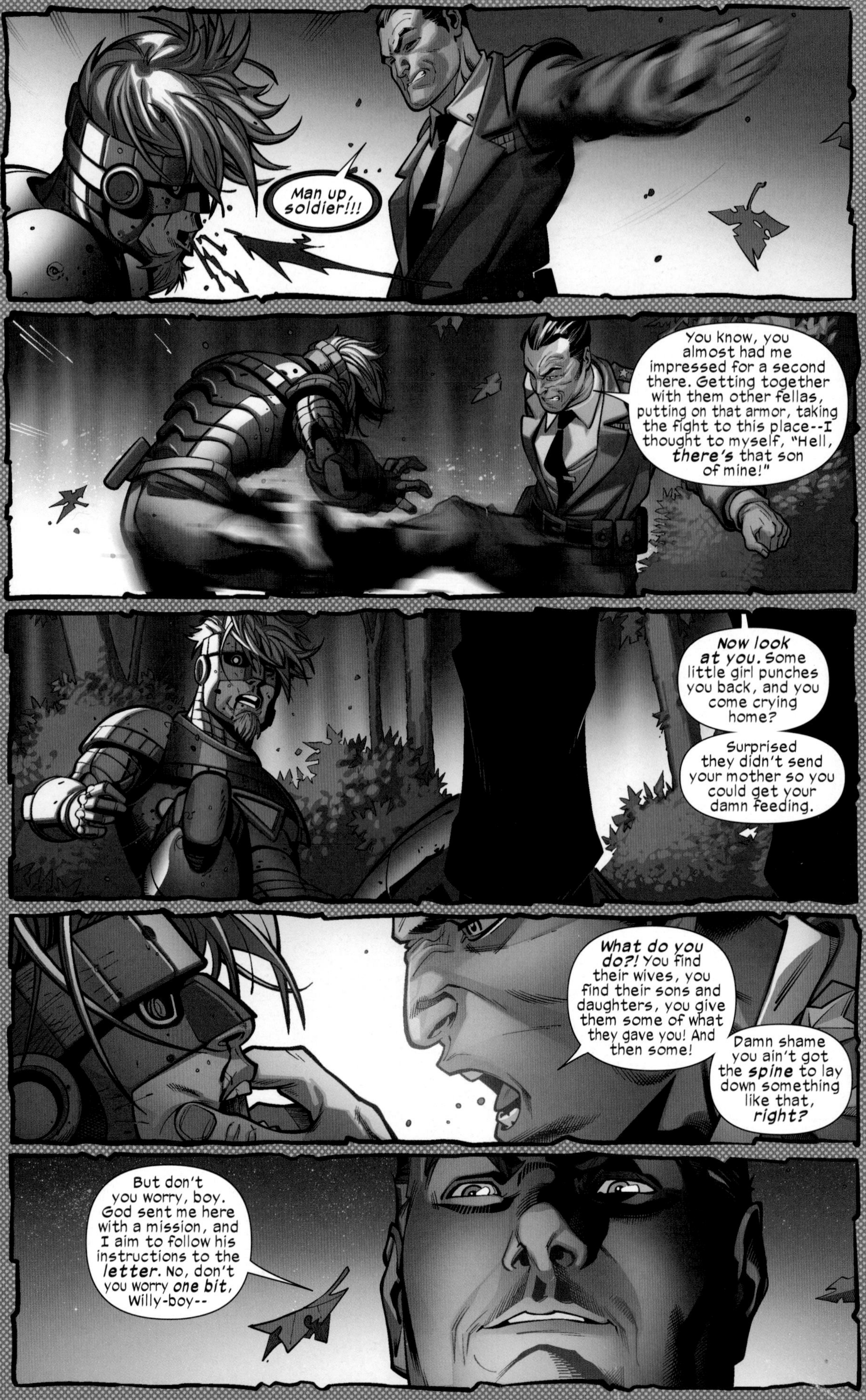
Man up, soldier!!!
You know, you almost had me impressed for a second there. Getting together with them other fellas, putting on that armor, taking the fight to this place--I thought to myself, "Hell, there's that son of mine!"
Now look at you. Some little girl punches you back, and you come crying home?
Surprised they didn't send your mother so you could get your damn feeding.
What do you do?! You find their wives, you find their sons and daughters, you give them some of what they gave you! And then some!
Damn shame you ain't got the spine to lay down something like that, right?
But don't you worry, boy. God sent me here with a mission, and I aim to follow his instructions to the letter. No, don't you worry one bit, Willy-boy--

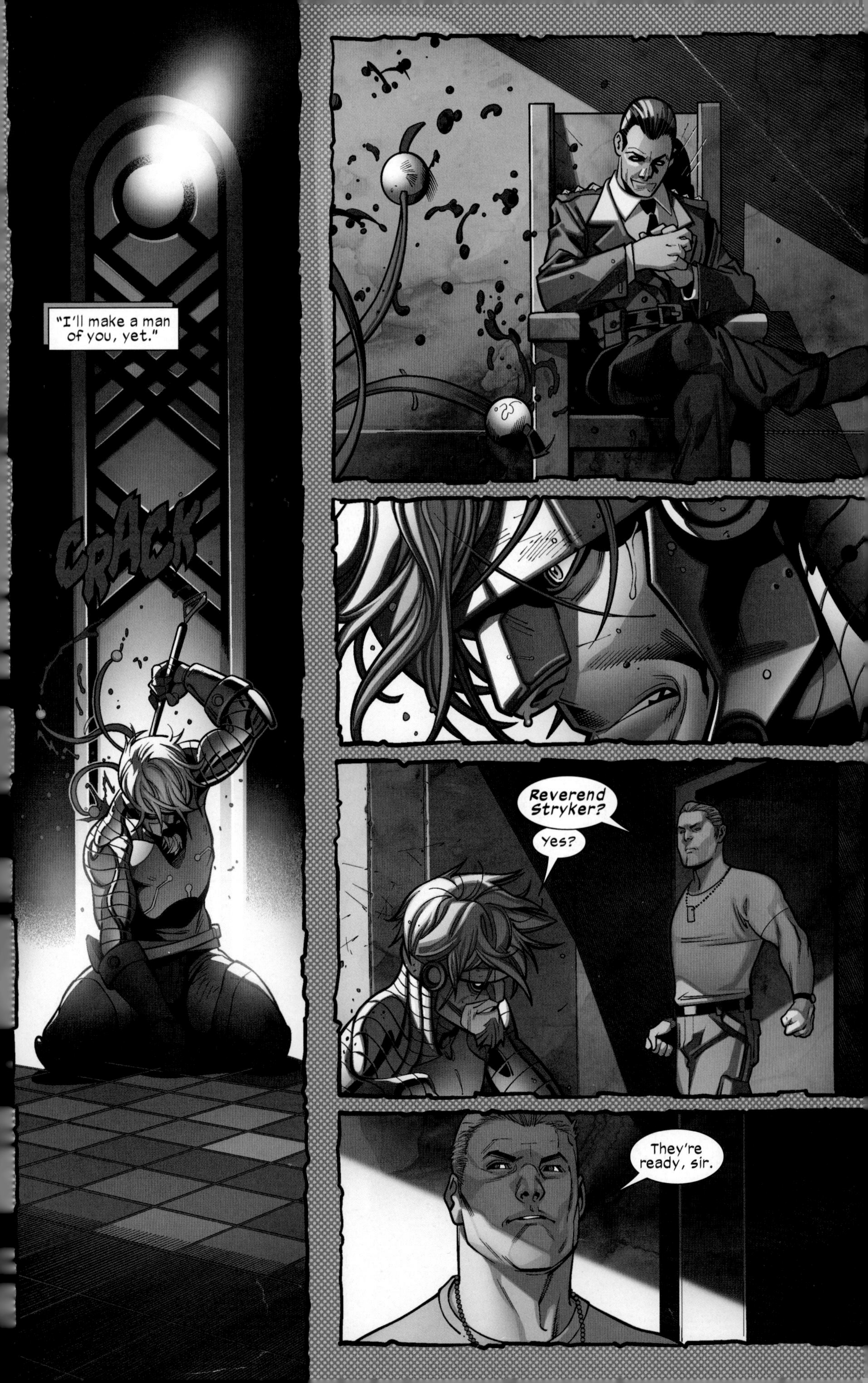

"I'll make a man of you, yet."
CRACK
Reverend Stryker?
Yes?
They're ready, sir.

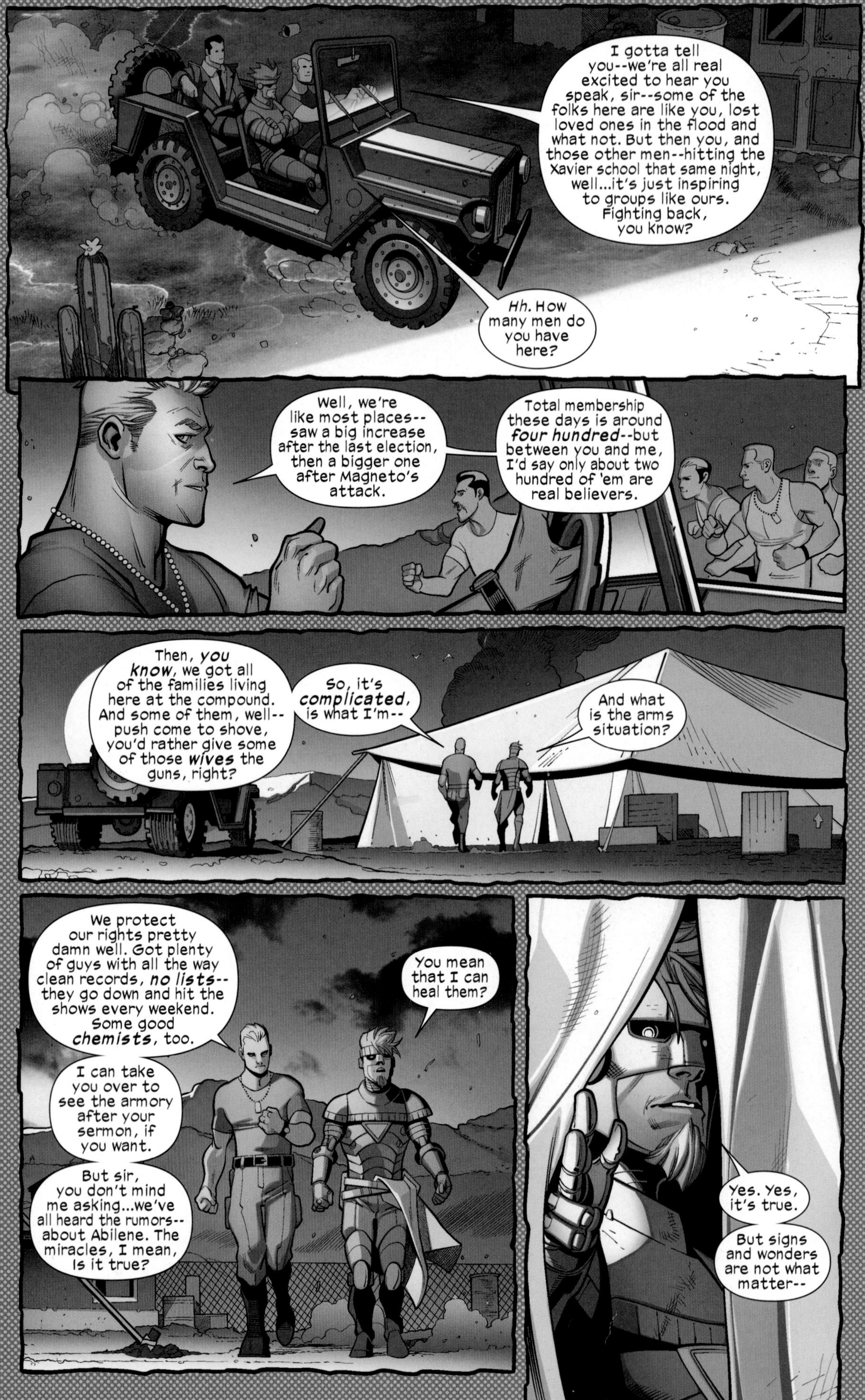
I gotta tell you--we're all real excited to hear you speak, sir--some of the folks here are like you, lost loved ones in the flood and what not. But then you, and those other men--hitting the Xavier school that same night, well...it's just inspiring to groups like ours. Fighting back, you know?
Hh. How many men do you have here?
Well, we're like most places--saw a big increase after the last election, then a bigger one after Magneto's attack.
Total membership these days is around four hundred--but between you and me, I'd say only about two hundred of 'em are real believers.
Then, you know, we got all of the families living here at the compound. And some of them, well--push come to shove, you'd rather give some of those wives the guns, right?
So, it's complicated, is what I'm--
And what is the arms situation?
We protect our rights pretty damn well. Got plenty of guys with all the way clean records, no lists--they go down and hit the shows every weekend. Some good chemists, too.
I can take you over to see the armory after your sermon, if you want.
But sir, you don't mind me asking...we've all heard the rumors--about Abilene. The miracles, I mean, Is it true?
You mean that I can heal them?
Yes. Yes, it's true.
But signs and wonders are not what matter--

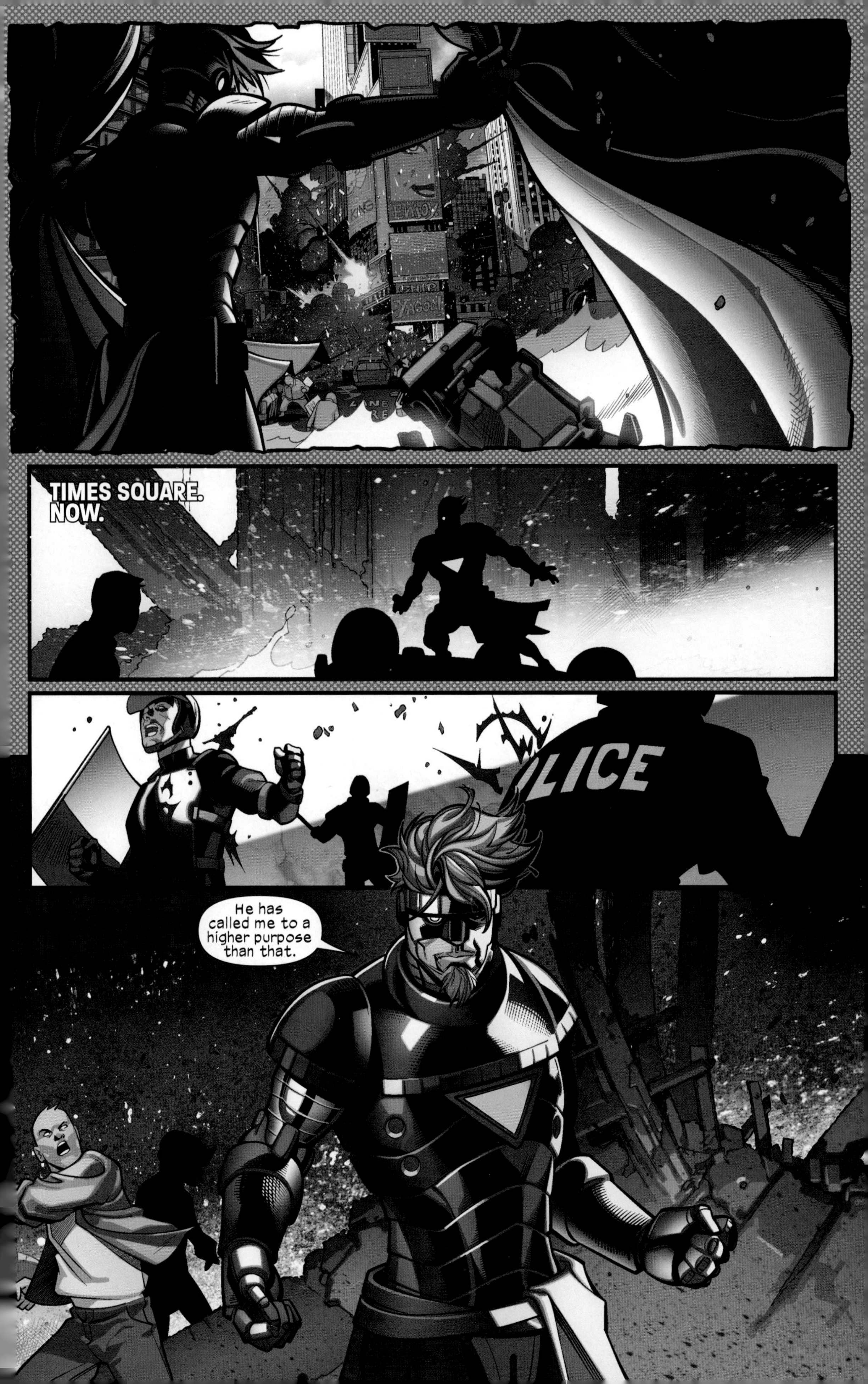
TIMES SQUARE.
NOW.
LICE
He has called me to a higher purpose than that.

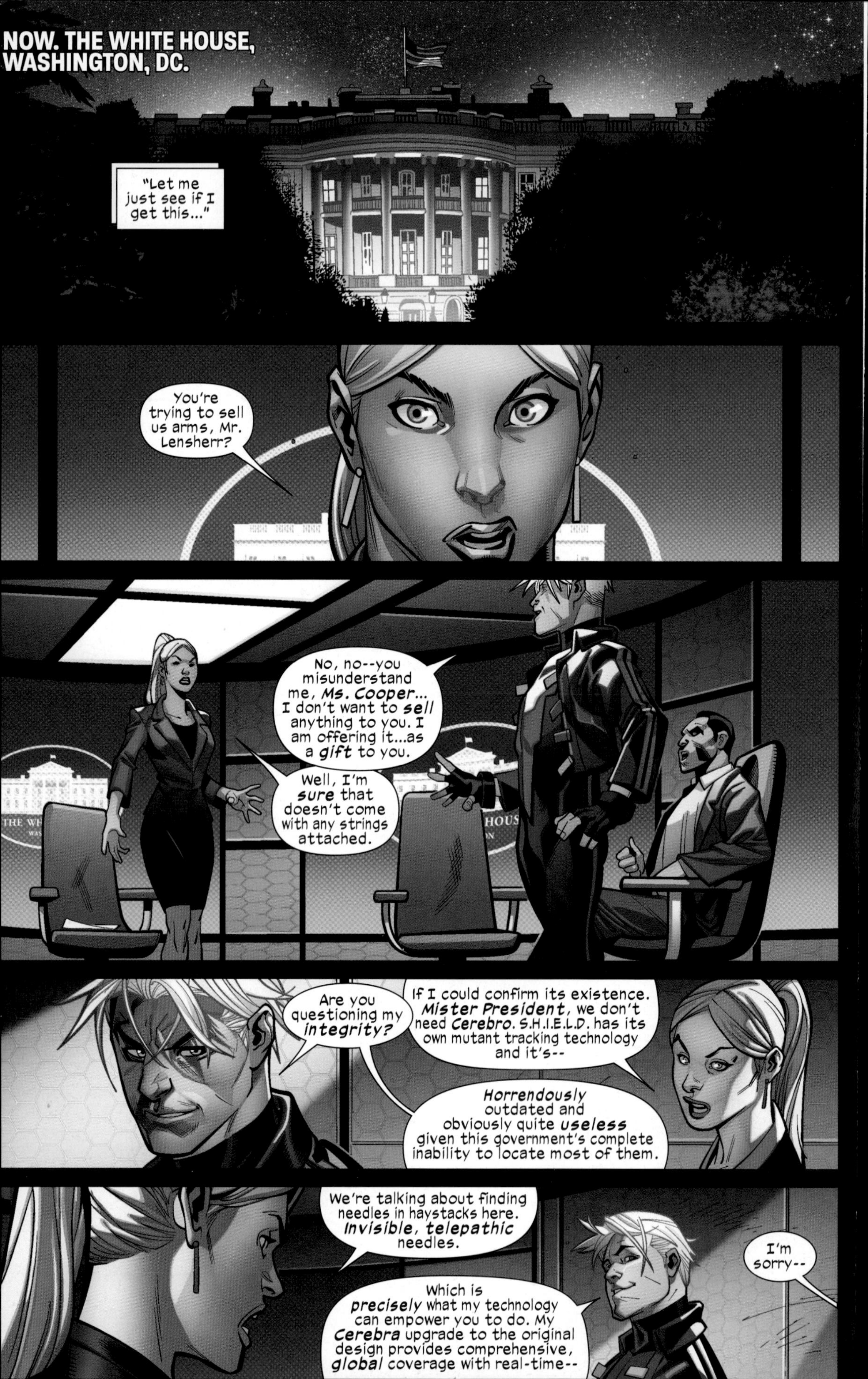
NOW. THE WHITE HOUSE, WASHINGTON, DC.
"Let me just see if I get this..."
You're trying to sell us arms, Mr. Lensherr?
No, no--you misunderstand me, Ms. Cooper... I don't want to sell anything to you. I am offering it...as a gift to you.
Well, I'm sure that doesn't come with any strings attached.
Are you questioning my integrity?
If I could confirm its existence. Mister President, we don't need Cerebro. S.H.I.E.L.D. has its own mutant tracking technology and it's--
Horrendously outdated and obviously quite useless given this government's complete inability to locate most of them.
We're talking about finding needles in haystacks here. Invisible, telepathic needles.
I'm sorry--
Which is precisely what my technology can empower you to do. My Cerebra upgrade to the original design provides comprehensive, global coverage with real-time--

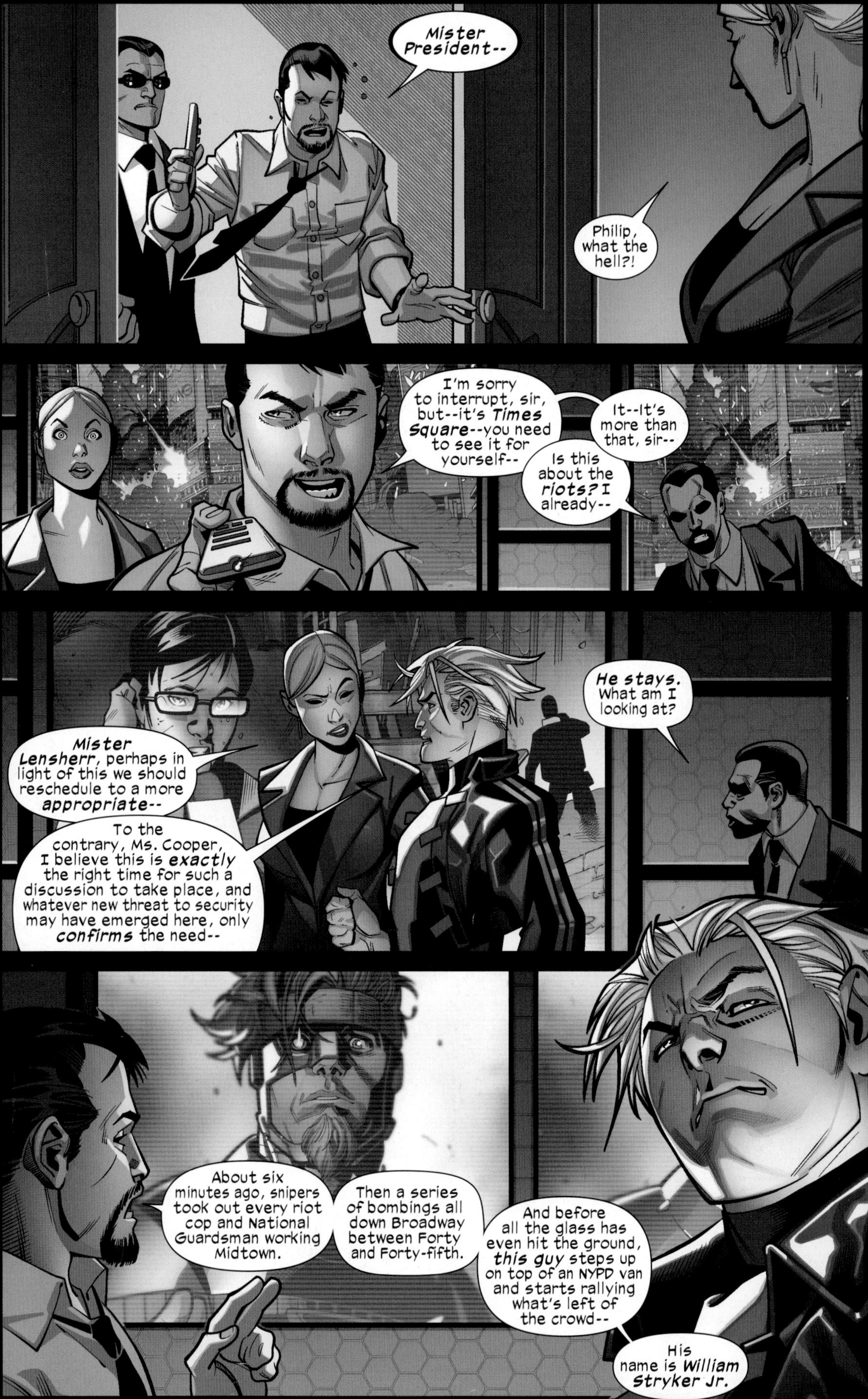
Mister President--
Philip, what the hell?!
I'm sorry to interrupt, sir, but--it's Times Square--you need to see it for yourself--
Is this about the riots? I already--
It--It's more than that, sir--
He stays. What am I looking at?
Mister Lensherr, perhaps in light of this we should reschedule to a more appropriate--
To the contrary, Ms. Cooper, I believe this is exactly the right time for such a discussion to take place, and whatever new threat to security may have emerged here, only confirms the need--
About six minutes ago, snipers took out every riot cop and National Guardsman working Midtown.
Then a series of bombings all down Broadway between Forty and Forty-fifth.
And before all the glass has even hit the ground, this guy steps up on top of an NYPD van and starts rallying what's left of the crowd--
His name is William Stryker Jr.

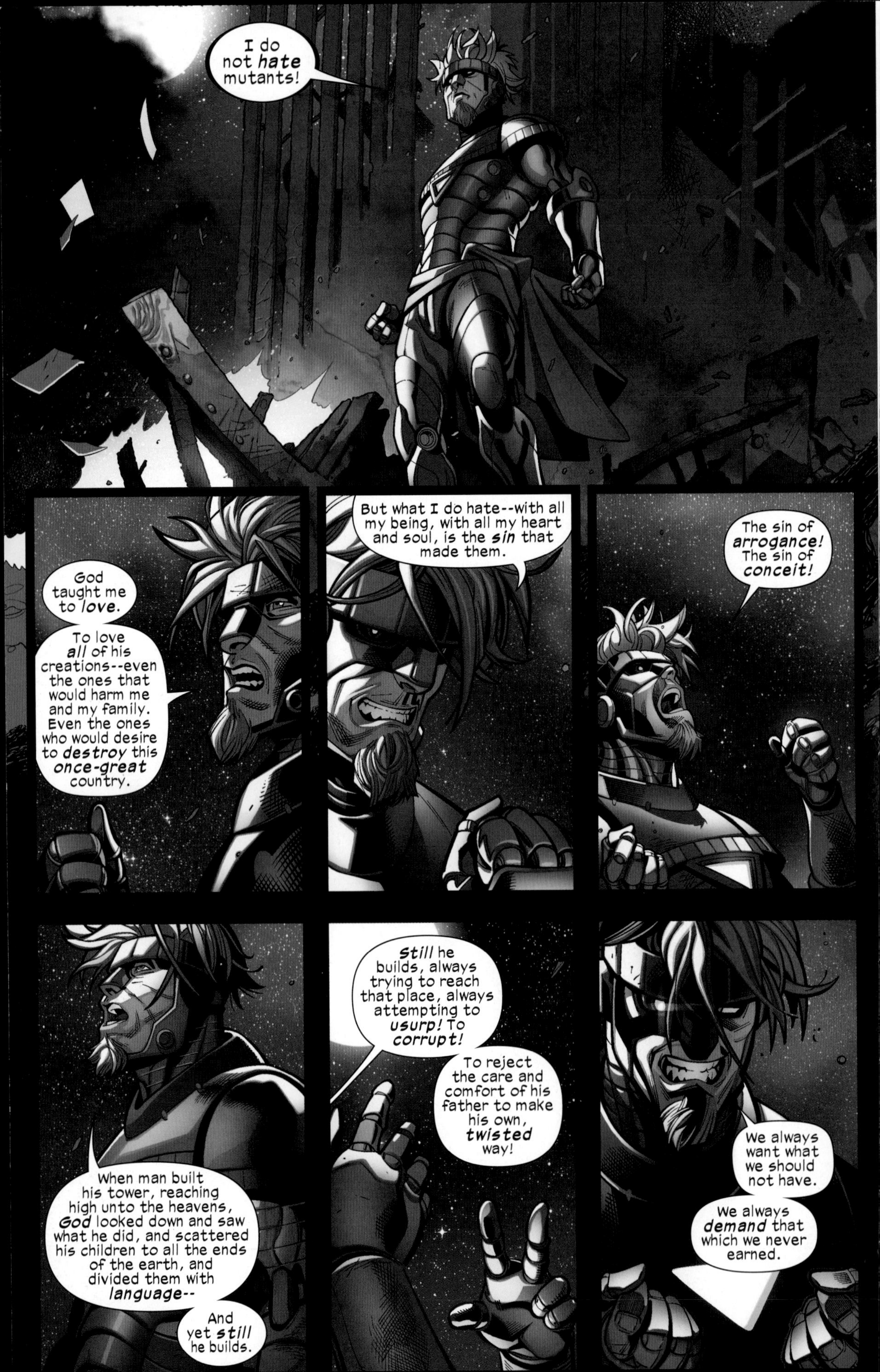
I do not *hate* mutants!
God taught me to *love*.
To love *all* of his creations--even the ones that would harm me and my family. Even the ones who would desire to *destroy* this *once-great* country.
But what I do hate--with all my being, with all my heart and soul, is the *sin* that made them.
The sin of *arrogance!* The sin of *conceit!*
When man built his tower, reaching high unto the heavens, *God* looked down and saw what he did, and scattered his children to all the ends of the earth, and divided them with *language*--
And yet *still* he builds.
Still he builds, always trying to reach that place, always attempting to *usurp!* To *corrupt!*
To reject the care and comfort of his father to make his own, *twisted* way!
We always want what we should not have.
We always *demand* that which we never earned.

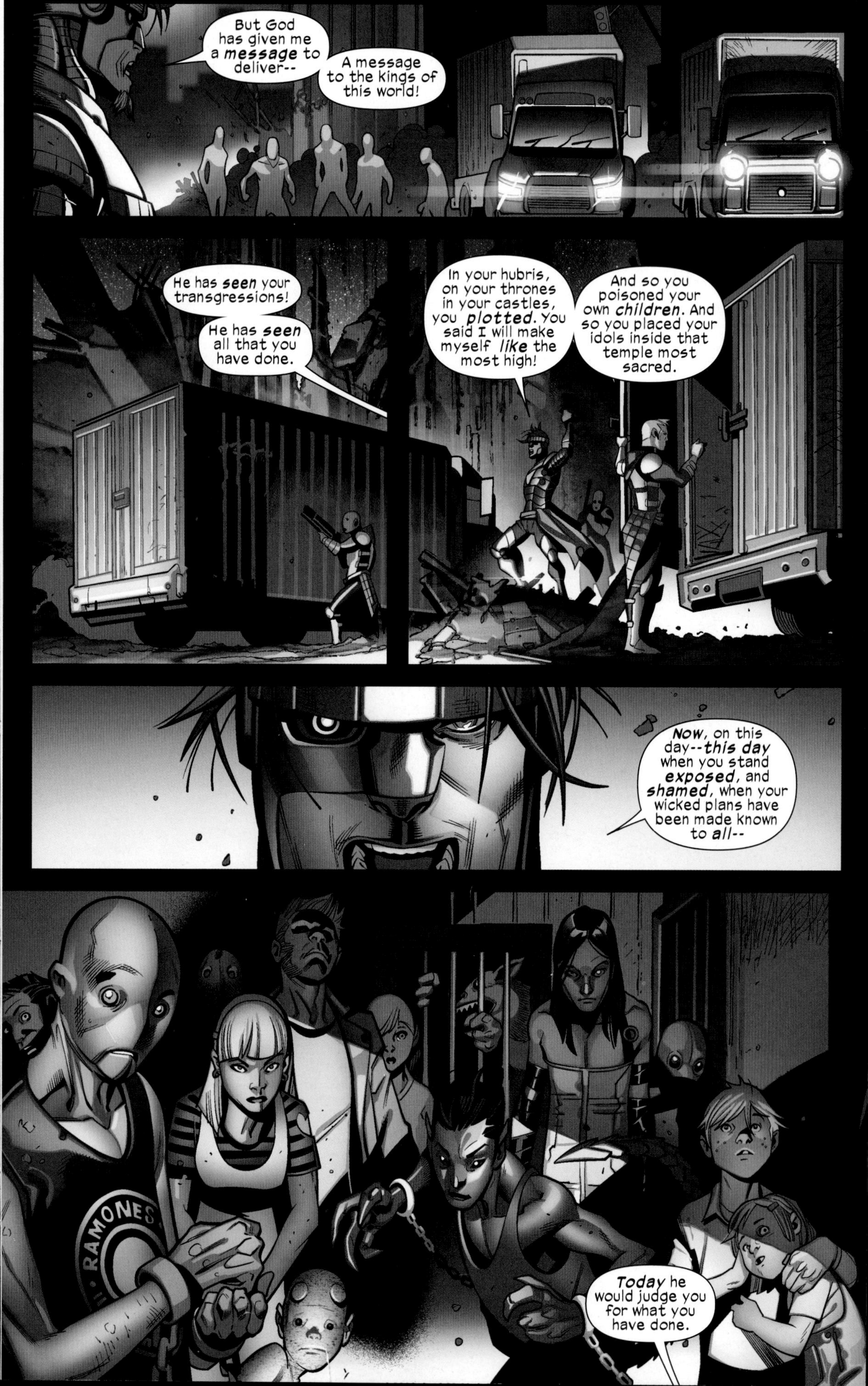

But God has given me a *message* to deliver--
A message to the kings of this world!
He has *seen* your transgressions!
He has *seen* all that you have done.
In your hubris, on your thrones in your castles, you *plotted*. You said I will make myself *like* the most high!
And so you poisoned your own *children*. And so you placed your idols inside that temple most sacred.
Now, on this day--*this day* when you stand *exposed*, and *shamed*, when your wicked plans have been made known to *all*--
RAMONES
Today he would judge you for what you have done.

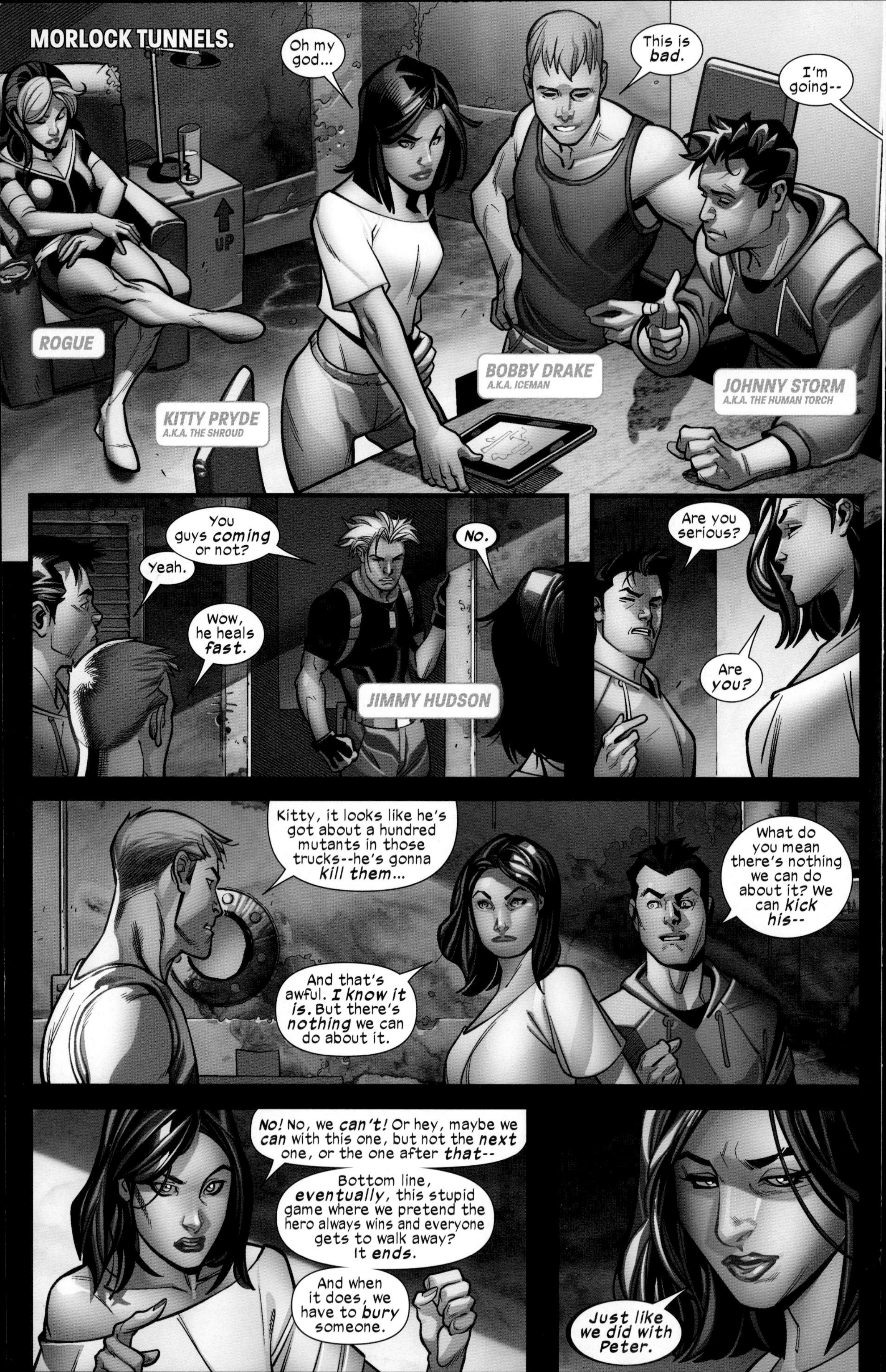

MORLOCK TUNNELS.
Oh my god...
This is bad.
I'm going--
ROGUE
KITTY PRYDE
A.K.A. THE SHROUD
BOBBY DRAKE
A.K.A. ICEMAN
JOHNNY STORM
A.K.A. THE HUMAN TORCH
You guys coming or not?
Yeah.
Wow, he heals fast.
No.
JIMMY HUDSON
Are you serious?
Are you?
Kitty, it looks like he's got about a hundred mutants in those trucks--he's gonna kill them...
And that's awful. I know it is. But there's nothing we can do about it.
What do you mean there's nothing we can do about it? We can kick his--
No! No, we can't! Or hey, maybe we can with this one, but not the next one, or the one after that--
Bottom line, eventually, this stupid game where we pretend the hero always wins and everyone gets to walk away? It ends.
And when it does, we have to bury someone.
Just like we did with Peter.

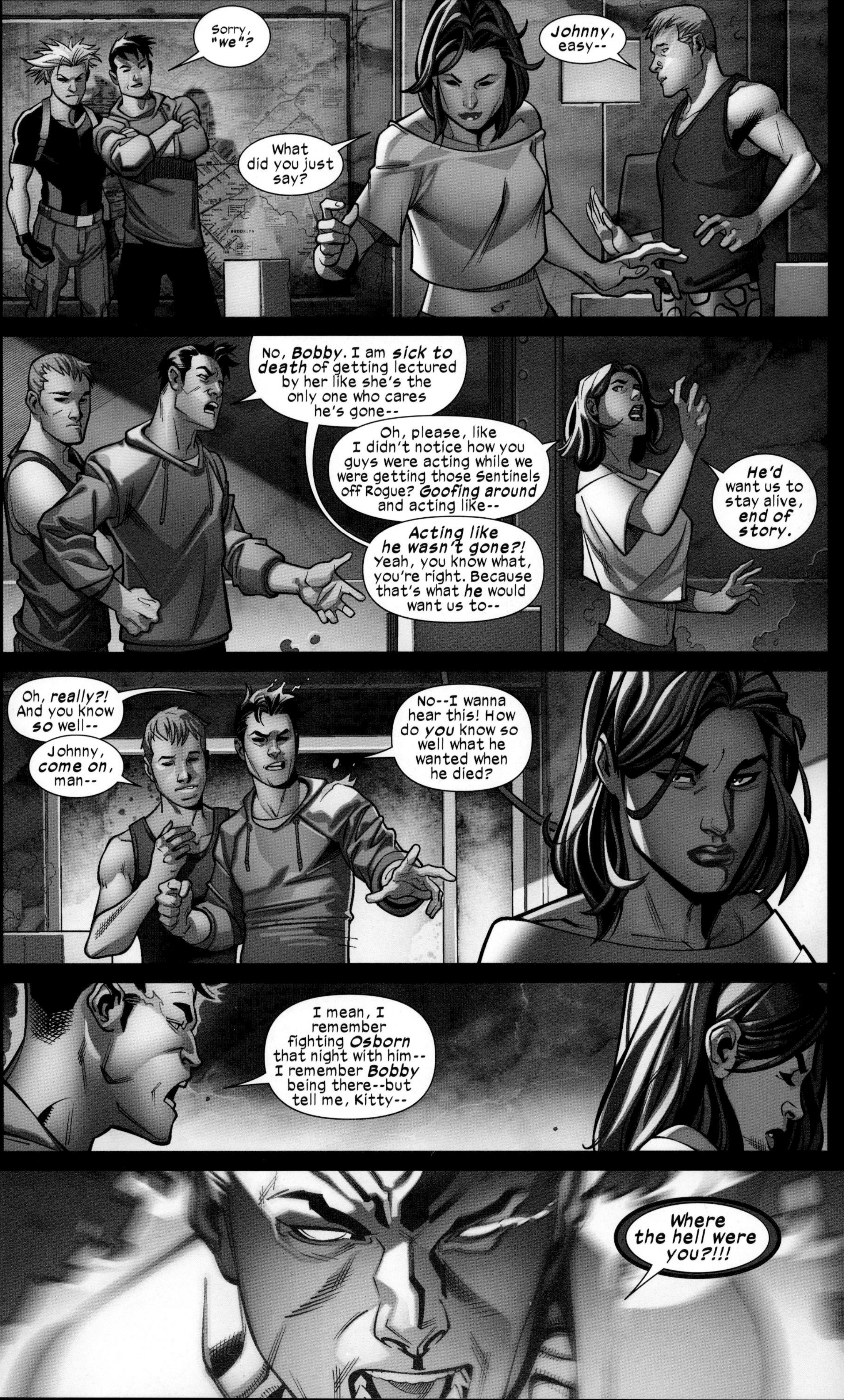

Sorry, "we"?
What did you just say?
Johnny, easy--
No, Bobby. I am sick to death of getting lectured by her like she's the only one who cares he's gone--
Oh, please, like I didn't notice how you guys were acting while we were getting those Sentinels off Rogue? Goofing around and acting like--
Acting like he wasn't gone?! Yeah, you know what, you're right. Because that's what he would want us to--
He'd want us to stay alive, end of story.
Oh, really?! And you know so well--
Johnny, come on, man--
No--I wanna hear this! How do you know so well what he wanted when he died?
I mean, I remember fighting Osborn that night with him--I remember Bobby being there--but tell me, Kitty--
Where the hell were you?!!!

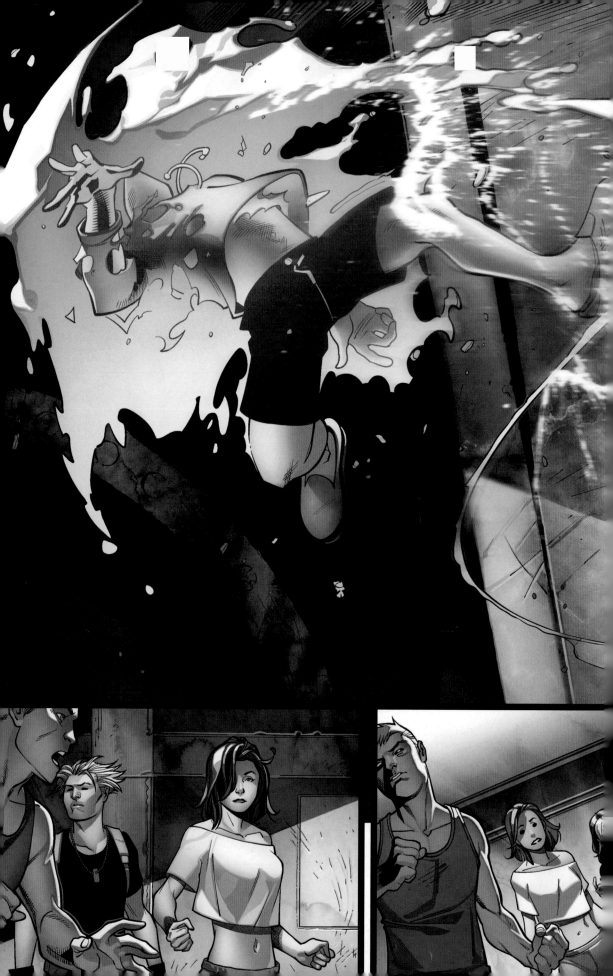

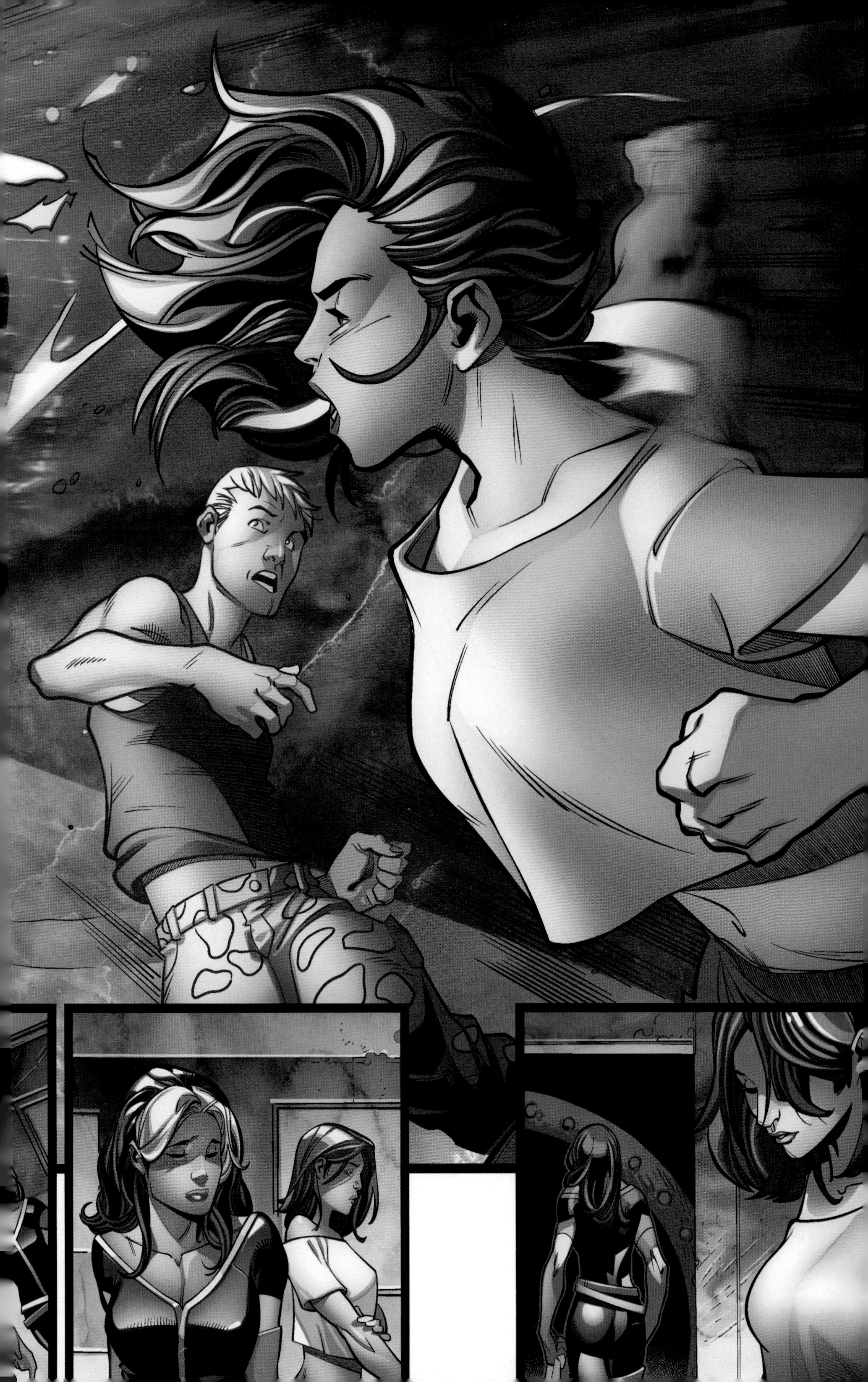

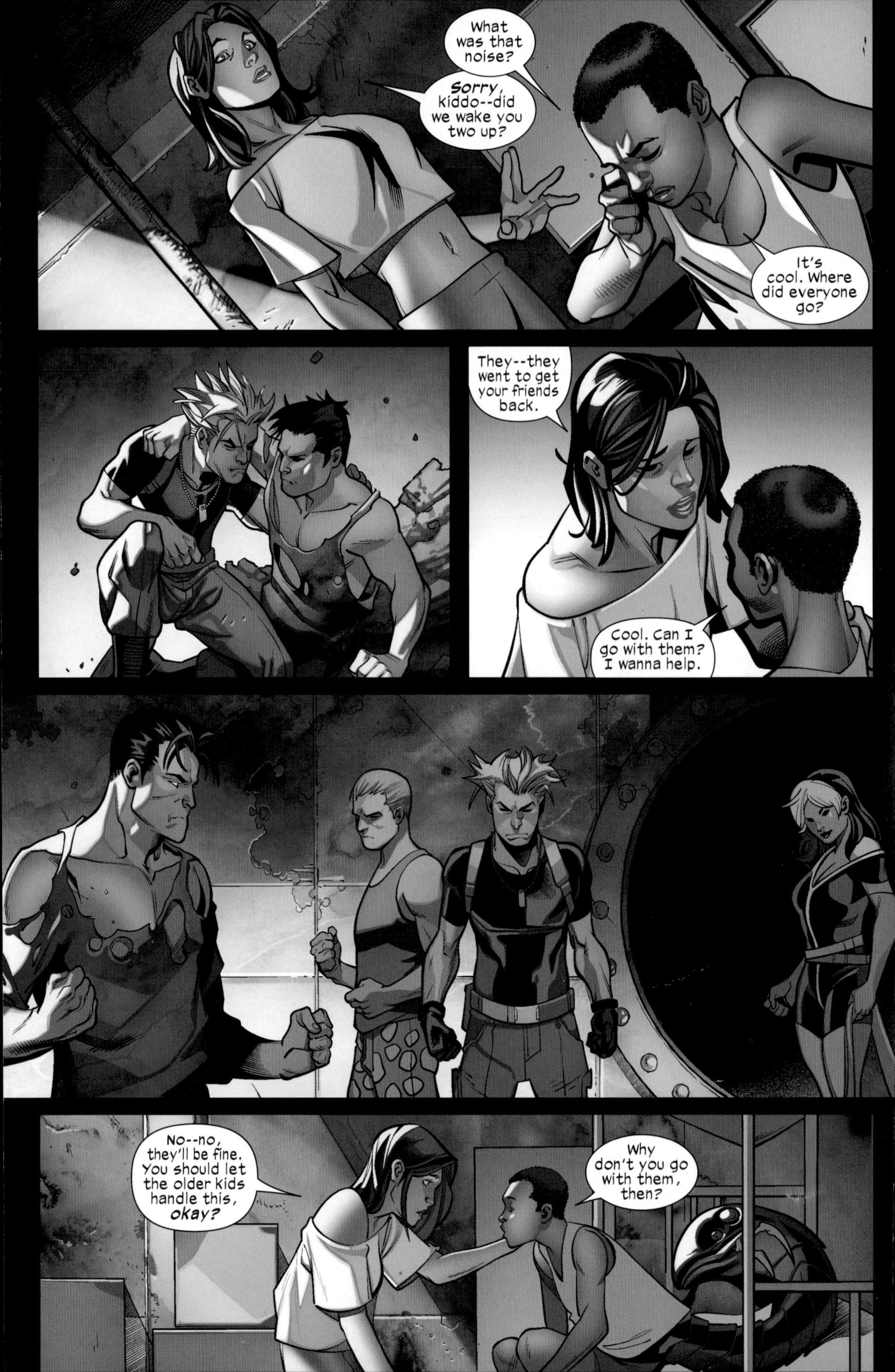
What was that noise?
Sorry, kiddo--did we wake you two up?
It's cool. Where did everyone go?
They--they went to get your friends back.
Cool. Can I go with them? I wanna help.
No--no, they'll be fine. You should let the older kids handle this, okay?
Why don't you go with them, then?

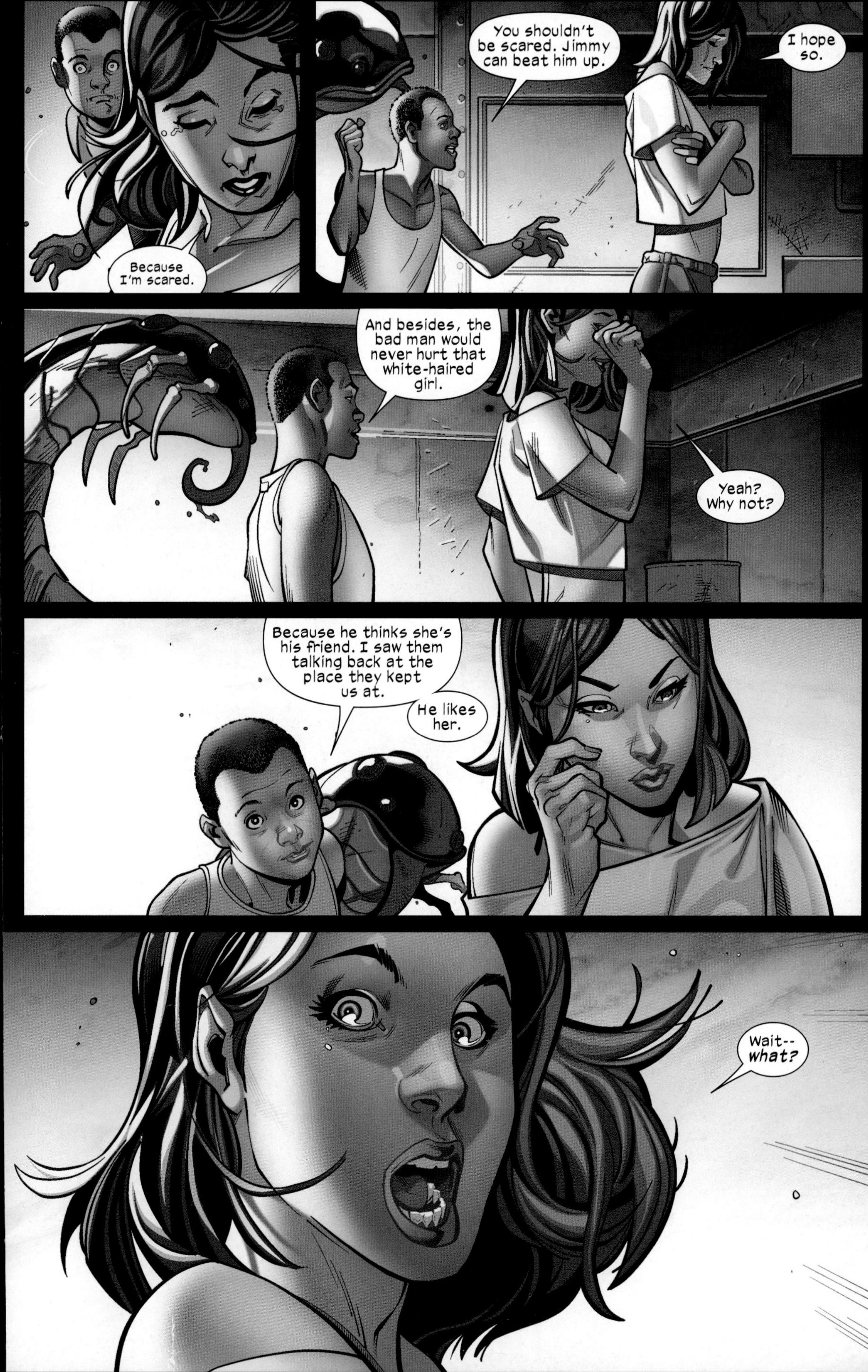

Because I'm scared.
You shouldn't be scared. Jimmy can beat him up.
I hope so.
And besides, the bad man would never hurt that white-haired girl.
Yeah? Why not?
Because he thinks she's his friend. I saw them talking back at the place they kept us at.
He likes her.
Wait-- what?

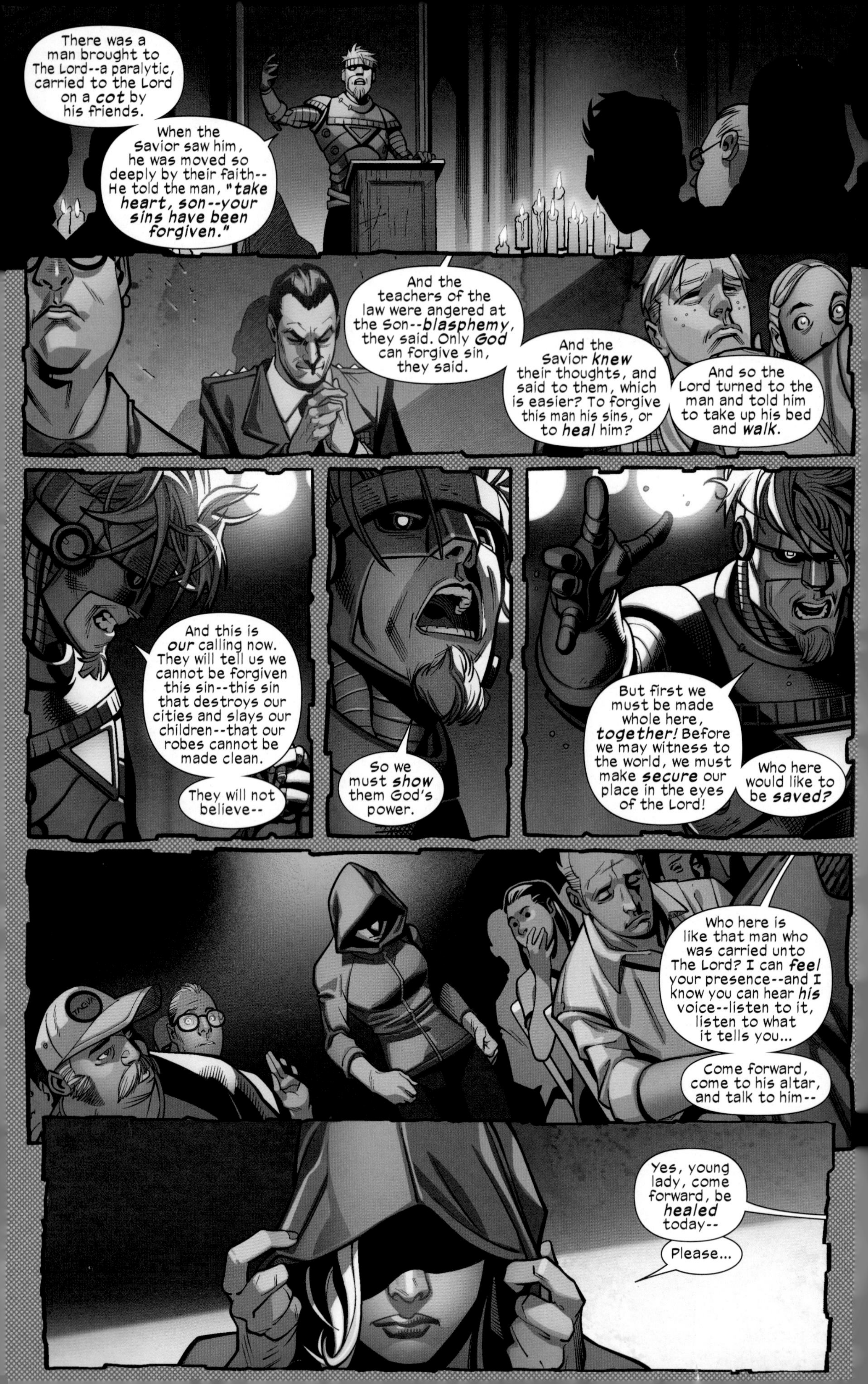
There was a man brought to The Lord--a paralytic, carried to the Lord on a *cot* by his friends.
When the Savior saw him, he was moved so deeply by their faith--He told the man, ***"take heart, son--your sins have been forgiven."***
And the teachers of the law were angered at the Son--*blasphemy*, they said. Only *God* can forgive sin, they said.
And the Savior *knew* their thoughts, and said to them, which is easier? To forgive this man his sins, or to *heal* him?
And so the Lord turned to the man and told him to take up his bed and *walk*.
And this is *our* calling now. They will tell us we cannot be forgiven this sin--this sin that destroys our cities and slays our children--that our robes cannot be made clean.
They will not believe--
So we must *show* them God's power.
But first we must be made whole here, *together!* Before we may witness to the world, we must make *secure* our place in the eyes of the Lord!
Who here would like to be *saved?*
Who here is like that man who was carried unto The Lord? I can *feel* your presence--and I know you can hear *his* voice--listen to it, listen to what it tells you...
Come forward, come to his altar, and talk to him--
Yes, young lady, come forward, be *healed* today--
Please...

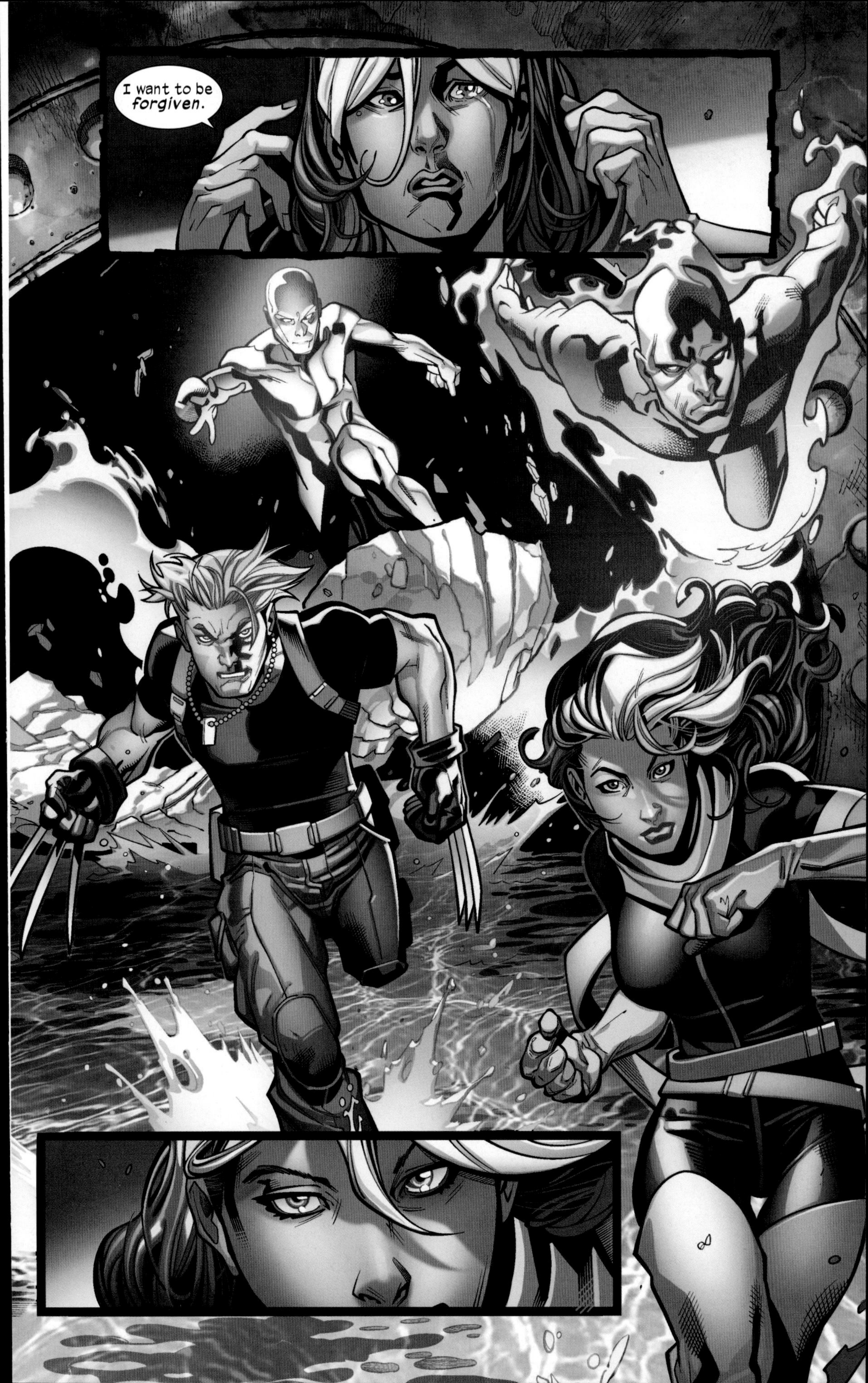
I want to be *forgiven*.

5

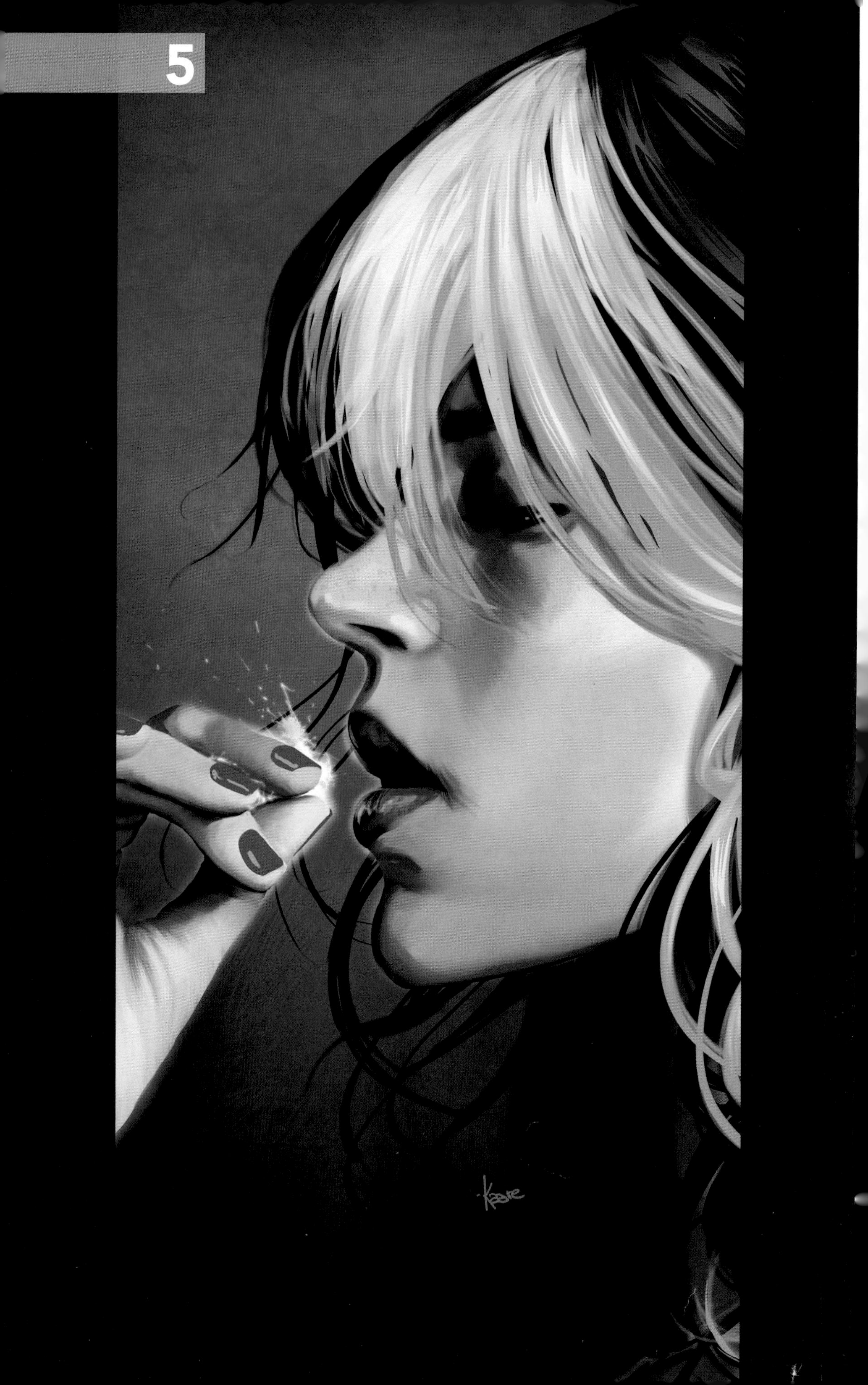
Kaare

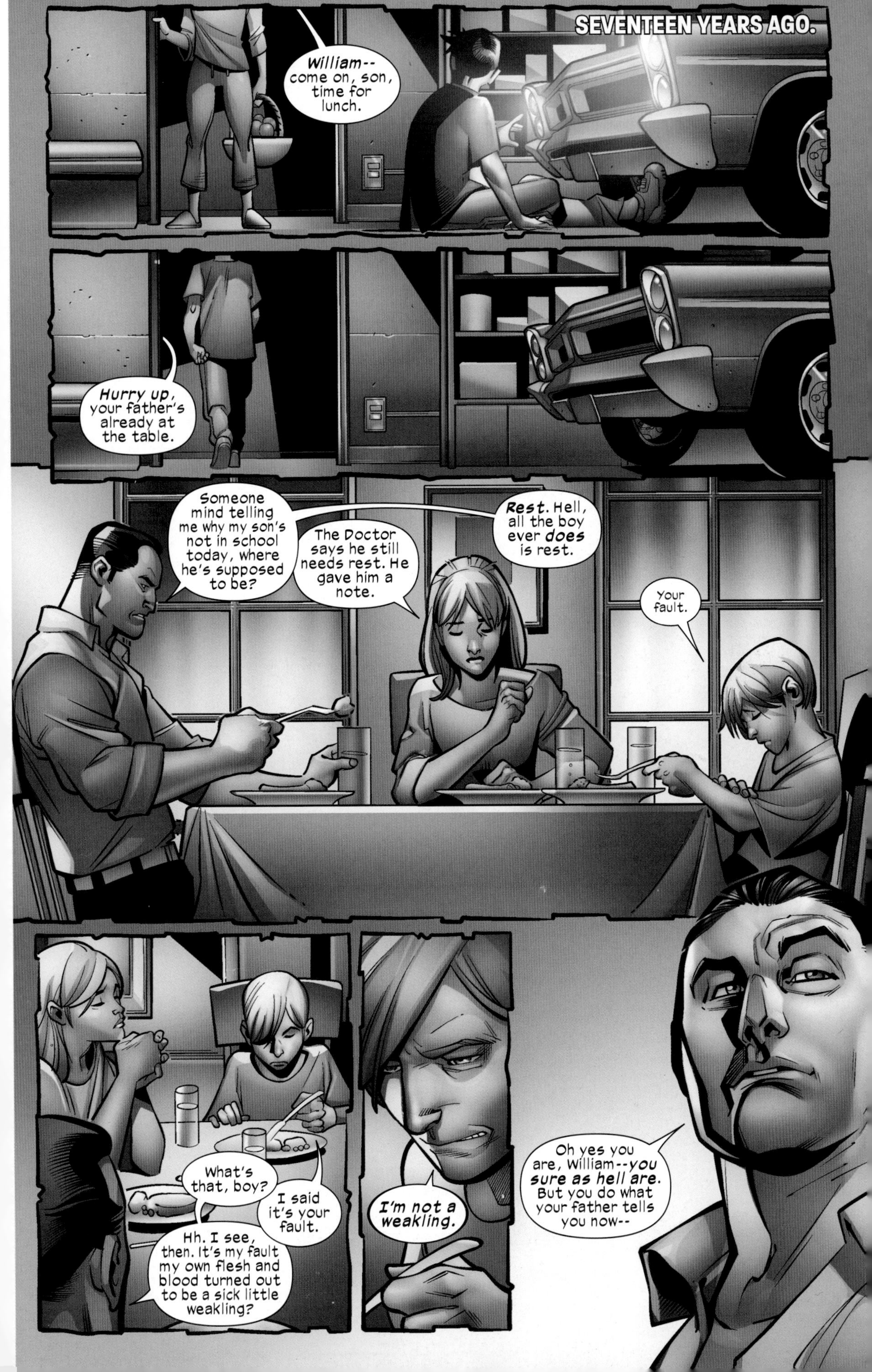
SEVENTEEN YEARS AGO.
William-- come on, son, time for lunch.
Hurry up, your father's already at the table.
Someone mind telling me why my son's not in school today, where he's supposed to be?
The Doctor says he still needs rest. He gave him a note.
Rest. Hell, all the boy ever does is rest.
Your fault.
What's that, boy?
I said it's your fault.
Hh. I see, then. It's my fault my own flesh and blood turned out to be a sick little weakling?
I'm not a weakling.
Oh yes you are, William--you sure as hell are. But you do what your father tells you now--

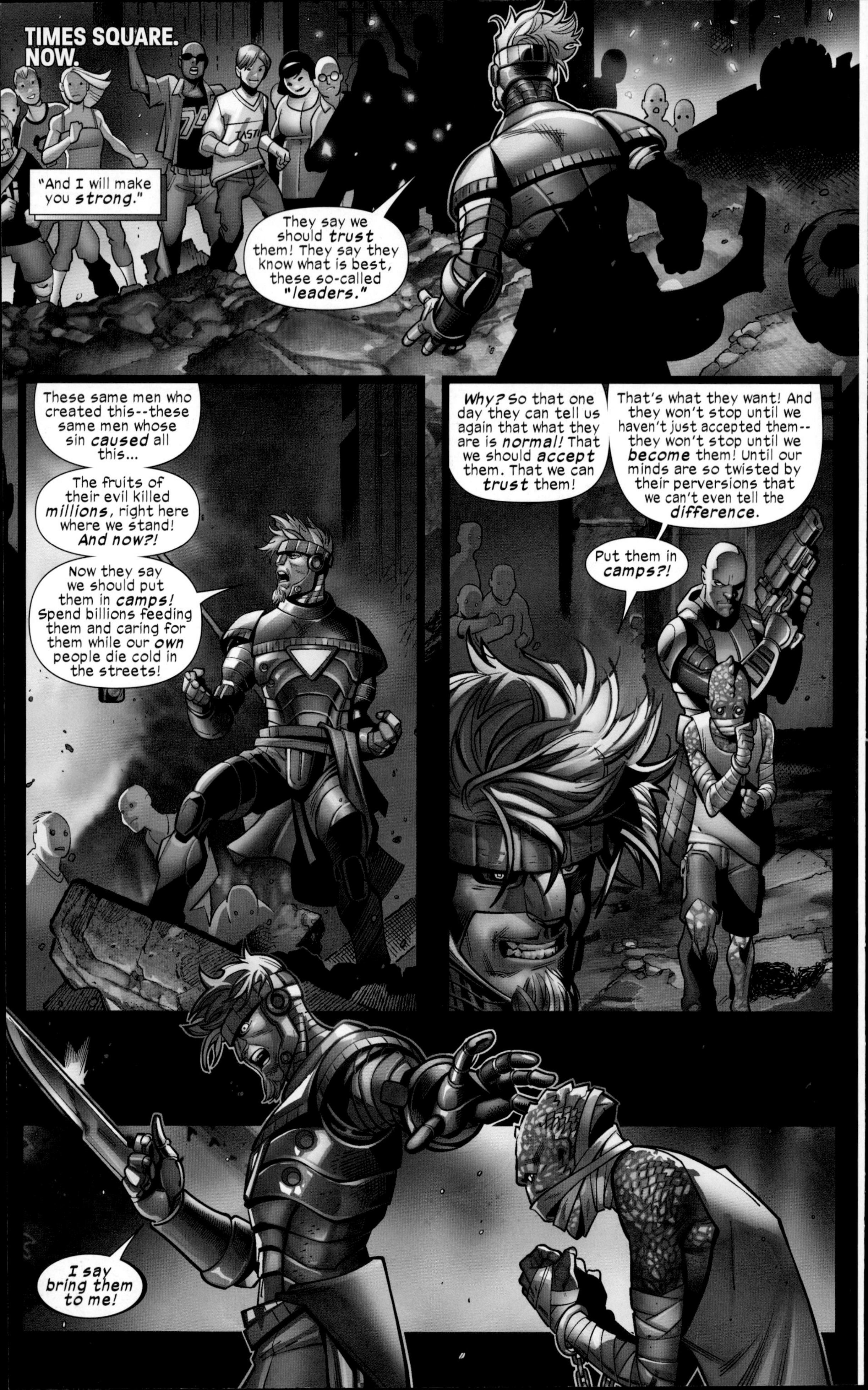
TIMES SQUARE. NOW.
"And I will make you strong."
They say we should trust them! They say they know what is best, these so-called "leaders."
These same men who created this--these same men whose sin caused all this...
The fruits of their evil killed millions, right here where we stand! And now?!
Now they say we should put them in camps! Spend billions feeding them and caring for them while our own people die cold in the streets!
Why? So that one day they can tell us again that what they are is normal! That we should accept them. That we can trust them!
That's what they want! And they won't stop until we haven't just accepted them-- they won't stop until we become them! Until our minds are so twisted by their perversions that we can't even tell the difference.
Put them in camps?!
I say bring them to me!

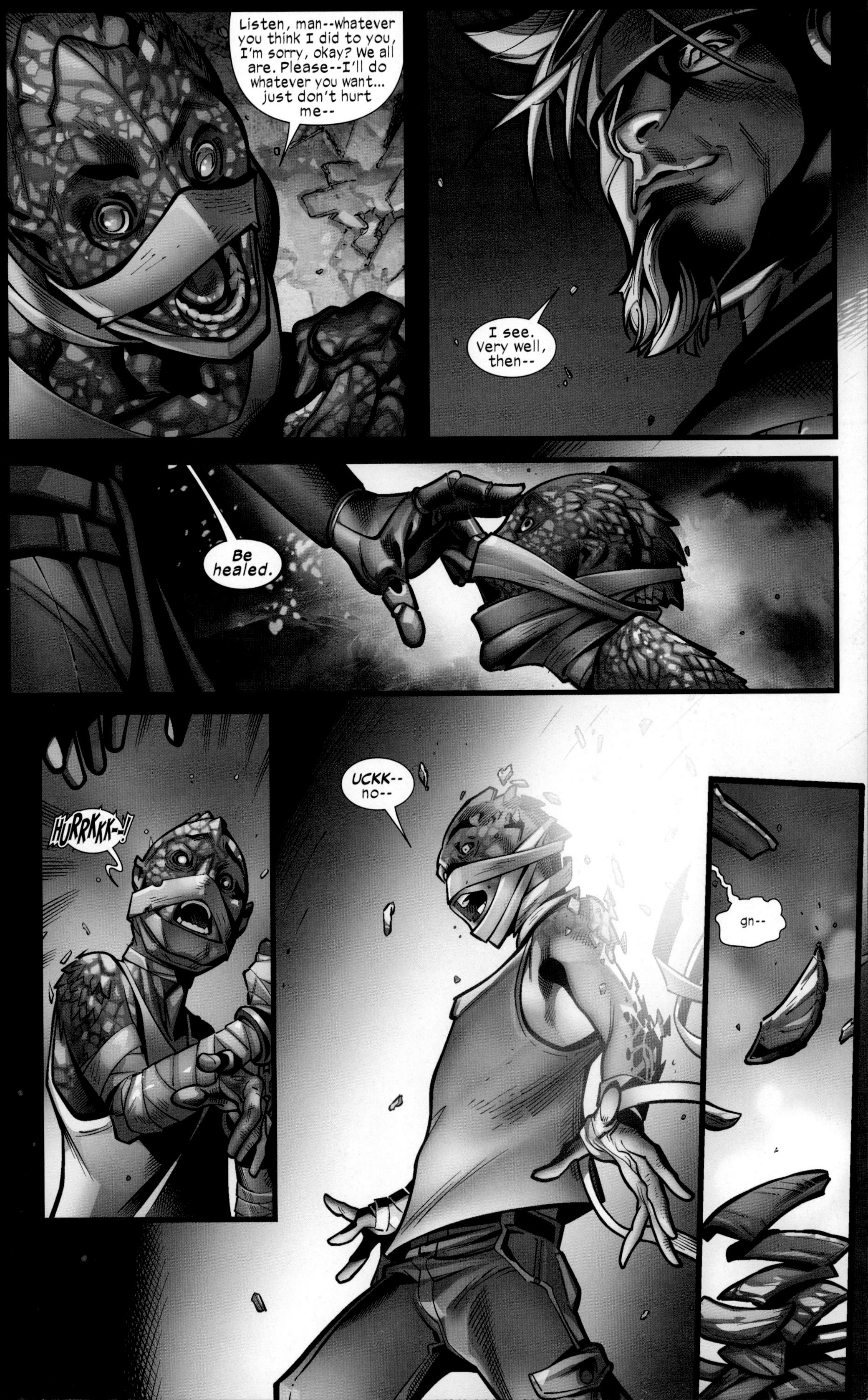
Listen, man--whatever you think I did to you, I'm sorry, okay? We all are. Please--I'll do whatever you want... just don't hurt me--
I see. Very well, then--
Be healed.
HURRKKK--!
UCKK-- no--
gn--

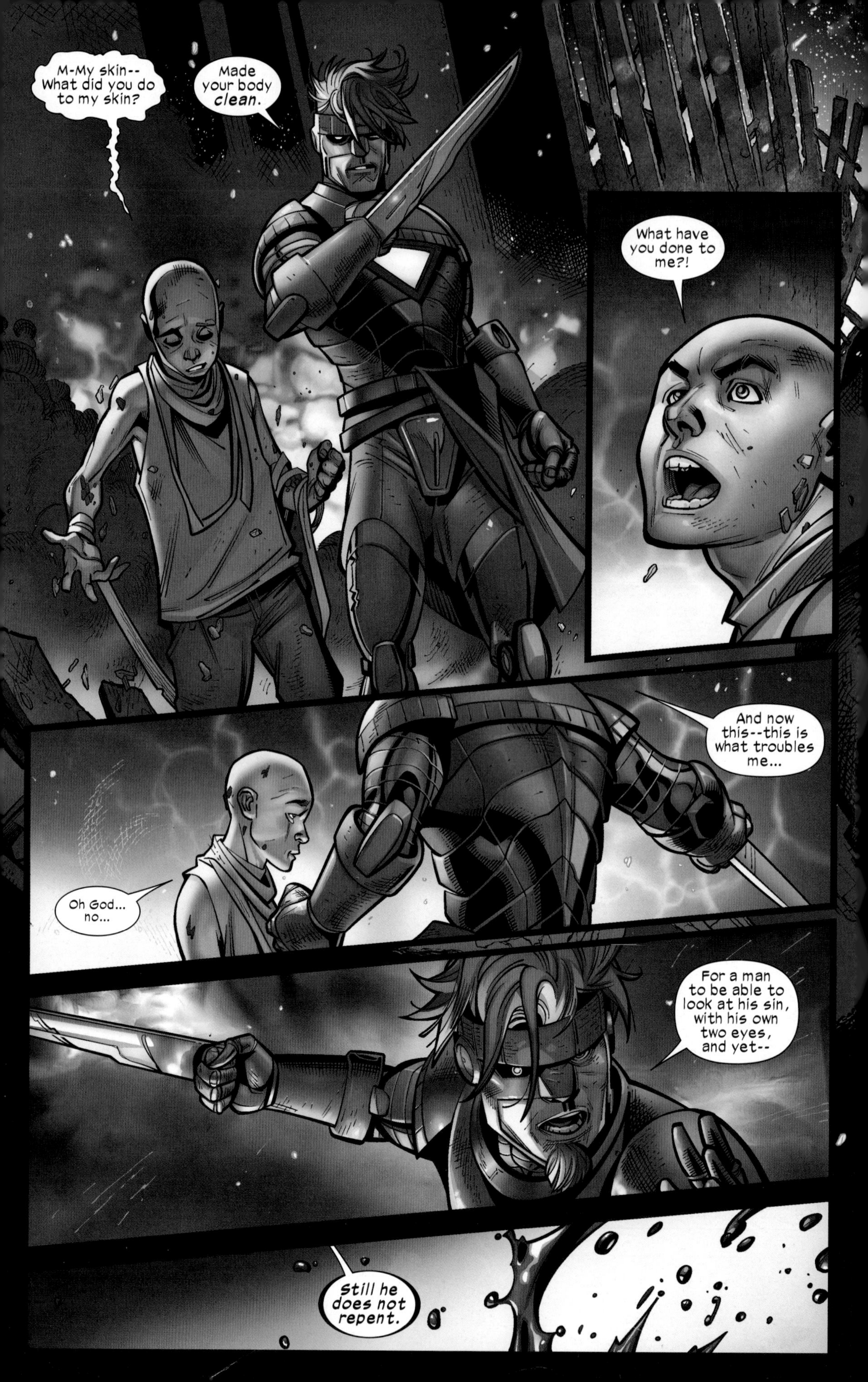
M-My skin-- What did you do to my skin?
Made your body *clean*.
What have you done to me?!
And now this--this is what troubles me...
Oh God... no...
For a man to be able to look at his sin, with his own two eyes, and yet--
Still he does not repent.

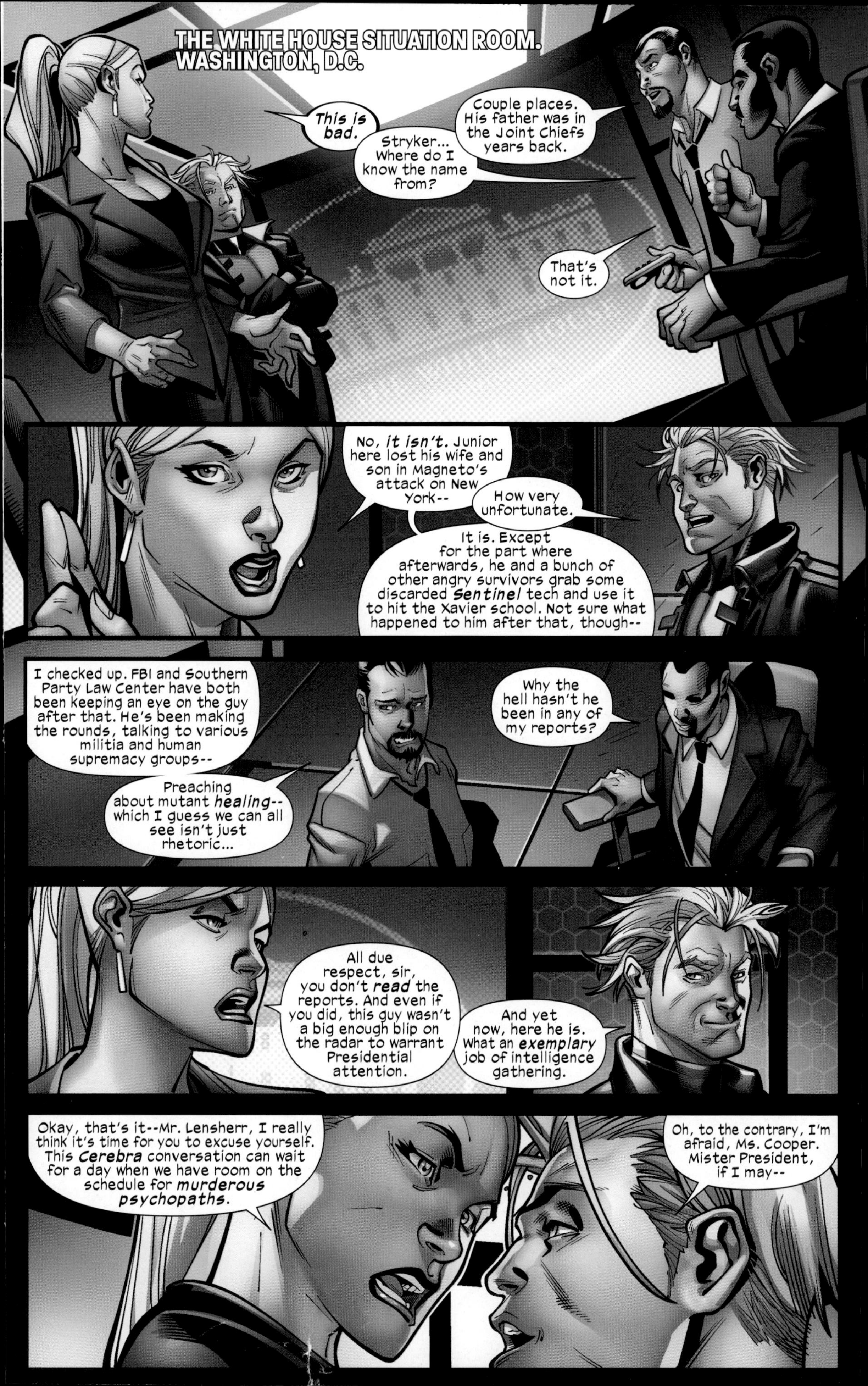
THE WHITE HOUSE SITUATION ROOM. WASHINGTON, D.C.
This is bad.
Stryker... Where do I know the name from?
Couple places. His father was in the Joint Chiefs years back.
That's not it.
No, it isn't. Junior here lost his wife and son in Magneto's attack on New York--
How very unfortunate.
It is. Except for the part where afterwards, he and a bunch of other angry survivors grab some discarded Sentinel tech and use it to hit the Xavier school. Not sure what happened to him after that, though--
I checked up. FBI and Southern Party Law Center have both been keeping an eye on the guy after that. He's been making the rounds, talking to various militia and human supremacy groups--
Preaching about mutant healing-- which I guess we can all see isn't just rhetoric...
Why the hell hasn't he been in any of my reports?
All due respect, sir, you don't read the reports. And even if you did, this guy wasn't a big enough blip on the radar to warrant Presidential attention.
And yet now, here he is. What an exemplary job of intelligence gathering.
Okay, that's it--Mr. Lensherr, I really think it's time for you to excuse yourself. This Cerebra conversation can wait for a day when we have room on the schedule for murderous psychopaths.
Oh, to the contrary, I'm afraid, Ms. Cooper. Mister President, if I may--

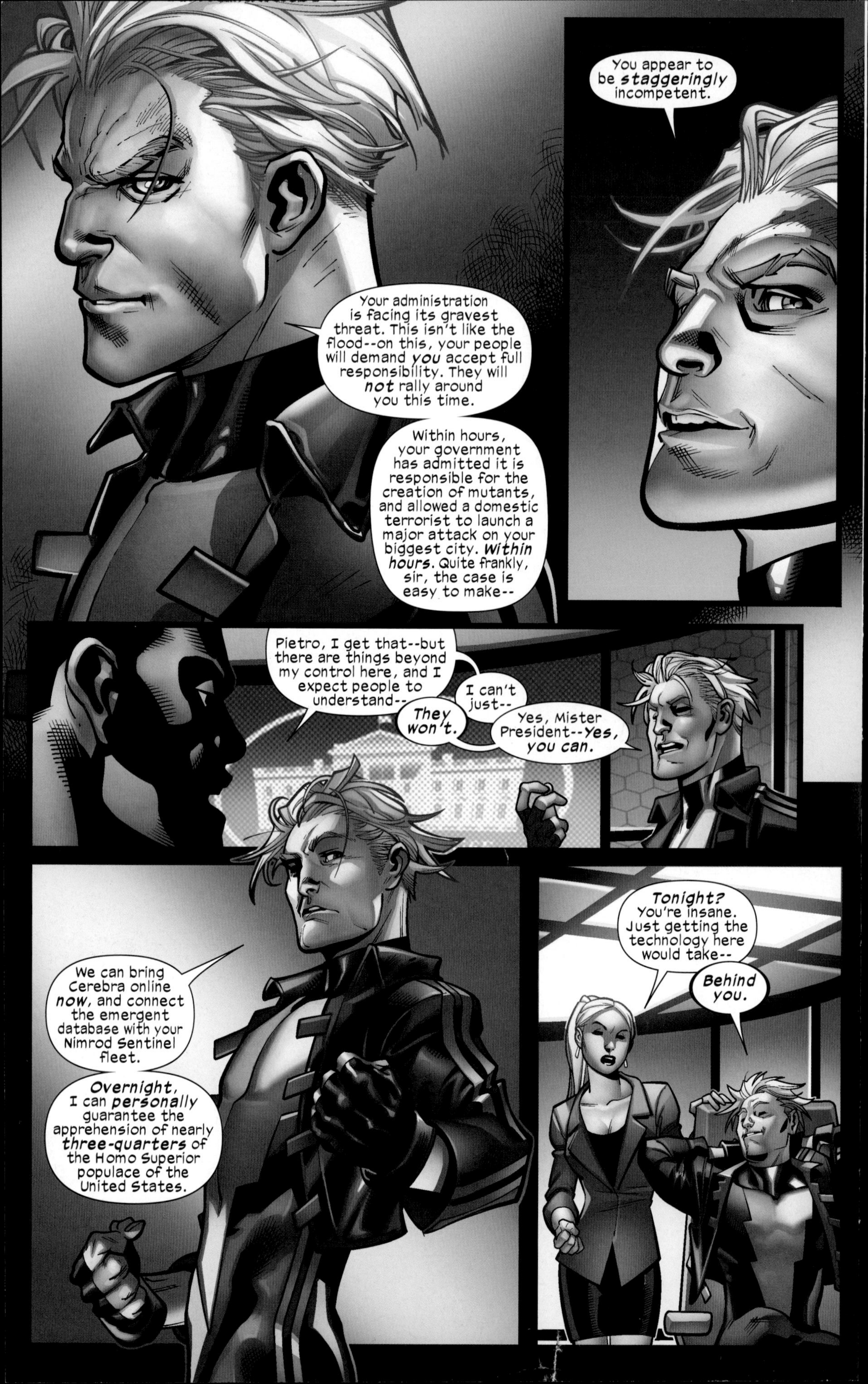
You appear to be staggeringly incompetent.
Your administration is facing its gravest threat. This isn't like the flood--on this, your people will demand you accept full responsibility. They will not rally around you this time.
Within hours, your government has admitted it is responsible for the creation of mutants, and allowed a domestic terrorist to launch a major attack on your biggest city. Within hours. Quite frankly, sir, the case is easy to make--
Pietro, I get that--but there are things beyond my control here, and I expect people to understand--
They won't.
I can't just--
Yes, Mister President--Yes, you can.
We can bring Cerebra online now, and connect the emergent database with your Nimrod Sentinel fleet.
Overnight, I can personally guarantee the apprehension of nearly three-quarters of the Homo Superior populace of the United States.
Tonight? You're insane. Just getting the technology here would take--
Behind you.

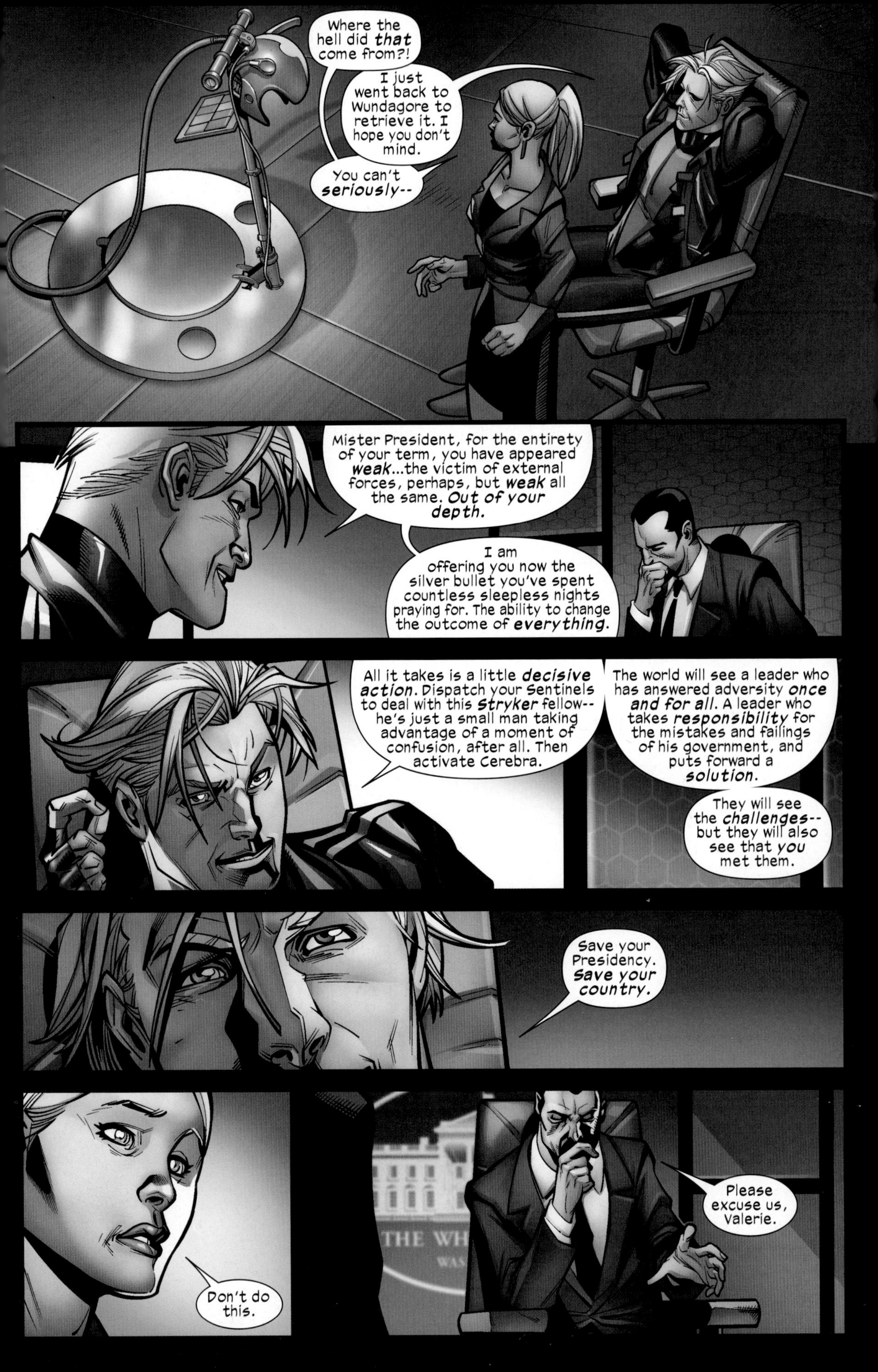
Where the hell did that come from?!
I just went back to Wundagore to retrieve it. I hope you don't mind.
You can't seriously--
Mister President, for the entirety of your term, you have appeared weak...the victim of external forces, perhaps, but weak all the same. Out of your depth.
I am offering you now the silver bullet you've spent countless sleepless nights praying for. The ability to change the outcome of everything.
All it takes is a little decisive action. Dispatch your Sentinels to deal with this Stryker fellow--he's just a small man taking advantage of a moment of confusion, after all. Then activate Cerebra.
The world will see a leader who has answered adversity once and for all. A leader who takes responsibility for the mistakes and failings of his government, and puts forward a solution.
They will see the challenges--but they will also see that you met them.
Save your Presidency. Save your country.
Don't do this.
Please excuse us, Valerie.

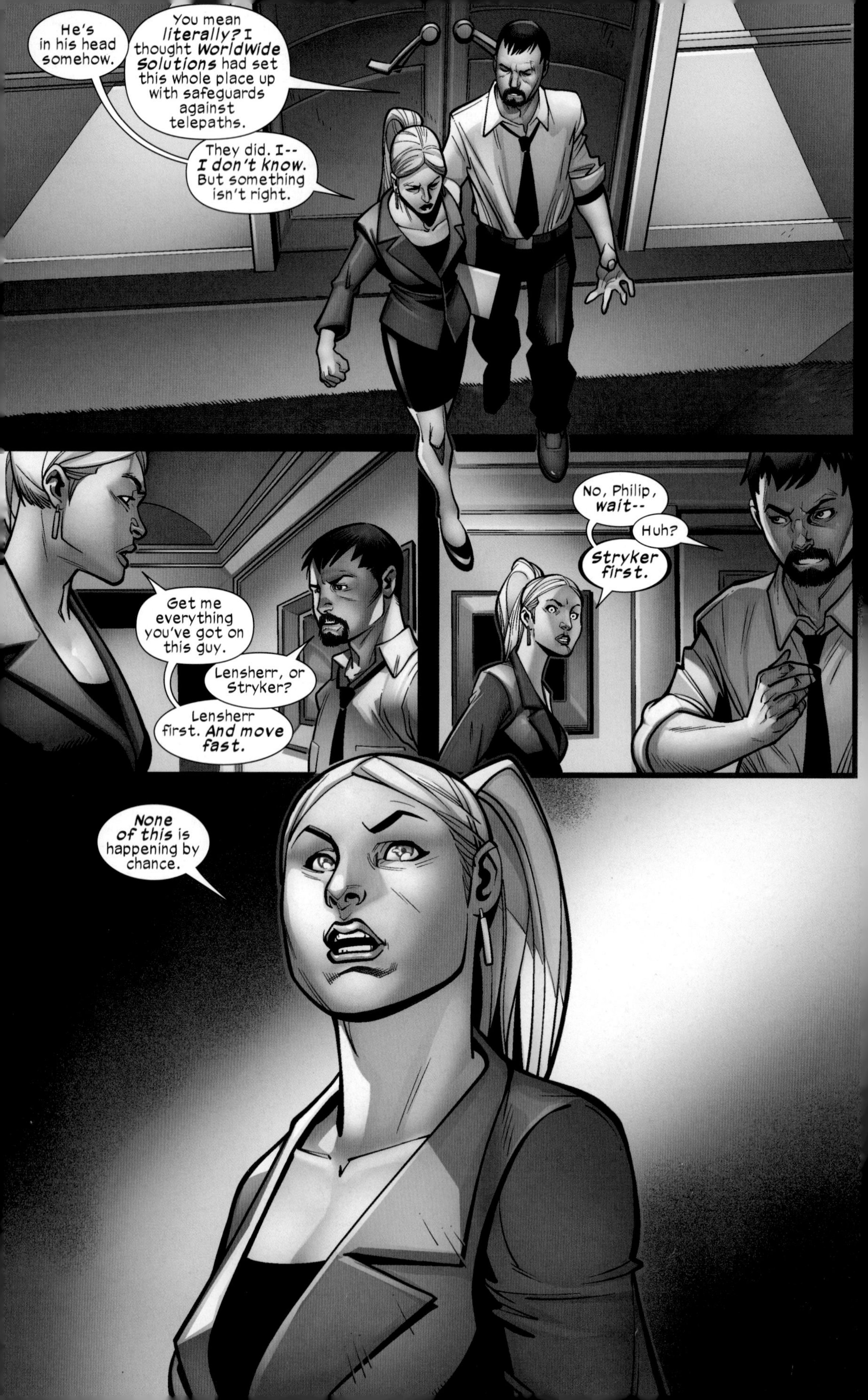
He's in his head somehow.
You mean *literally?* I thought *WorldWide Solutions* had set this whole place up with safeguards against telepaths.
They did. I-- *I don't know.* But something isn't right.
Get me everything you've got on this guy.
Lenssherr, or Stryker?
Lensherr first. *And move fast.*
No, Philip, *wait--*
Huh?
Stryker first.
None of this is happening by chance.

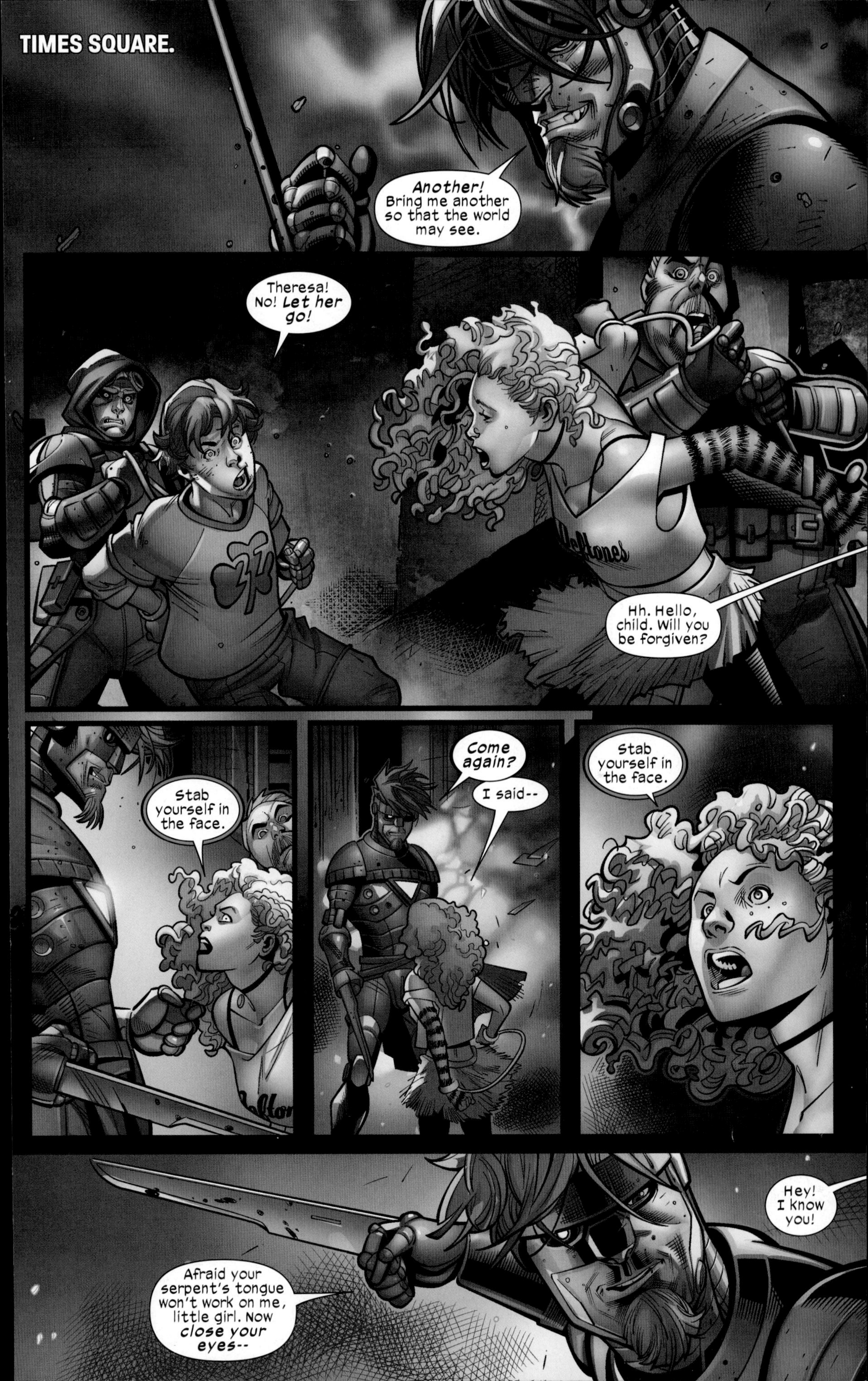
TIMES SQUARE.
Another! Bring me another so that the world may see.
Theresa! No! Let her go!
Hh. Hello, child. Will you be forgiven?
Stab yourself in the face.
Come again?
I said--
Stab yourself in the face.
Hey! I know you!
Afraid your serpent's tongue won't work on me, little girl. Now close your eyes--

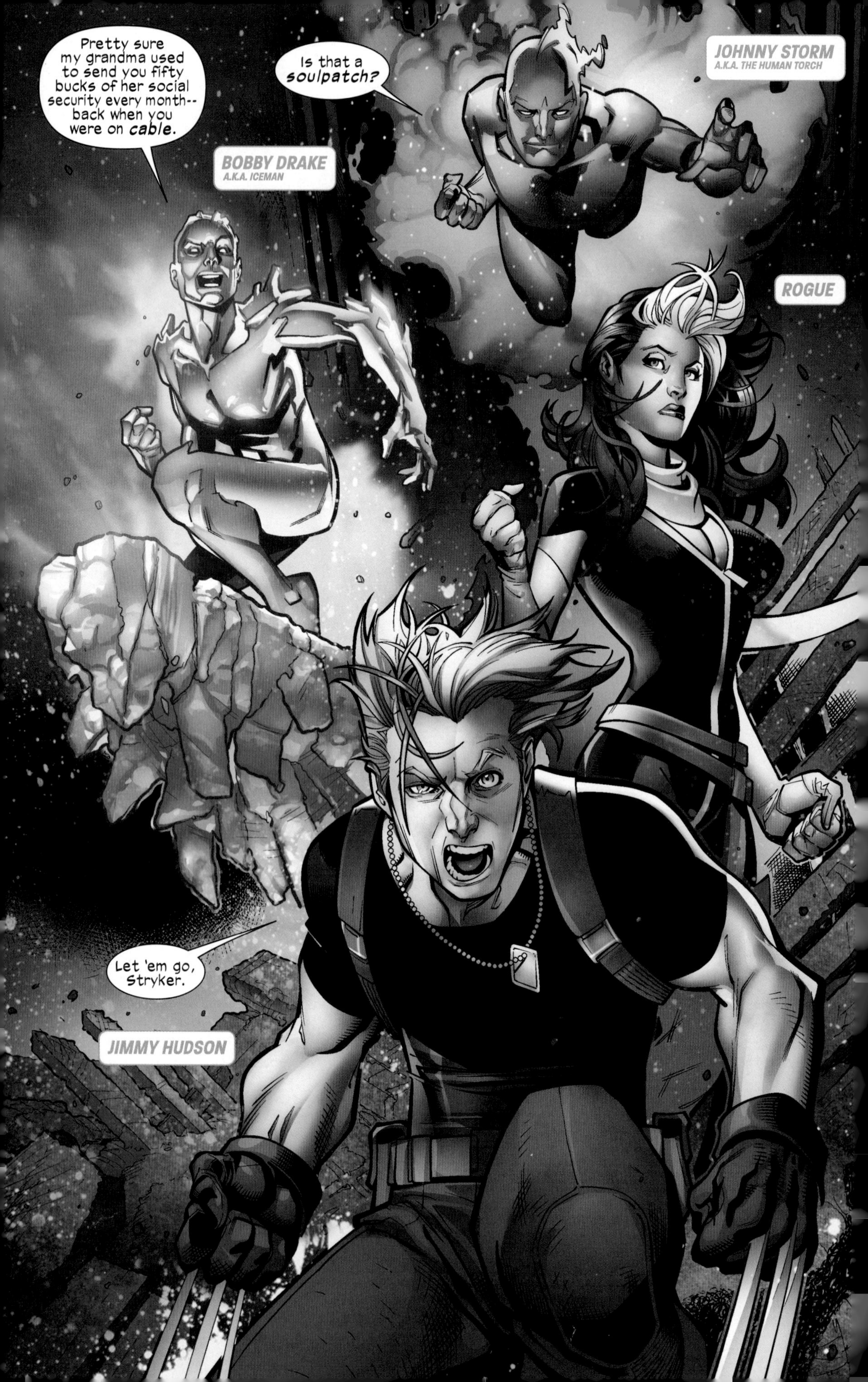
Pretty sure my grandma used to send you fifty bucks of her social security every month-- back when you were on cable.
Is that a soulpatch?
JOHNNY STORM
A.K.A. THE HUMAN TORCH
BOBBY DRAKE
A.K.A. ICEMAN
ROGUE
Let 'em go, Stryker.
JIMMY HUDSON

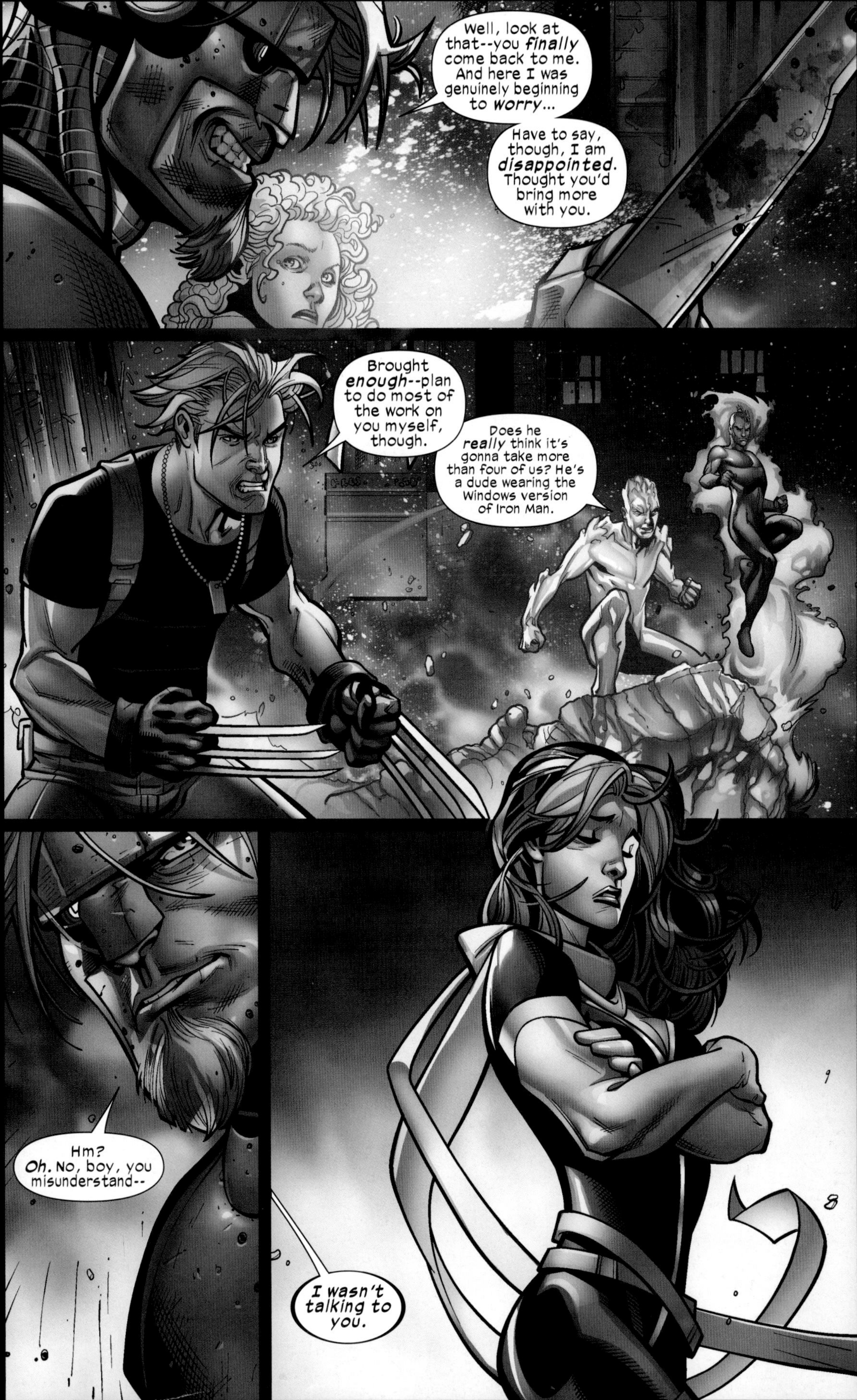

Well, look at that--you *finally* come back to me. And here I was genuinely beginning to *worry*...
Have to say, though, I am *disappointed*. Thought you'd bring more with you.
Brought *enough*--plan to do most of the work on you myself, though.
Does he *really* think it's gonna take more than four of us? He's a dude wearing the Windows version of Iron Man.
Hm? *Oh.* No, boy, you misunderstand--
I wasn't talking to you.

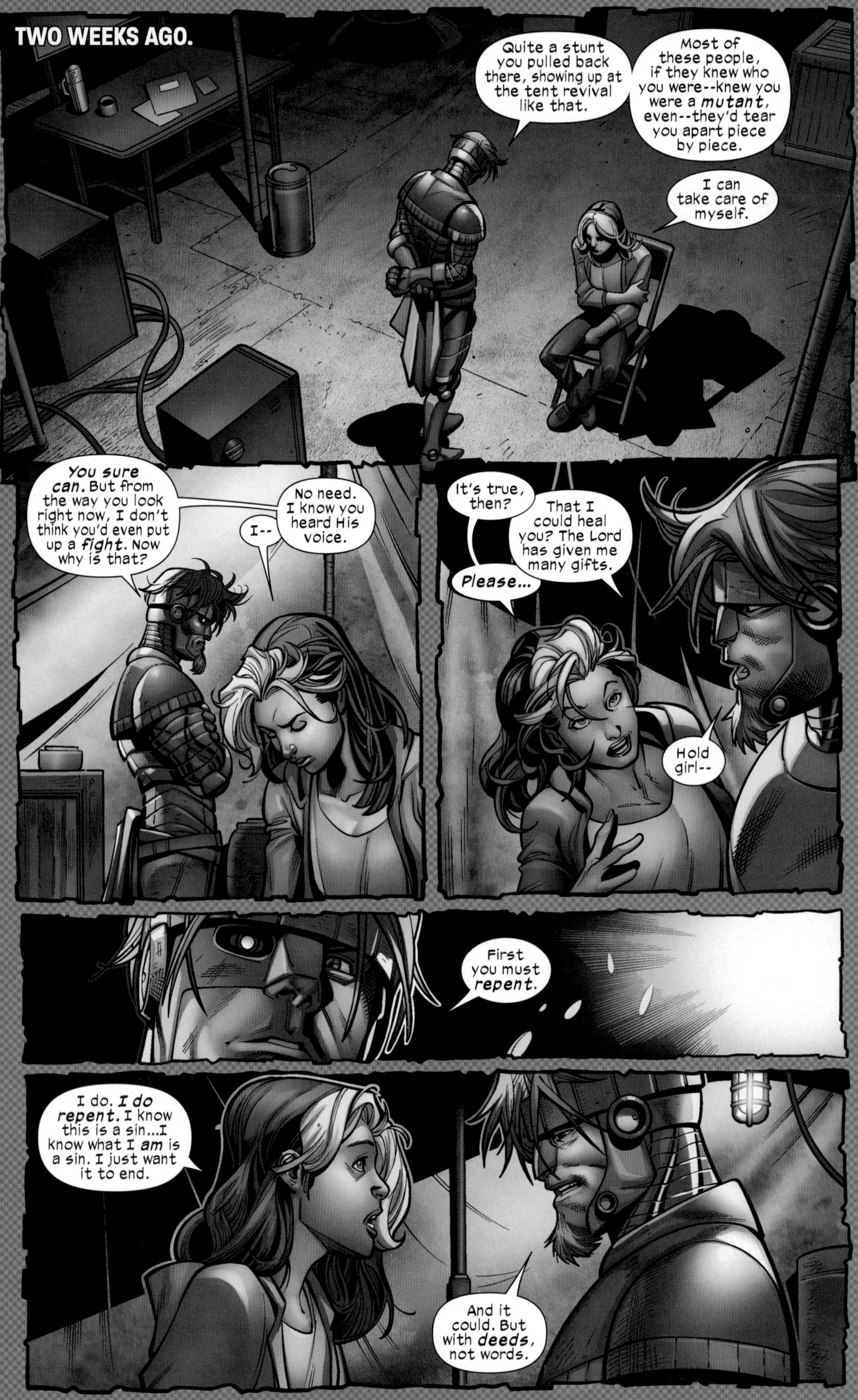
TWO WEEKS AGO.
Quite a stunt you pulled back there, showing up at the tent revival like that.
Most of these people, if they knew who you were--knew you were a *mutant*, even--they'd tear you apart piece by piece.
I can take care of myself.
You sure can. But from the way you look right now, I don't think you'd even put up a *fight*. Now why is that?
I--
No need. I know you heard His voice.
It's true, then?
That I could heal you? The Lord has given me many gifts.
Please...
Hold girl--
First you must *repent*.
I do. *I do repent.* I know this is a sin...I know what I *am* is a sin. I just want it to end.
And it could. But with *deeds*, not words.

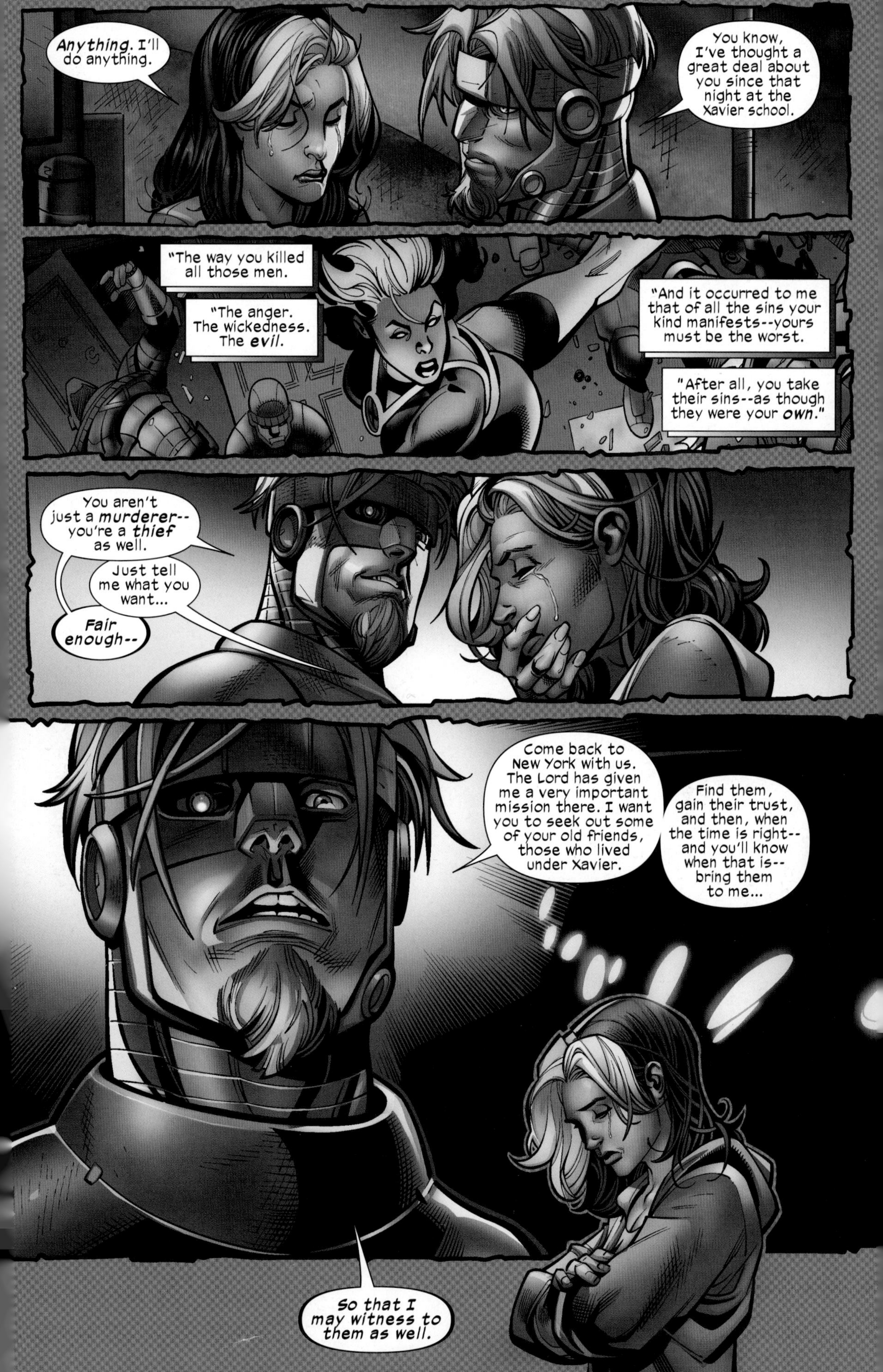

Anything. I'll do anything.
You know, I've thought a great deal about you since that night at the Xavier school.
"The way you killed all those men.
"The anger. The wickedness. The *evil*.
"And it occurred to me that of all the sins your kind manifests--yours must be the worst.
"After all, you take their sins--as though they were your *own*."
You aren't just a *murderer*--you're a *thief* as well.
Just tell me what you want...
Fair enough--
Come back to New York with us. The Lord has given me a very important mission there. I want you to seek out some of your old friends, those who lived under Xavier.
Find them, gain their trust, and then, when the time is right--and you'll know when that is--bring them to me...
So that I may witness to them as well.

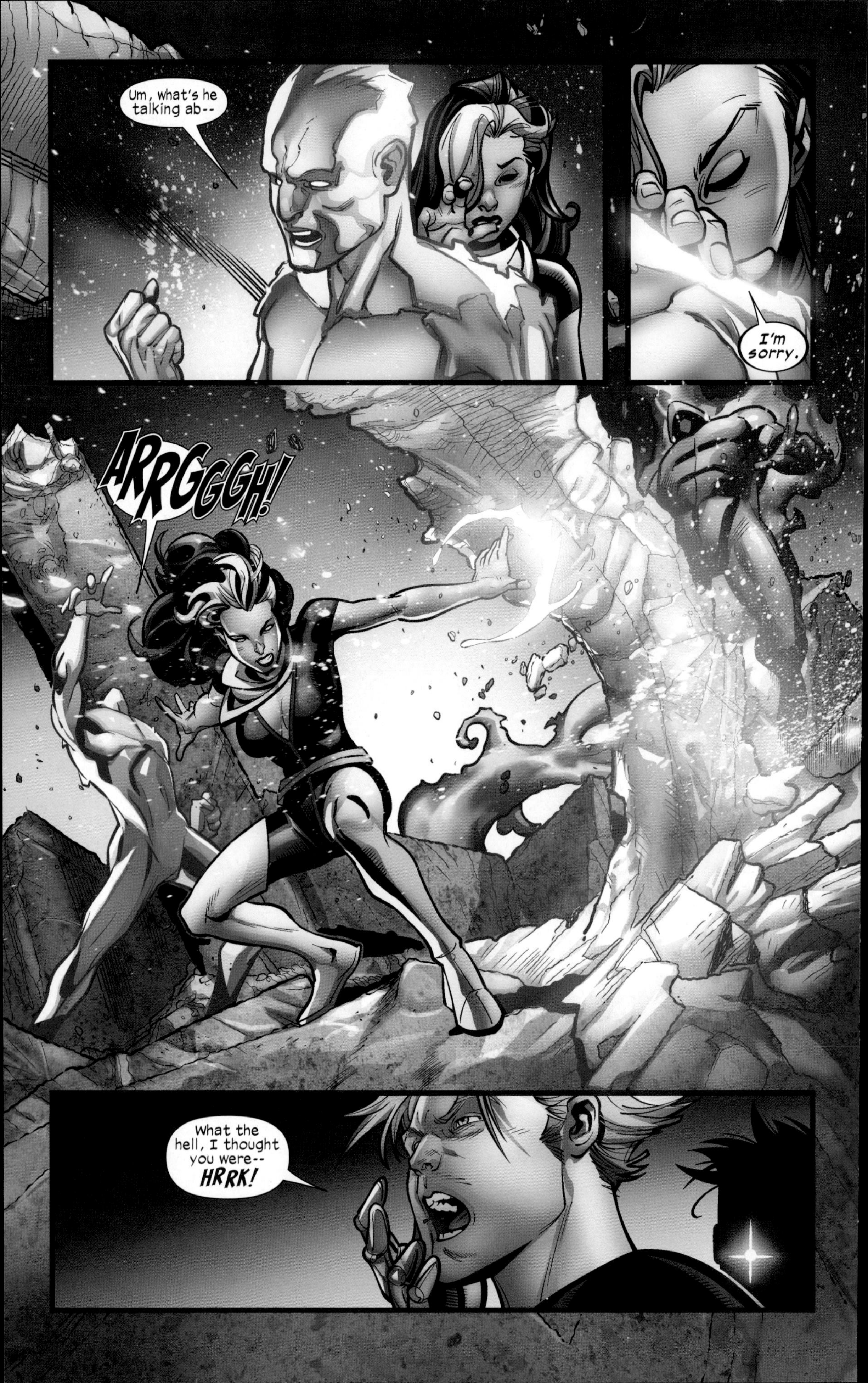
Um, what's he talking ab--
I'm sorry.
ARRGGGH!
What the hell, I thought you were-- HRRK!

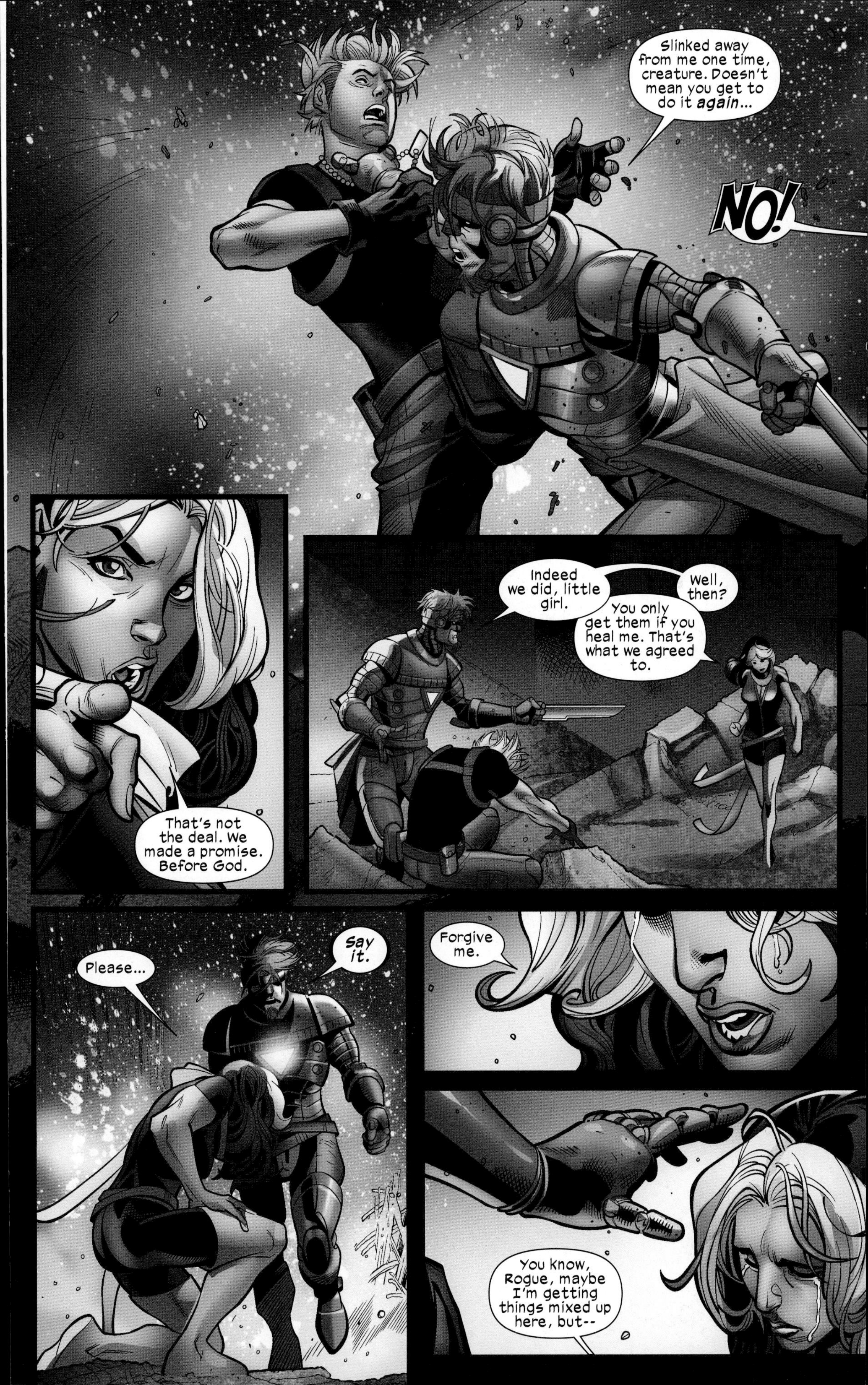
Slinked away from me one time, creature. Doesn't mean you get to do it *again*...
NO!
That's not the deal. We made a promise. Before God.
Indeed we did, little girl.
Well, then?
You only get them if you heal me. That's what we agreed to.
Please...
Say it.
Forgive me.
You know, Rogue, maybe I'm getting things mixed up here, but--

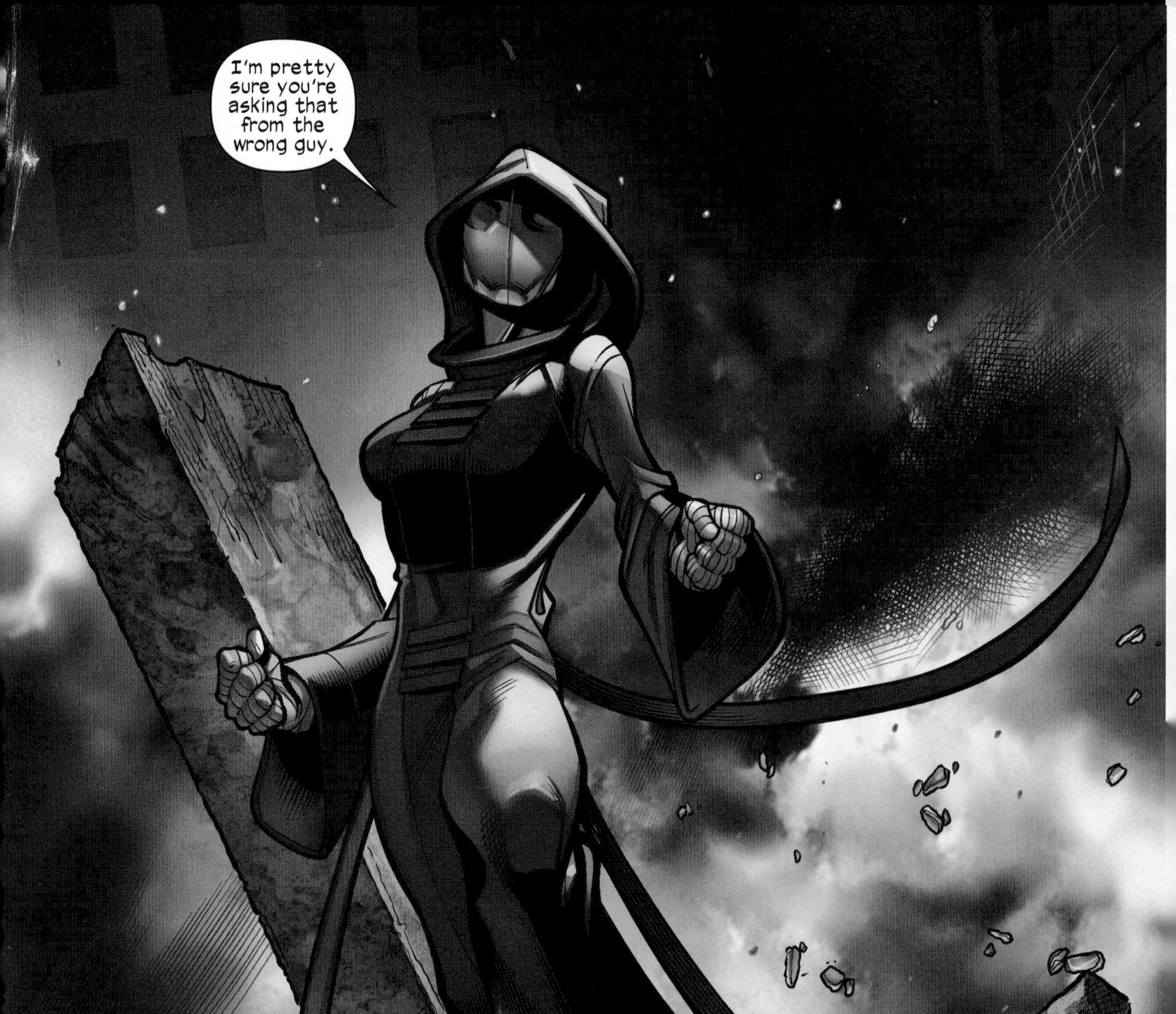
I'm pretty sure you're asking that from the wrong guy.

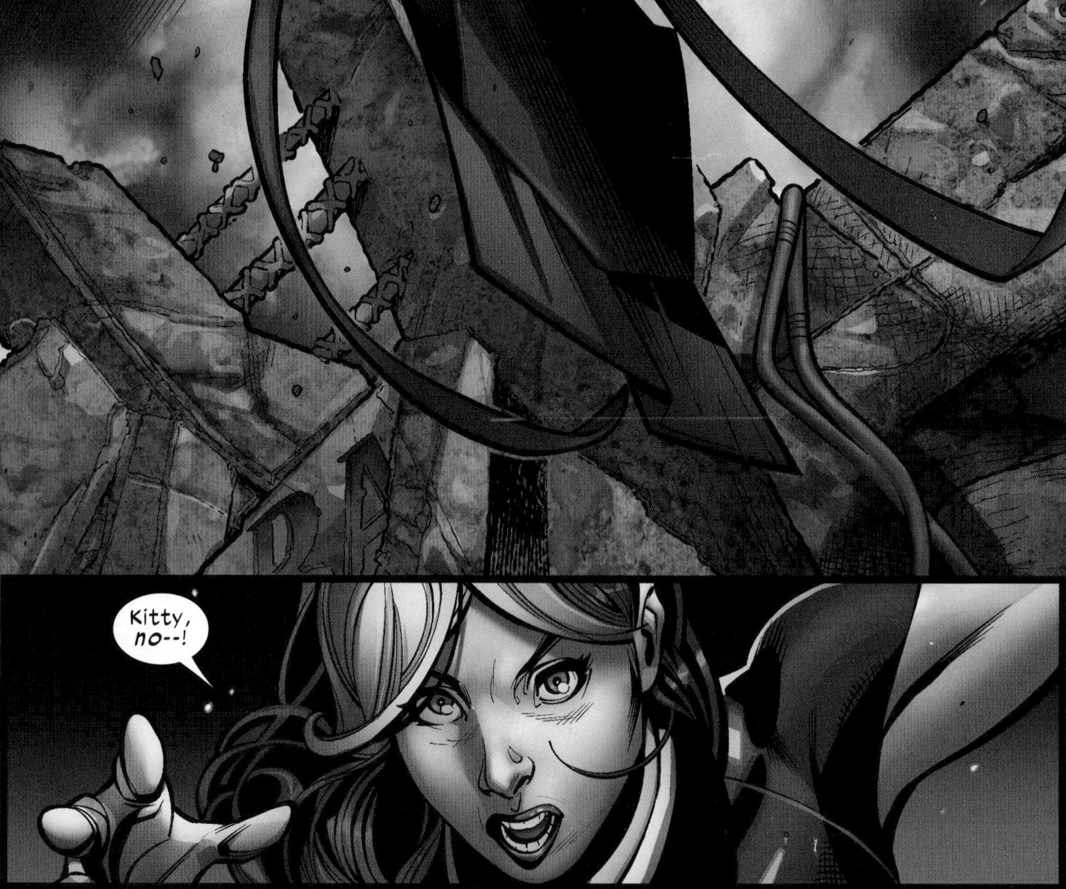
Kitty, no--!

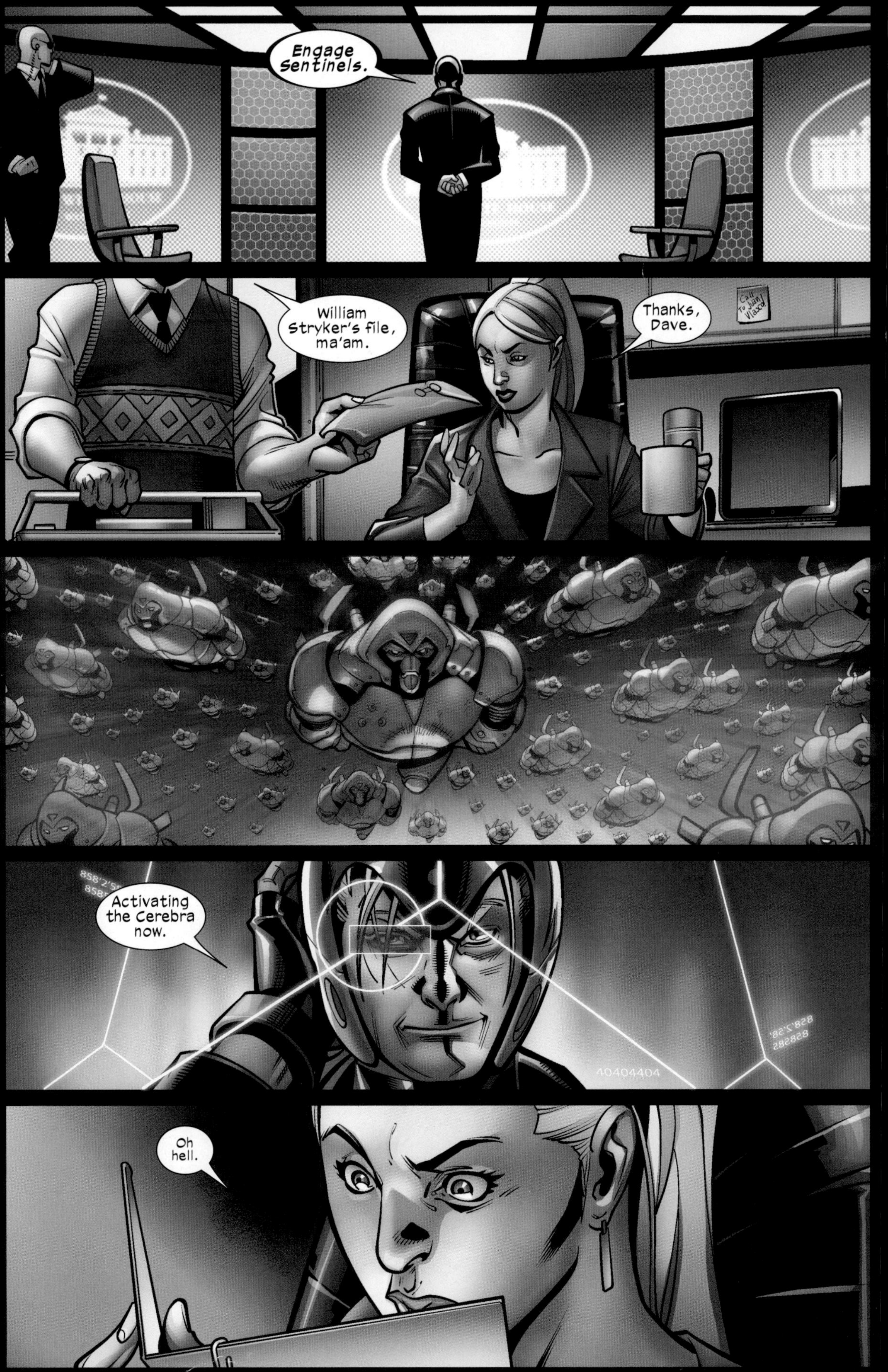
Engage Sentinels.
William Stryker's file, ma'am.
Thanks, Dave.
Activating the Cerebra now.
40404404
Oh hell.

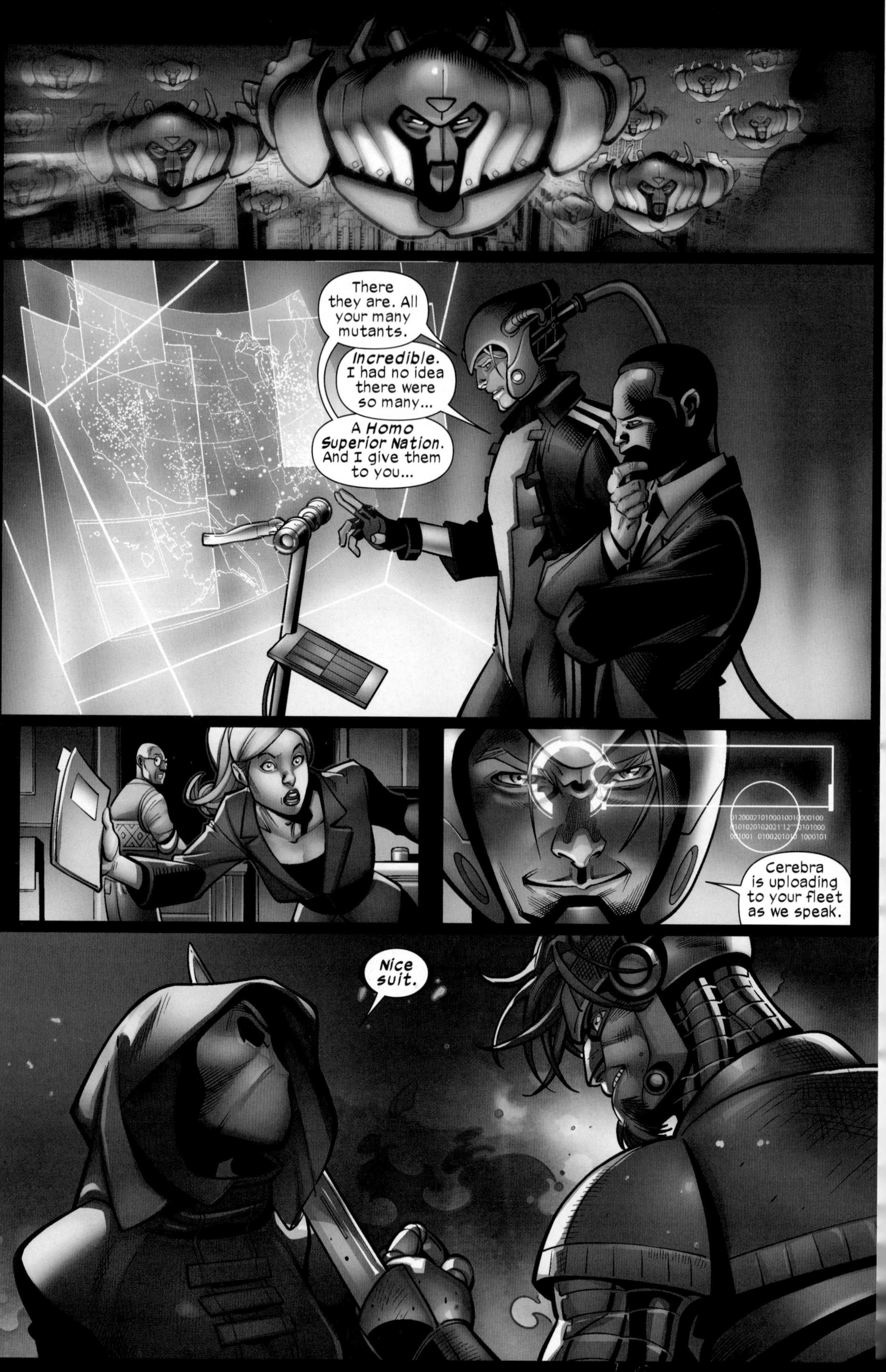
There they are. All your many mutants.
Incredible. I had no idea there were so many...
A Homo Superior Nation. And I give them to you...
Cerebra is uploading to your fleet as we speak.
Nice suit.

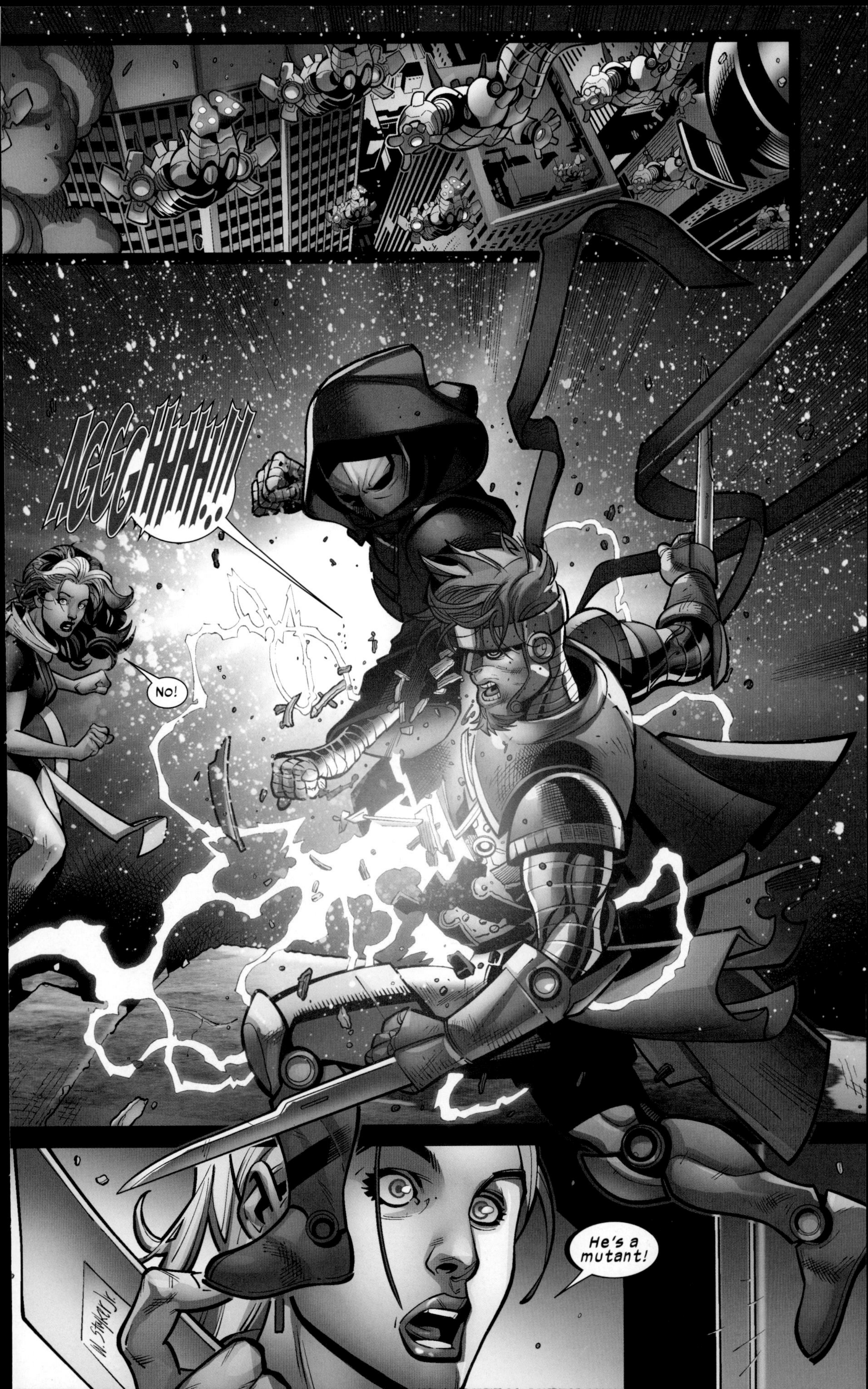
AGGGHHHH!!!
NO!
He's a mutant!

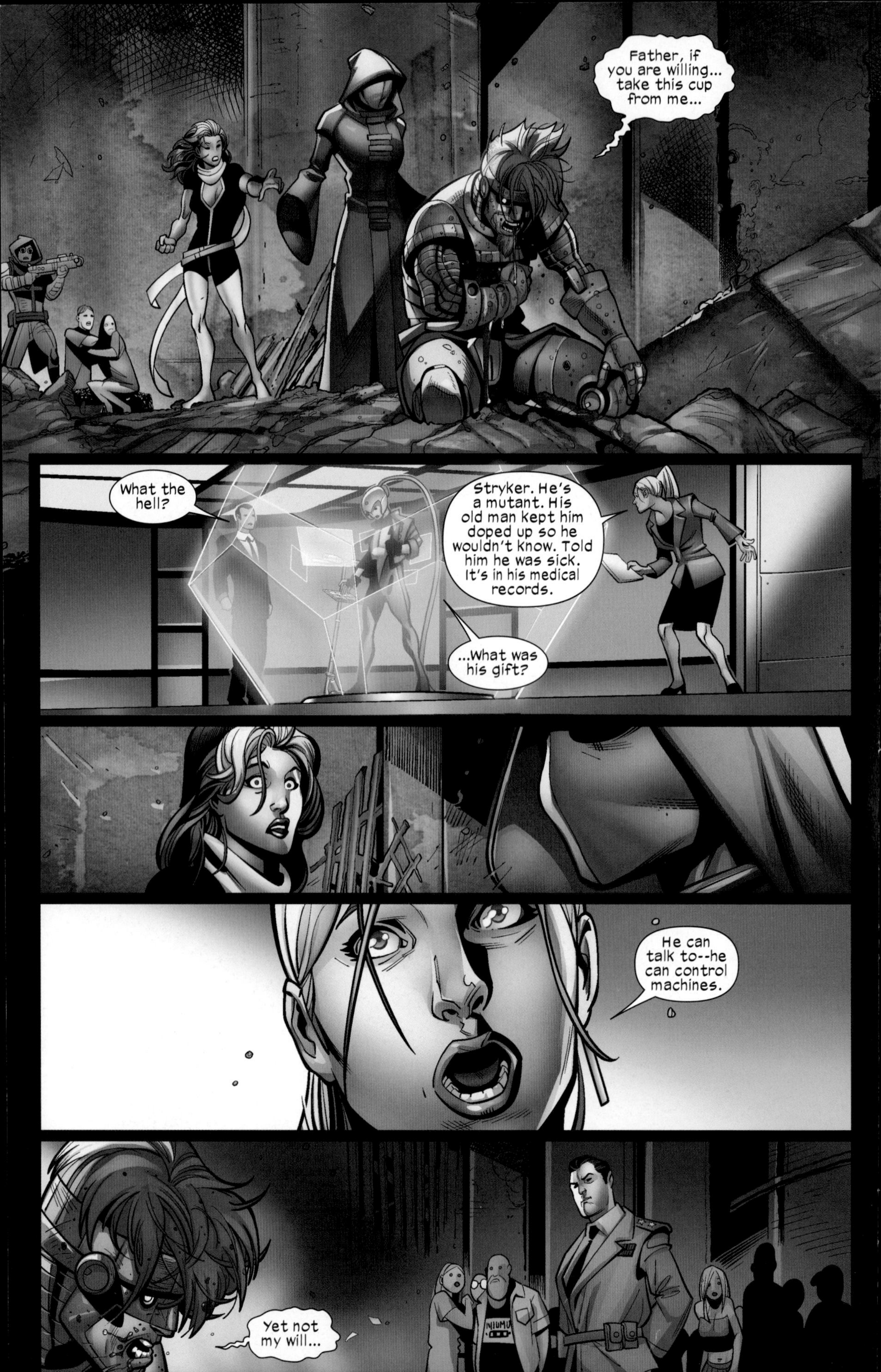
Father, if you are willing... take this cup from me...
What the hell?
Stryker. He's a mutant. His old man kept him doped up so he wouldn't know. Told him he was sick. It's in his medical records.
...What was his gift?
He can talk to--he can control machines.
Yet not my will...

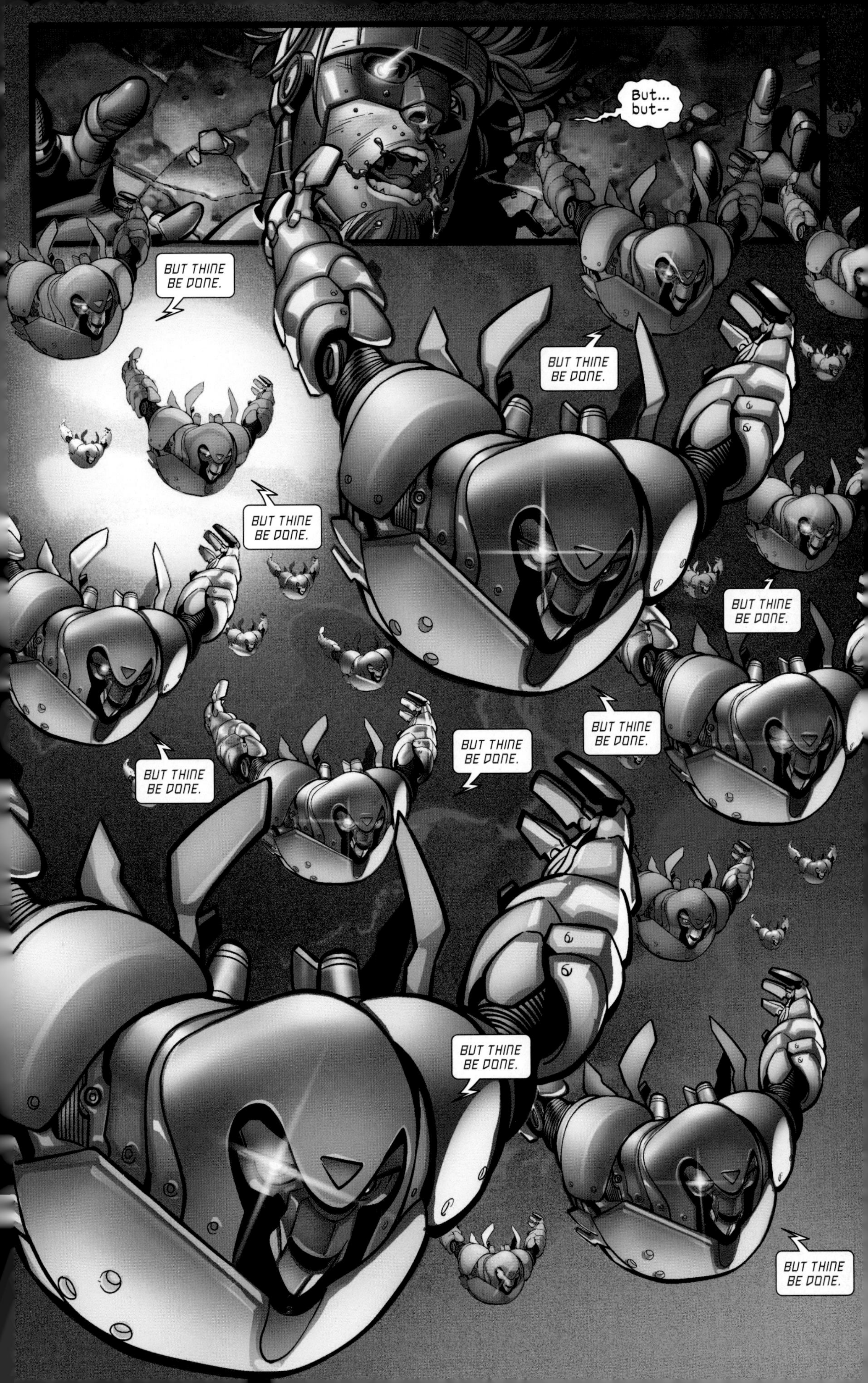
But... but--
BUT THINE BE DONE.
BUT THINE BE DONE.
BUT THINE BE DONE.
BUT THINE BE DONE.
BUT THINE BE DONE.
BUT THINE BE DONE.
BUT THINE BE DONE.
BUT THINE BE DONE.
BUT THINE BE DONE.

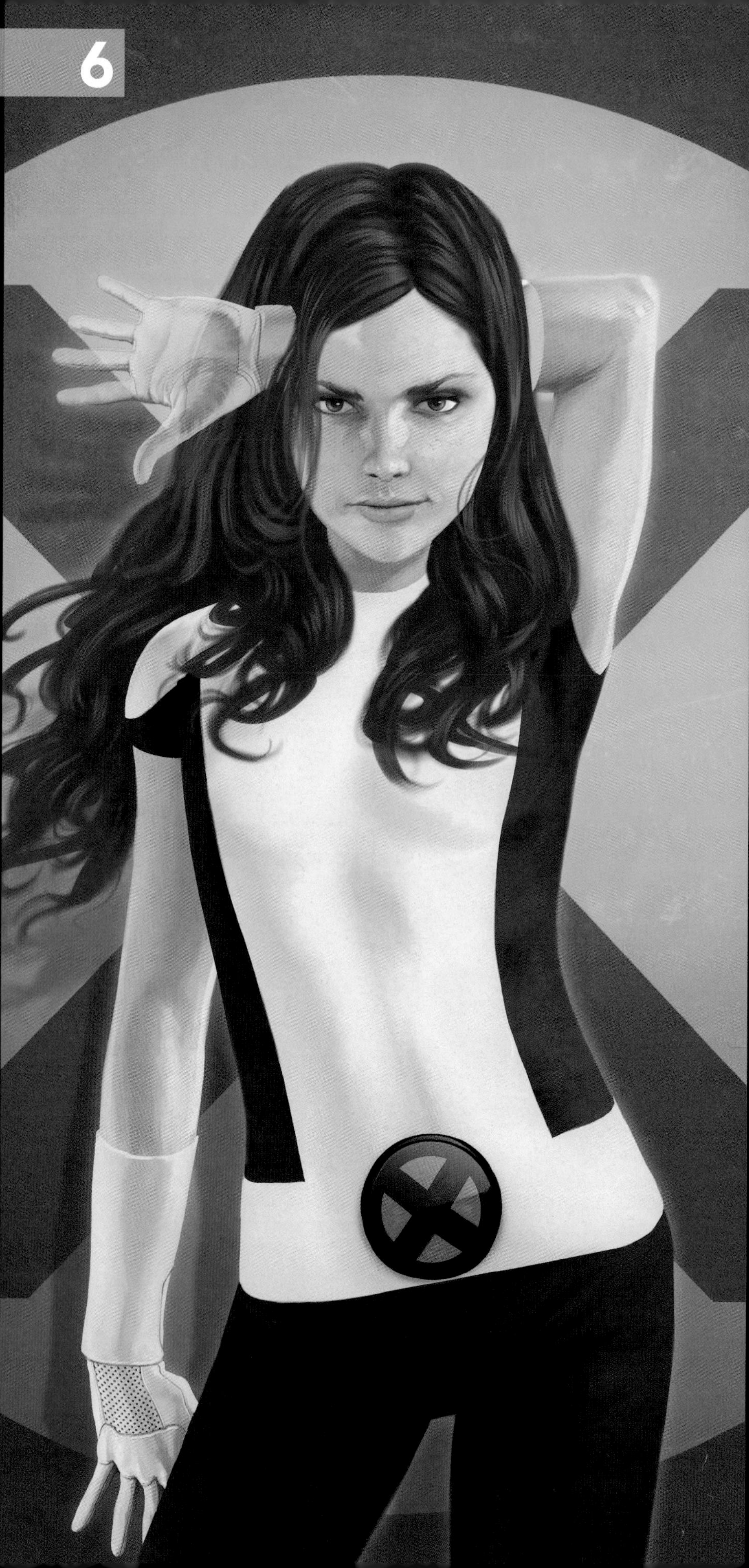

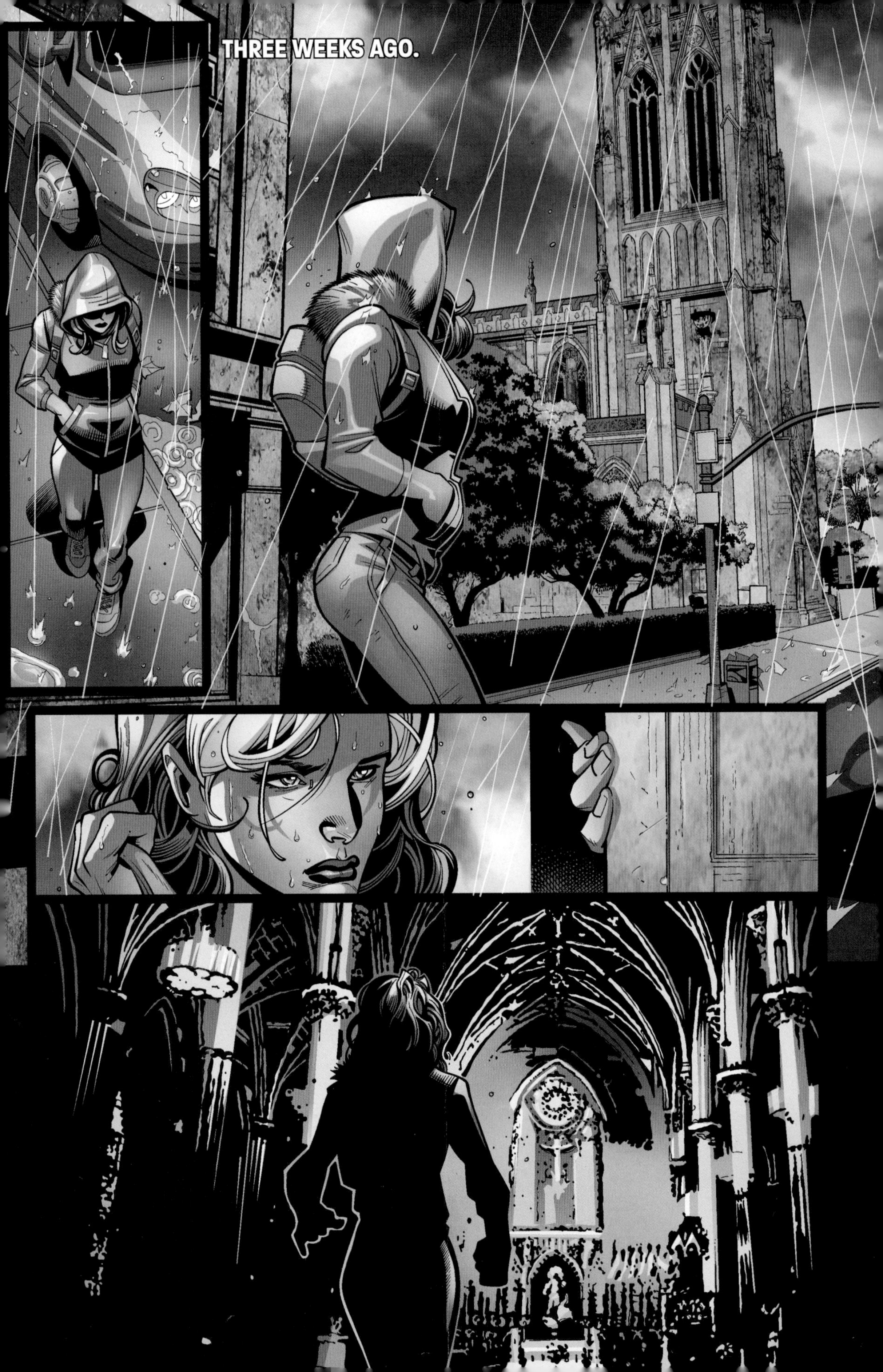
THREE WEEKS AGO.

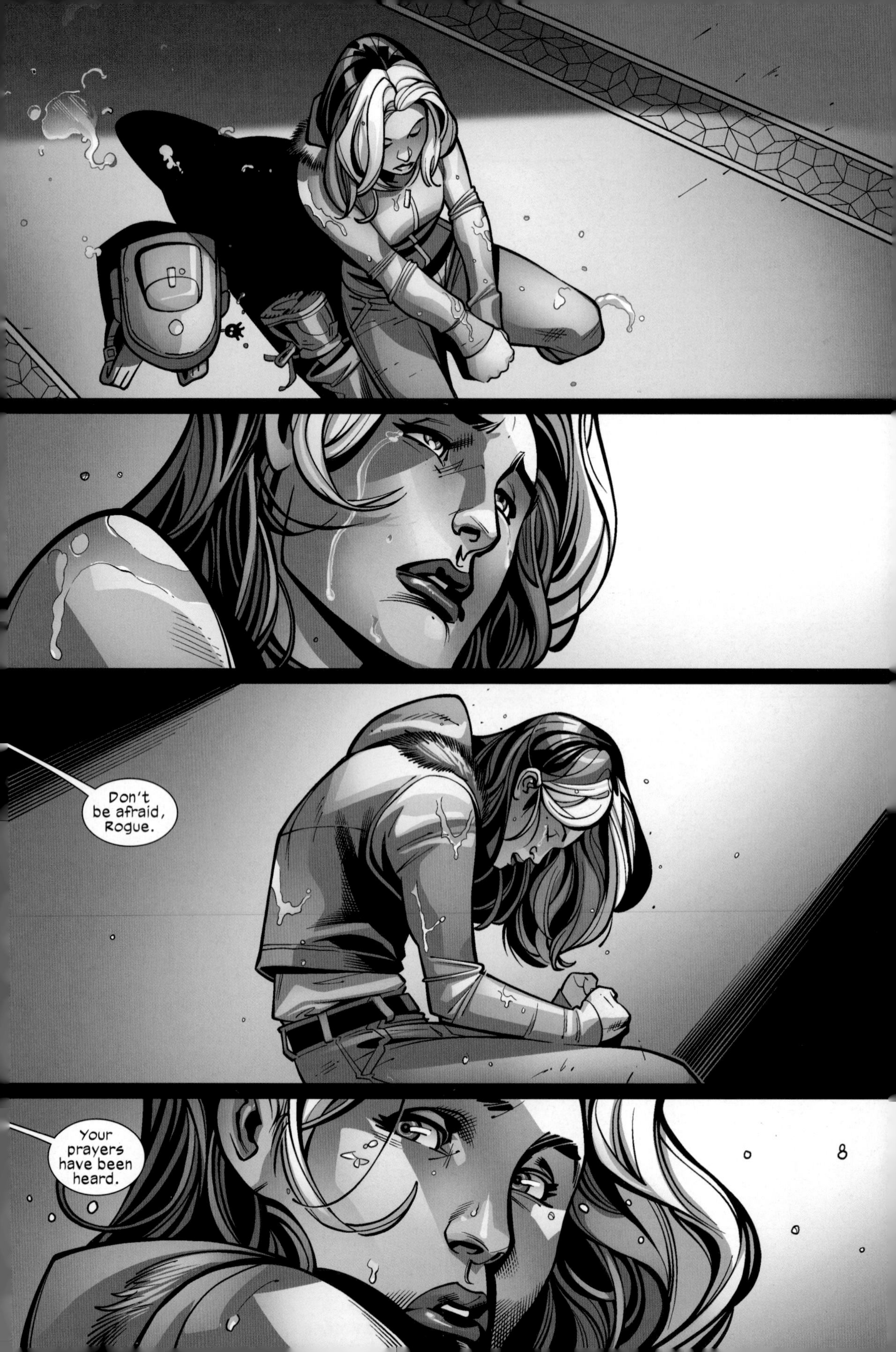
Don't be afraid, Rogue.
Your prayers have been heard.

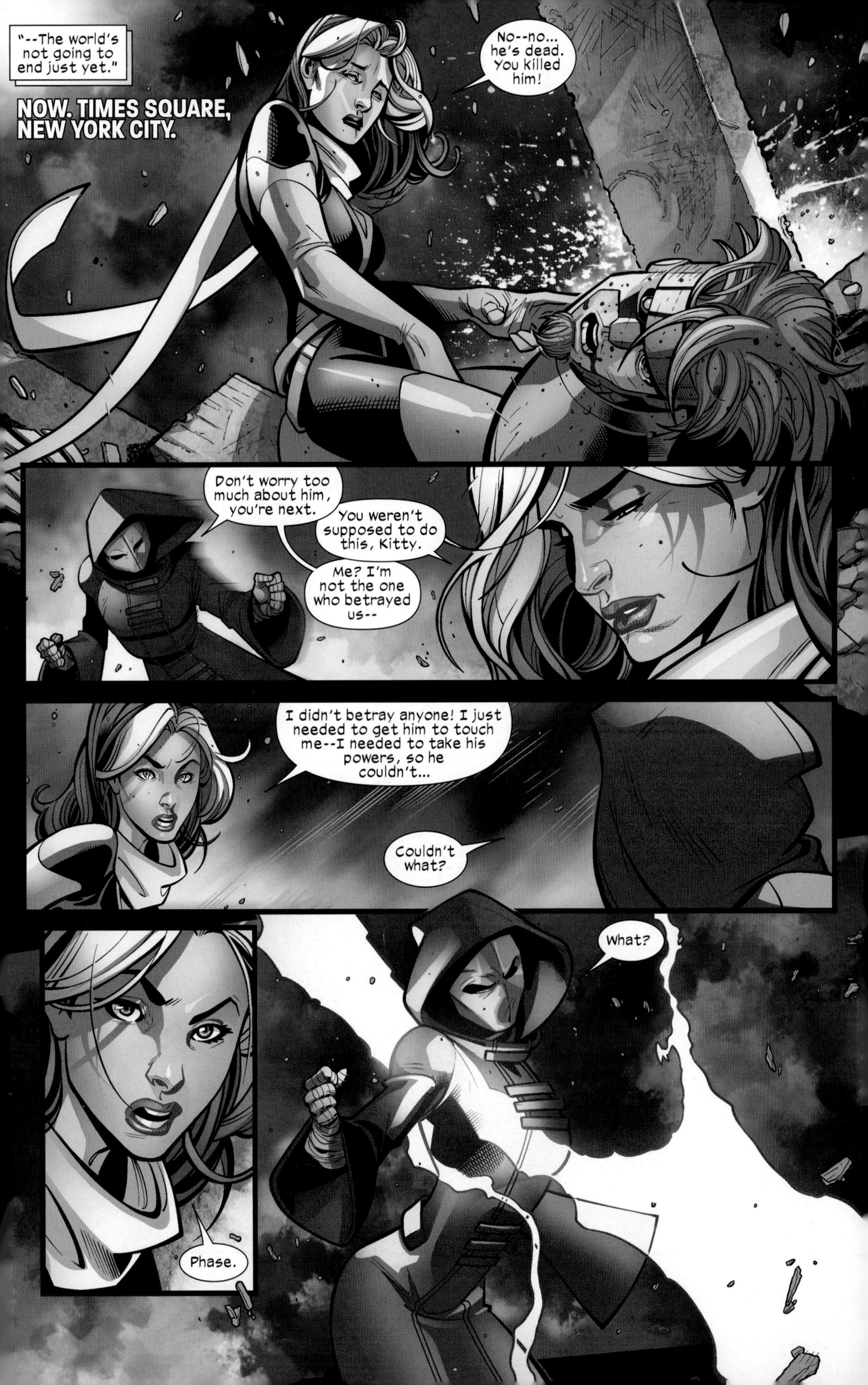
"--The world's not going to end just yet."
NOW. TIMES SQUARE, NEW YORK CITY.
No--no... he's dead. You killed him!
Don't worry too much about him, you're next.
You weren't supposed to do this, Kitty.
Me? I'm not the one who betrayed us--
I didn't betray anyone! I just needed to get him to touch me--I needed to take his powers, so he couldn't...
Couldn't what?
What?
Phase.

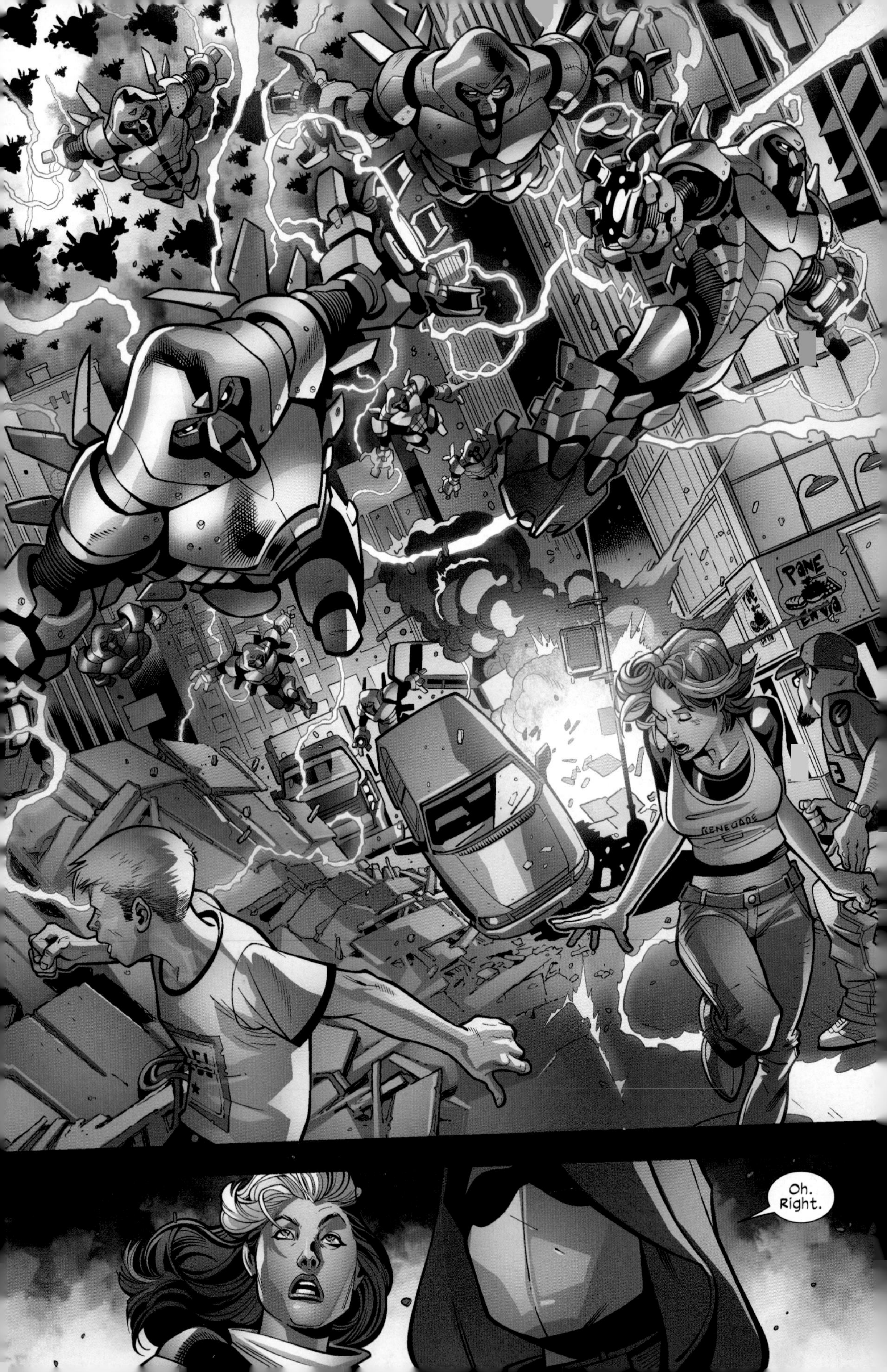
Oh. Right.

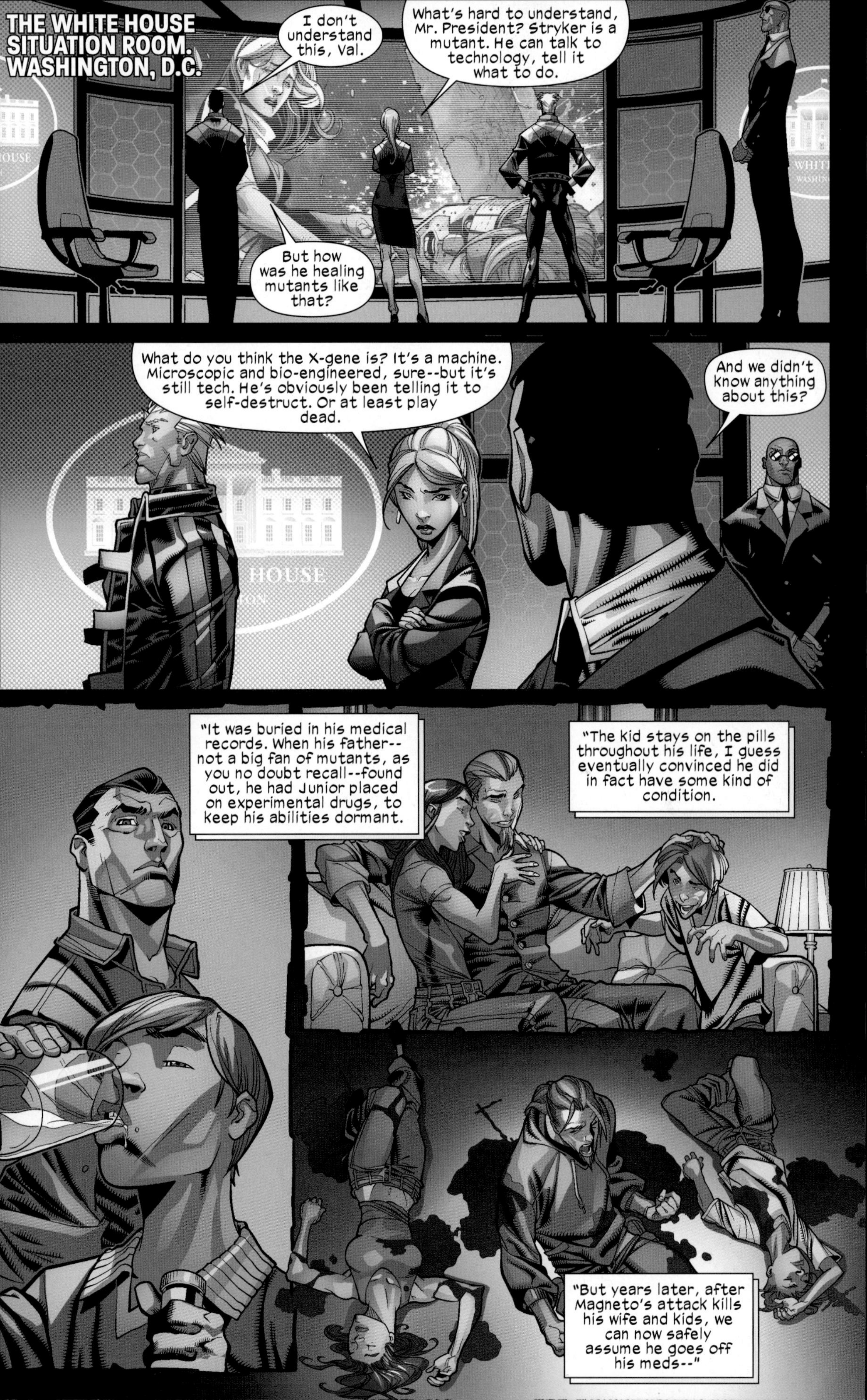
THE WHITE HOUSE SITUATION ROOM. WASHINGTON, D.C.
I don't understand this, Val.
What's hard to understand, Mr. President? Stryker is a mutant. He can talk to technology, tell it what to do.
But how was he healing mutants like that?
What do you think the X-gene is? It's a machine. Microscopic and bio-engineered, sure--but it's still tech. He's obviously been telling it to self-destruct. Or at least play dead.
And we didn't know anything about this?
"It was buried in his medical records. When his father--not a big fan of mutants, as you no doubt recall--found out, he had Junior placed on experimental drugs, to keep his abilities dormant.
"The kid stays on the pills throughout his life, I guess eventually convinced he did in fact have some kind of condition.
"But years later, after Magneto's attack kills his wife and kids, we can now safely assume he goes off his meds--"

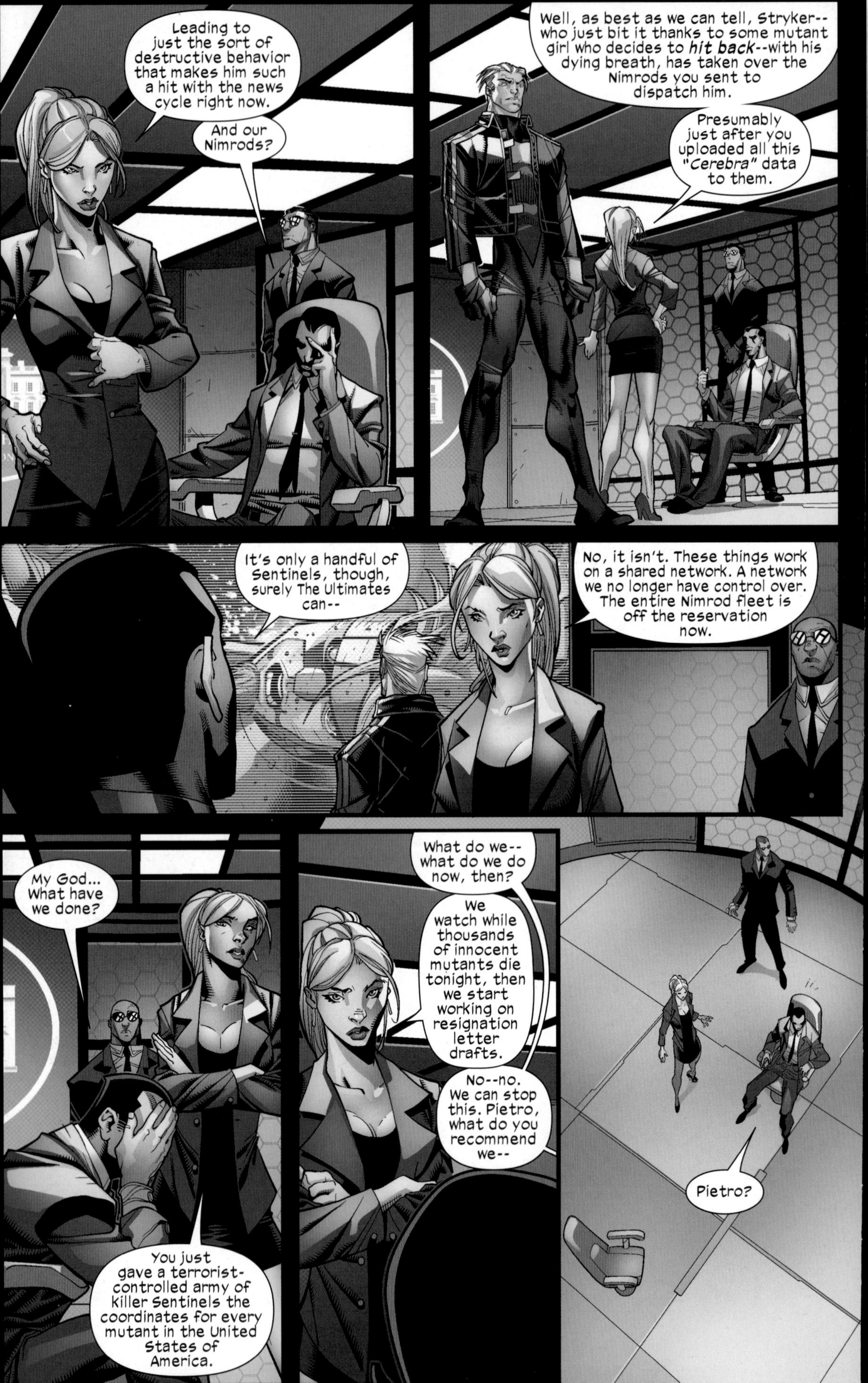

Leading to just the sort of destructive behavior that makes him such a hit with the news cycle right now.
And our Nimrods?
Well, as best as we can tell, Stryker--who just bit it thanks to some mutant girl who decides to *hit back*--with his dying breath, has taken over the Nimrods you sent to dispatch him.
Presumably just after you uploaded all this "*Cerebra*" data to them.
It's only a handful of Sentinels, though, surely The Ultimates can--
No, it isn't. These things work on a shared network. A network we no longer have control over. The entire Nimrod fleet is off the reservation now.
My God... What have we done?
You just gave a terrorist-controlled army of killer Sentinels the coordinates for every mutant in the United States of America.
What do we--what do we do now, then?
We watch while thousands of innocent mutants die tonight, then we start working on resignation letter drafts.
No--no. We can stop this. Pietro, what do you recommend we--
Pietro?

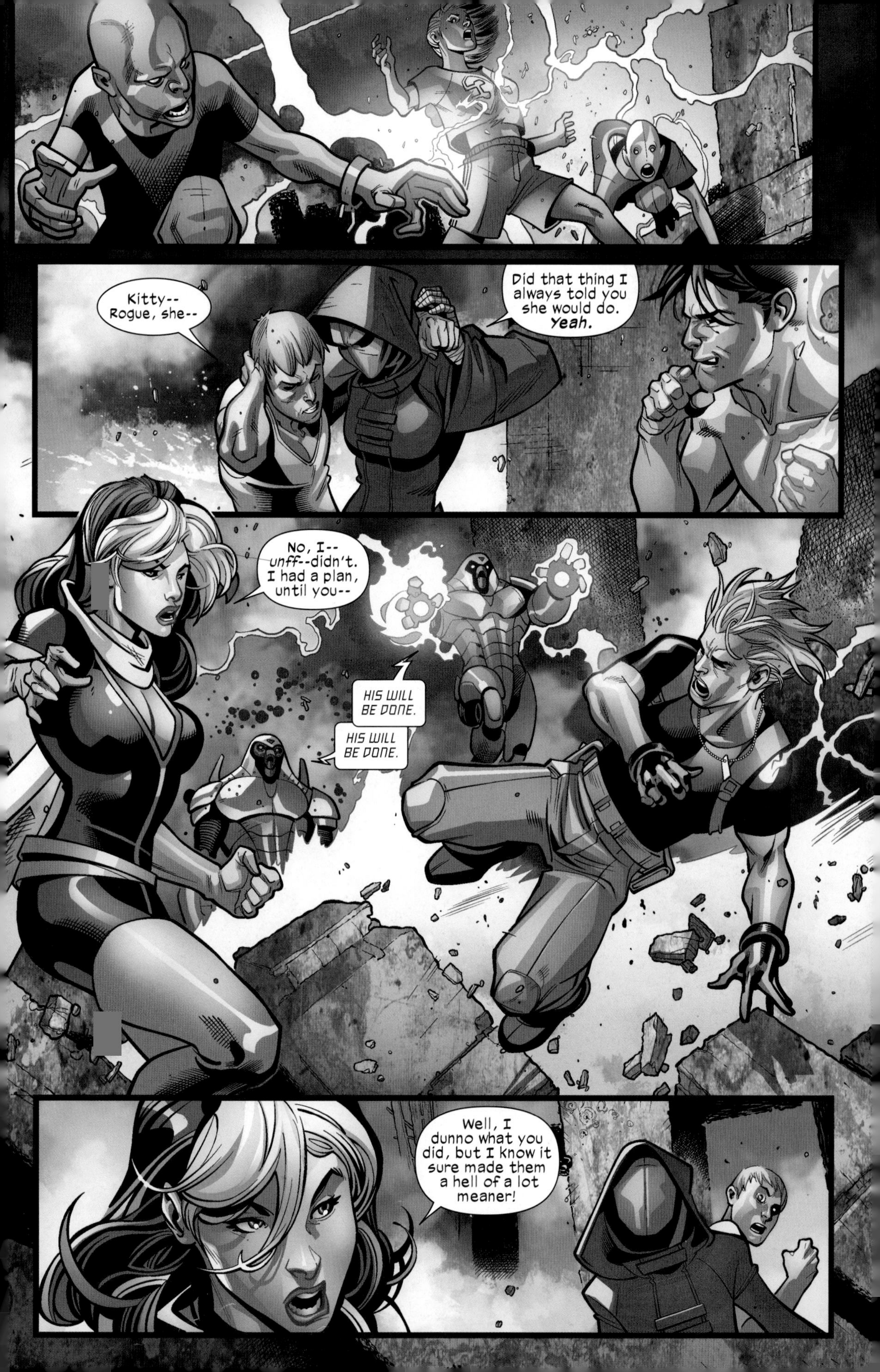

Kitty--
Rogue, she--
Did that thing I always told you she would do. *Yeah.*
No, I-- *unff*--didn't. I had a plan, until you--
HIS WILL BE DONE.
HIS WILL BE DONE.
Well, I dunno what you did, but I know it sure made them a hell of a lot meaner!

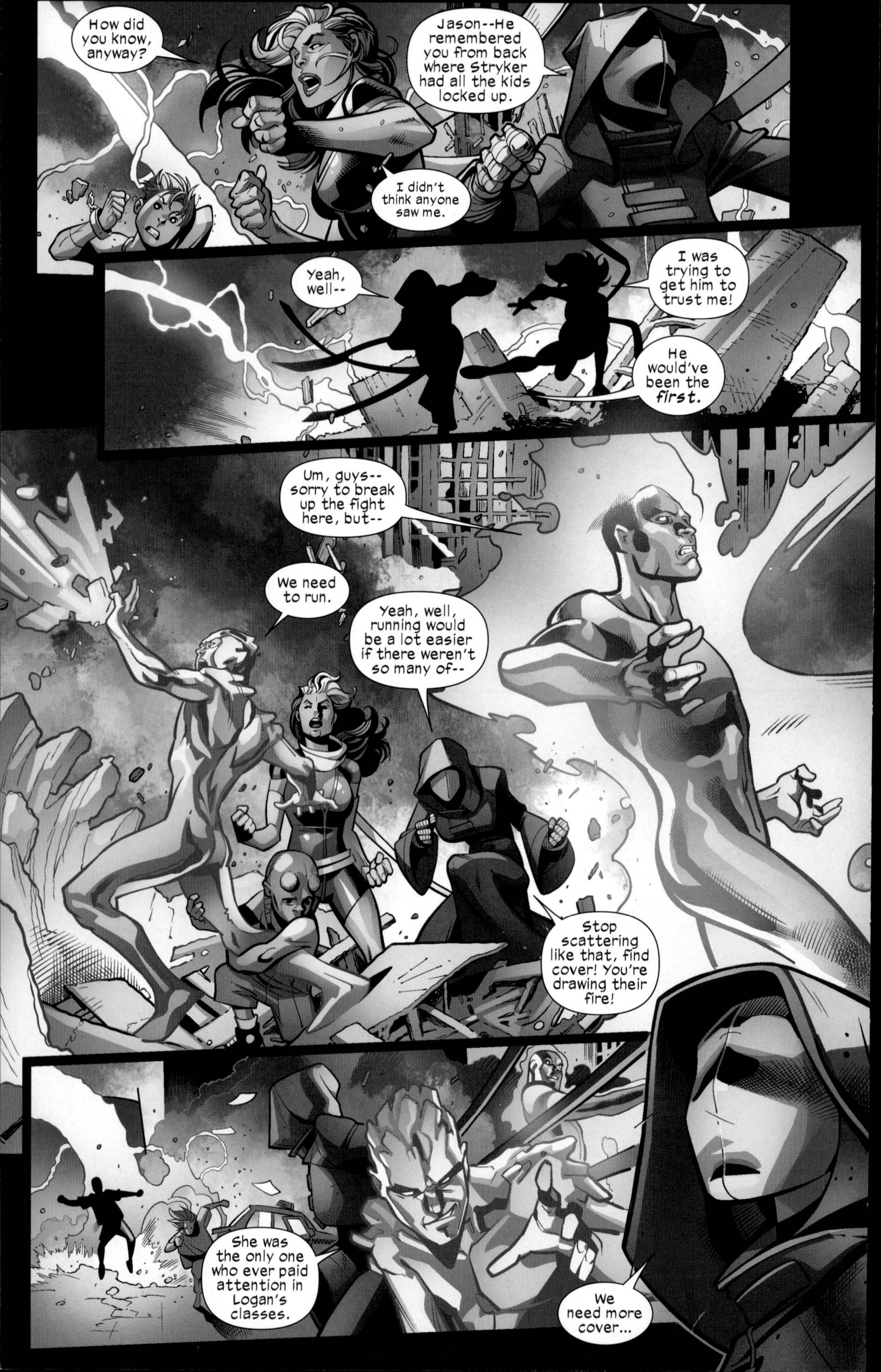
How did you know, anyway?
Jason--He remembered you from back where Stryker had all the kids locked up.
I didn't think anyone saw me.
Yeah, well--
I was trying to get him to trust me!
He would've been the *first.*
Um, guys-- sorry to break up the fight here, but--
We need to run.
Yeah, well, running would be a lot easier if there weren't so many of--
Stop scattering like that, find cover! You're drawing their fire!
She was the only one who ever paid attention in Logan's classes.
We need more cover...

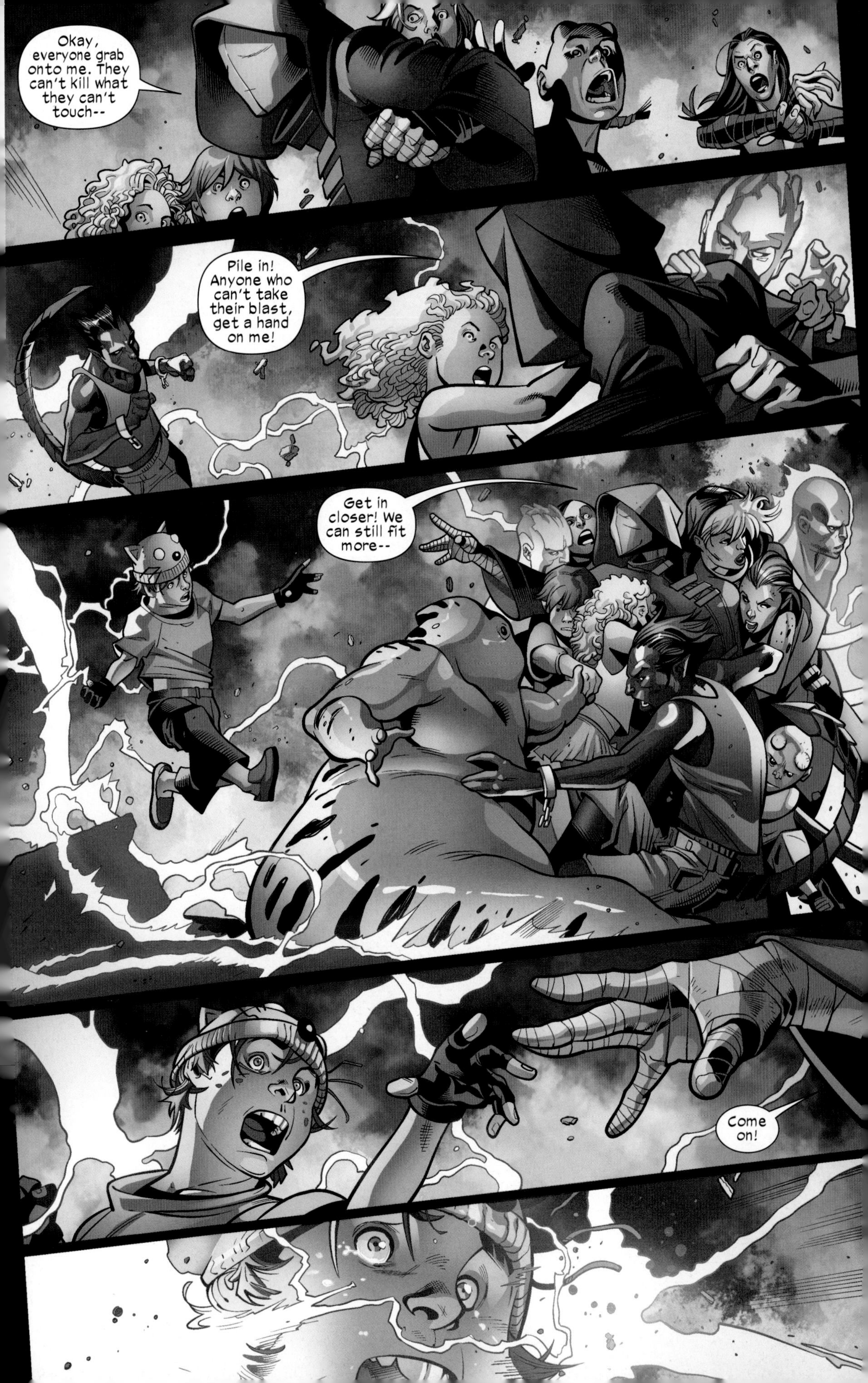
Okay, everyone grab onto me. They can't kill what they can't touch--
Pile in! Anyone who can't take their blast, get a hand on me!
Get in closer! We can still fit more--
Come on!

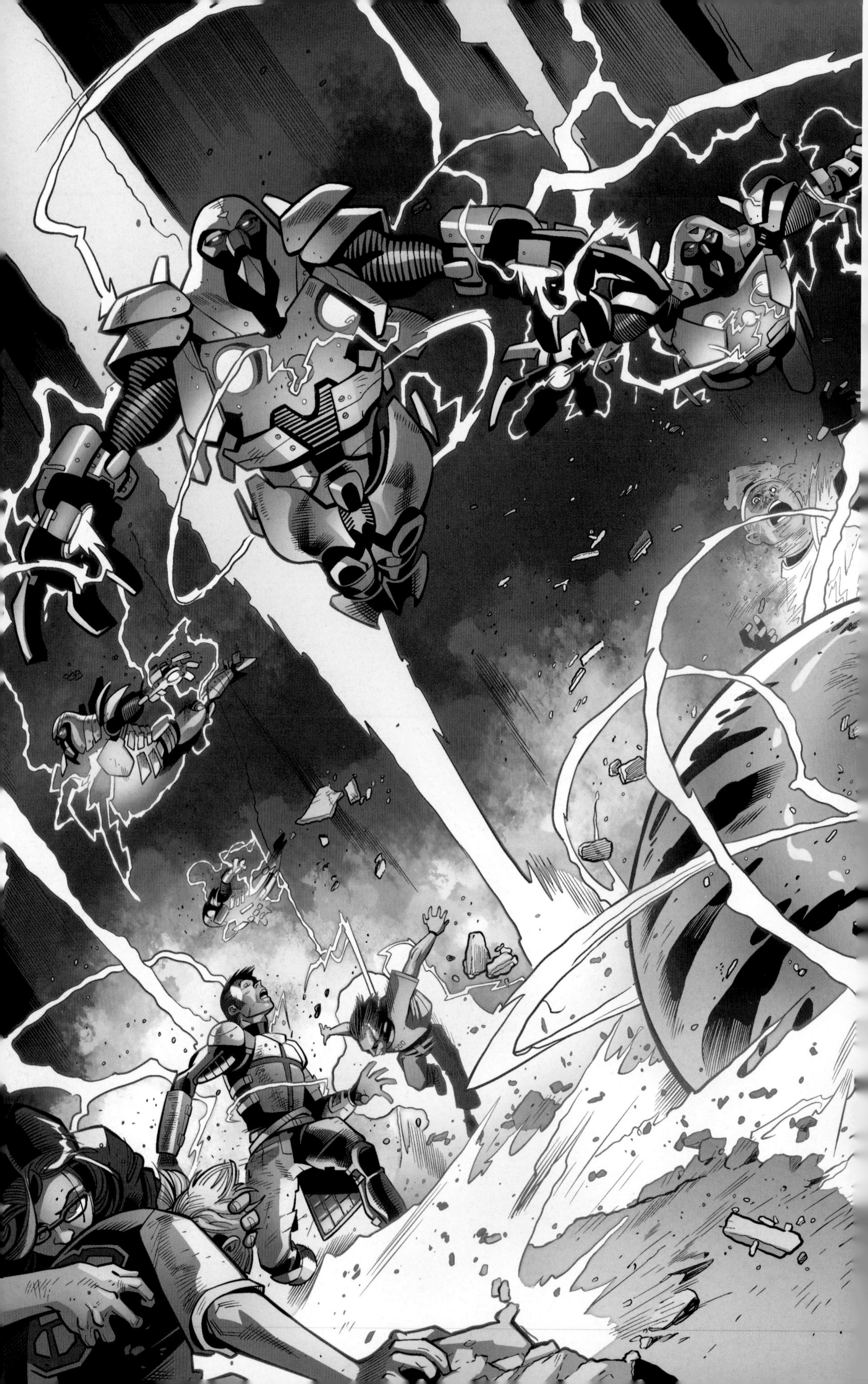

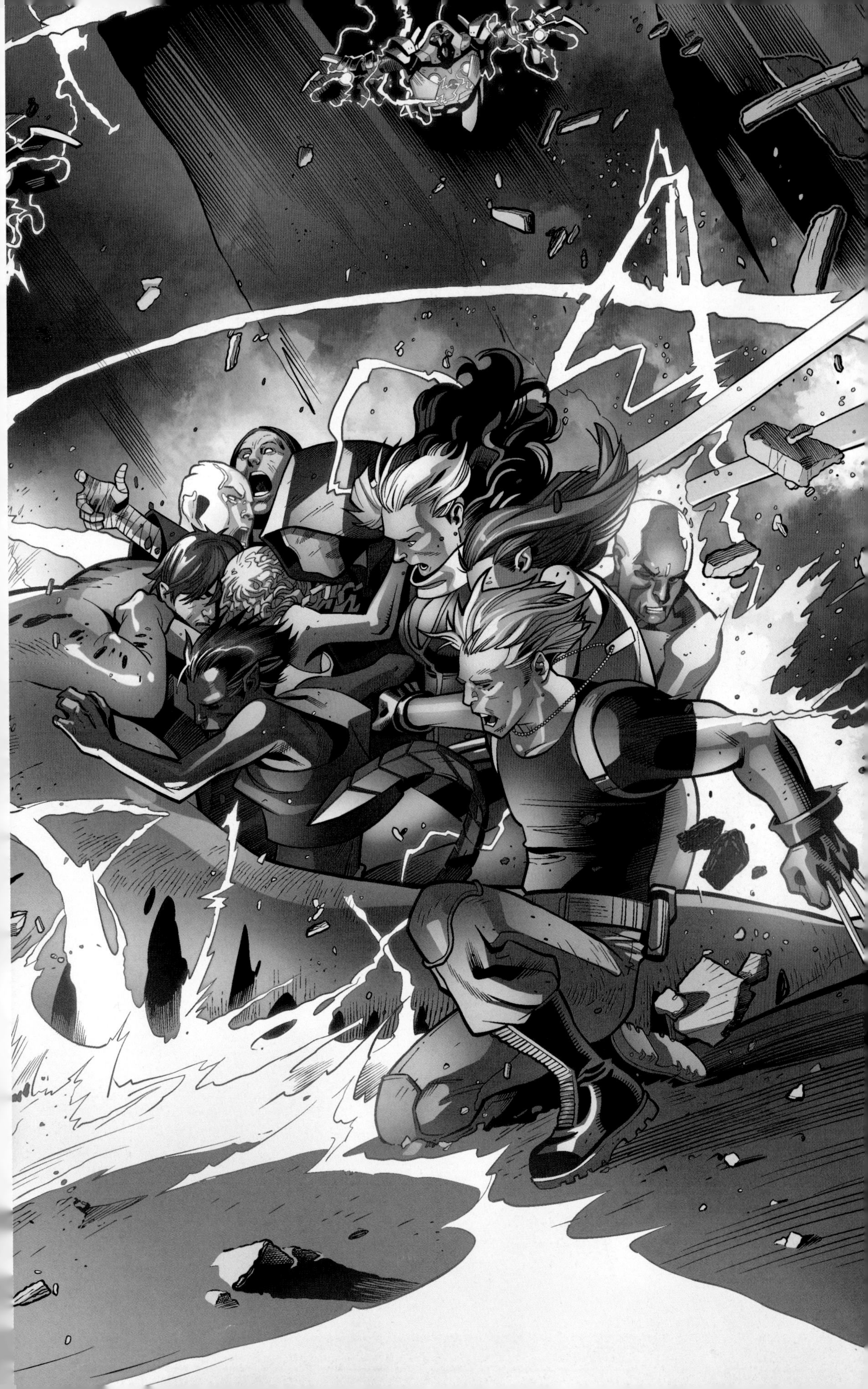

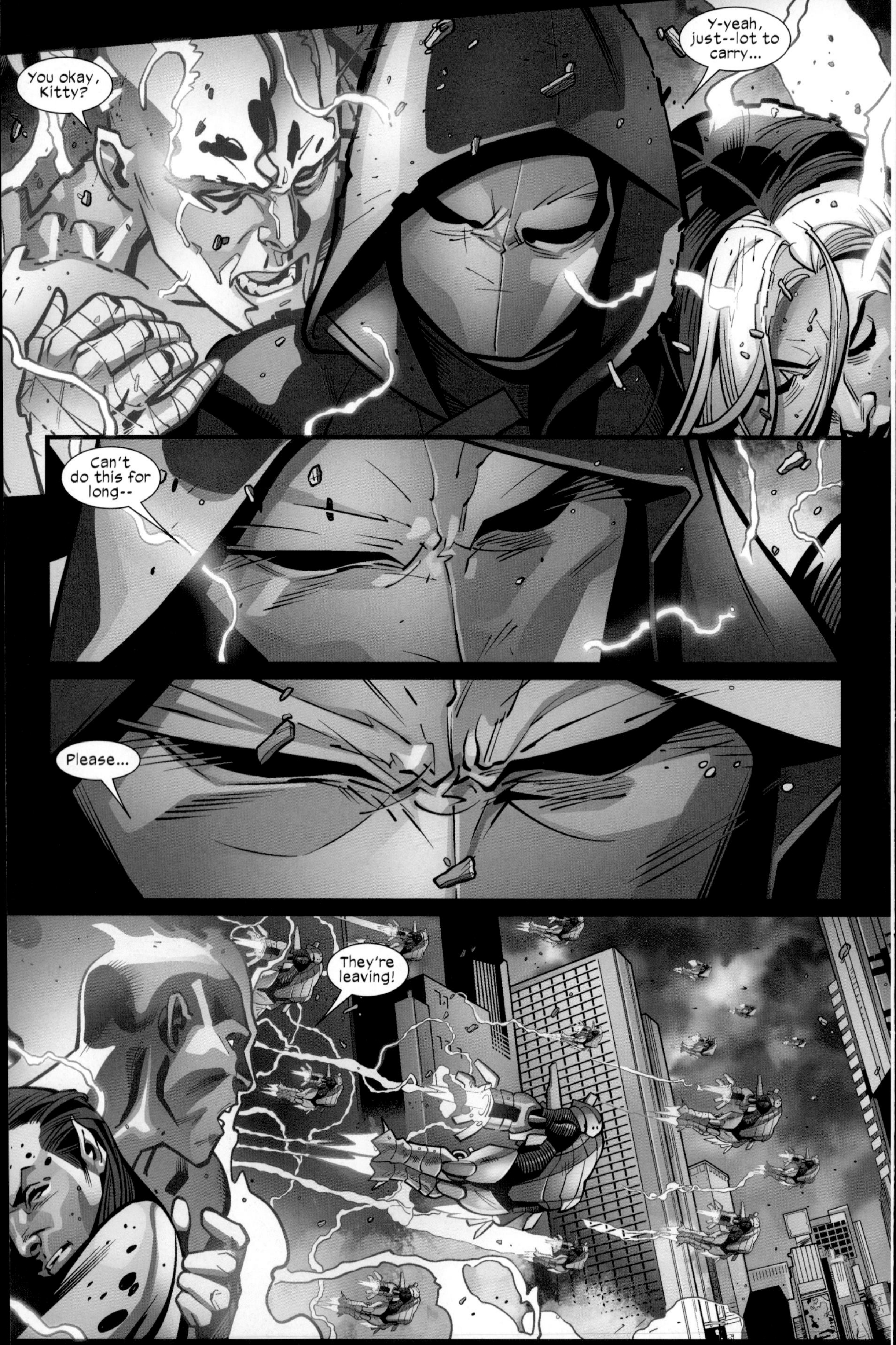
You okay, Kitty?
Y-yeah, just--lot to carry...
Can't do this for long--
Please...
They're leaving!

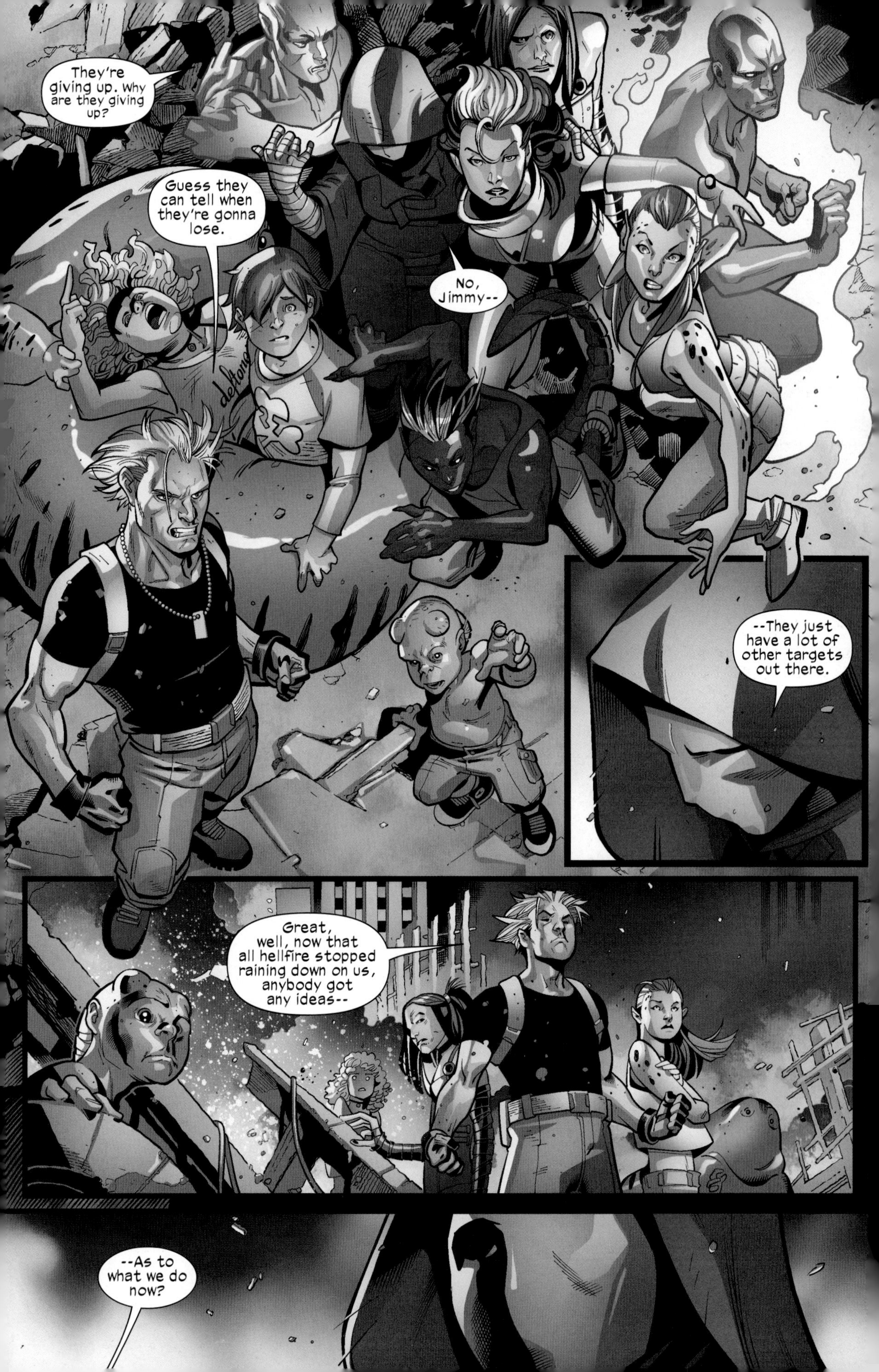
They're giving up. Why are they giving up?
Guess they can tell when they're gonna lose.
No, Jimmy--
--They just have a lot of other targets out there.
Great, well, now that all hellfire stopped raining down on us, anybody got any ideas--
--As to what we do now?

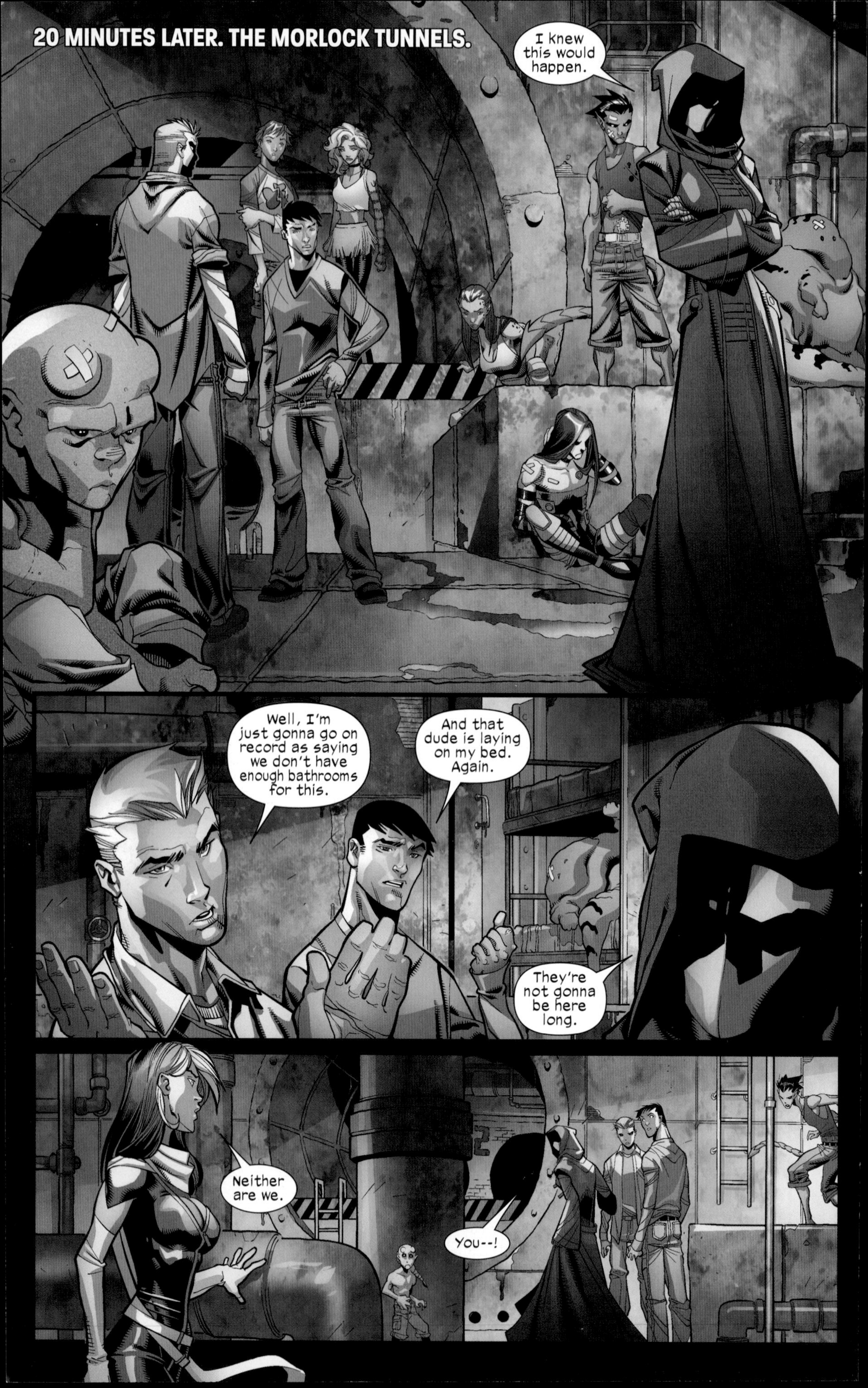
20 MINUTES LATER. THE MORLOCK TUNNELS.
I knew this would happen.
Well, I'm just gonna go on record as saying we don't have enough bathrooms for this.
And that dude is laying on my bed. Again.
They're not gonna be here long.
Neither are we.
You--!

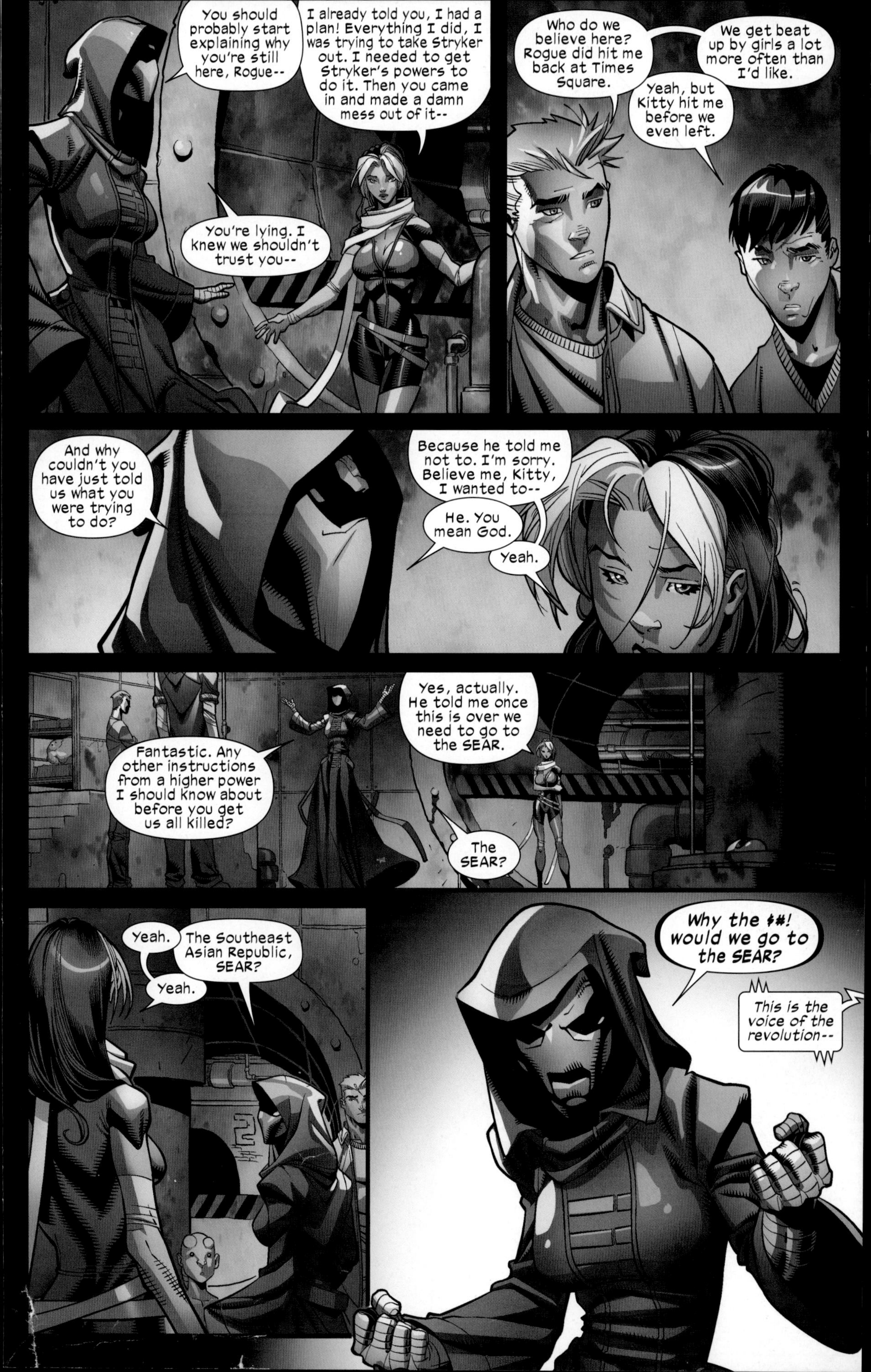
You should probably start explaining why you're still here, Rogue--
I already told you, I had a plan! Everything I did, I was trying to take Stryker out. I needed to get Stryker's powers to do it. Then you came in and made a damn mess out of it--
You're lying. I knew we shouldn't trust you--
Who do we believe here? Rogue did hit me back at Times Square.
We get beat up by girls a lot more often than I'd like.
Yeah, but Kitty hit me before we even left.
And why couldn't you have just told us what you were trying to do?
Because he told me not to. I'm sorry. Believe me, Kitty, I wanted to--
He. You mean God.
Yeah.
Fantastic. Any other instructions from a higher power I should know about before you get us all killed?
Yes, actually. He told me once this is over we need to go to the SEAR.
The SEAR?
Yeah.
The Southeast Asian Republic, SEAR?
Yeah.
Why the $#! would we go to the SEAR?
This is the voice of the revolution--

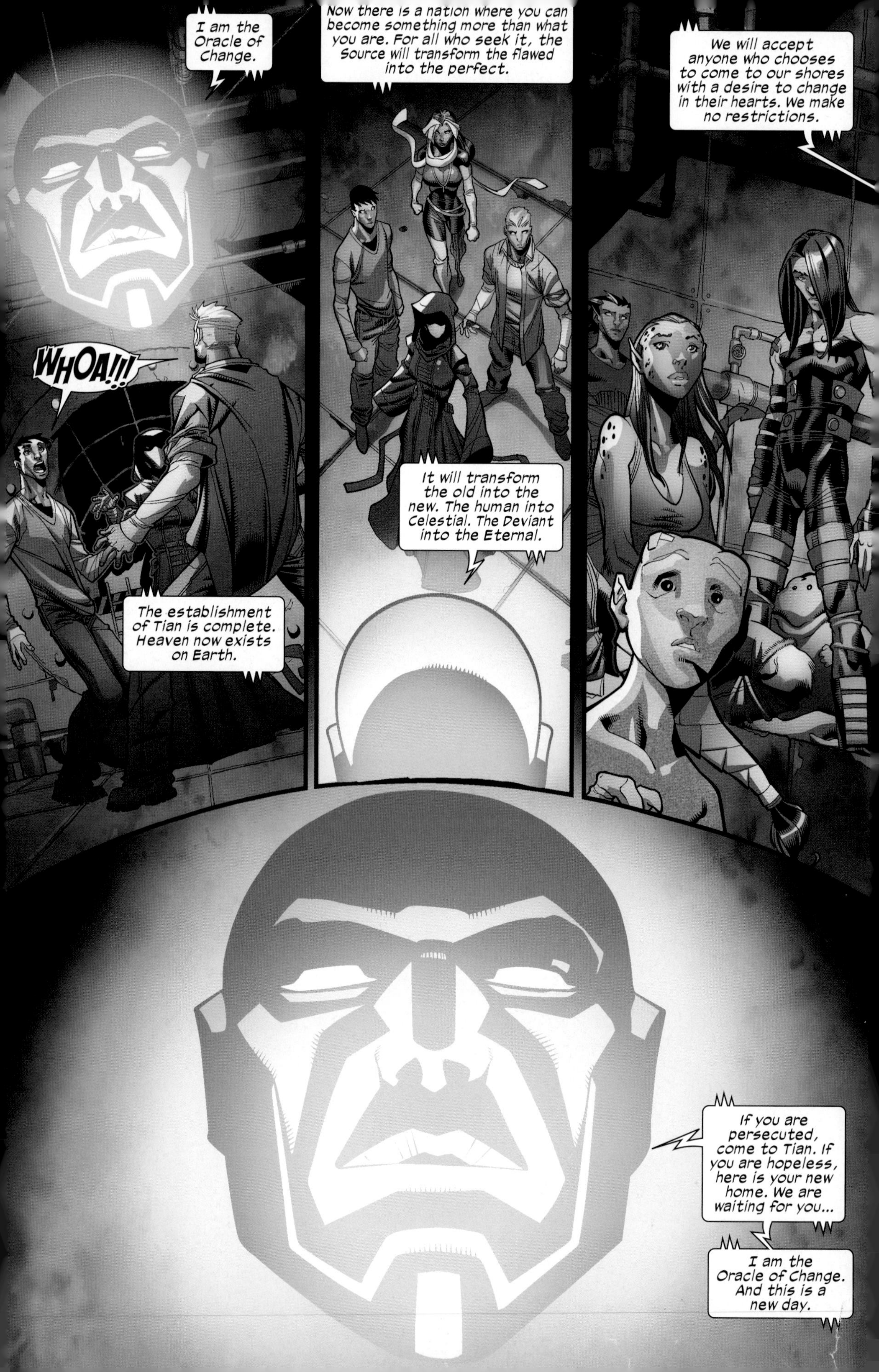
I am the Oracle of Change.
Now there is a nation where you can become something more than what you are. For all who seek it, the Source will transform the flawed into the perfect.
We will accept anyone who chooses to come to our shores with a desire to change in their hearts. We make no restrictions.
WHOA!!!
The establishment of Tian is complete. Heaven now exists on Earth.
It will transform the old into the new. The human into Celestial. The Deviant into the Eternal.
If you are persecuted, come to Tian. If you are hopeless, here is your new home. We are waiting for you...
I am the Oracle of Change. And this is a new day.

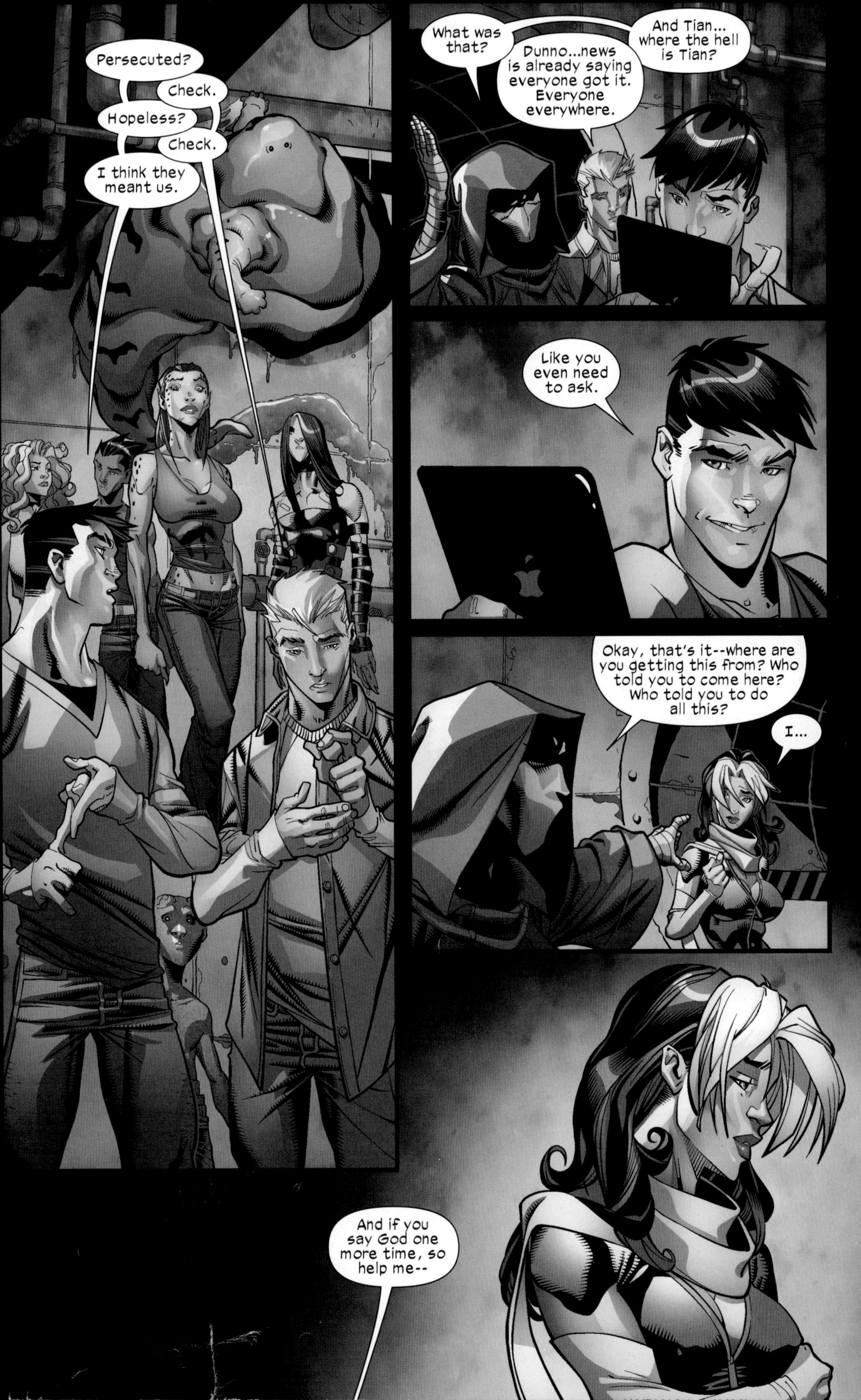
Persecuted?
Check.
Hopeless?
Check.
I think they meant us.
What was that?
Dunno...news is already saying everyone got it. Everyone everywhere.
And Tian... where the hell is Tian?
Like you even need to ask.
Okay, that's it--where are you getting this from? Who told you to come here? Who told you to do all this?
I...
And if you say God one more time, so help me--

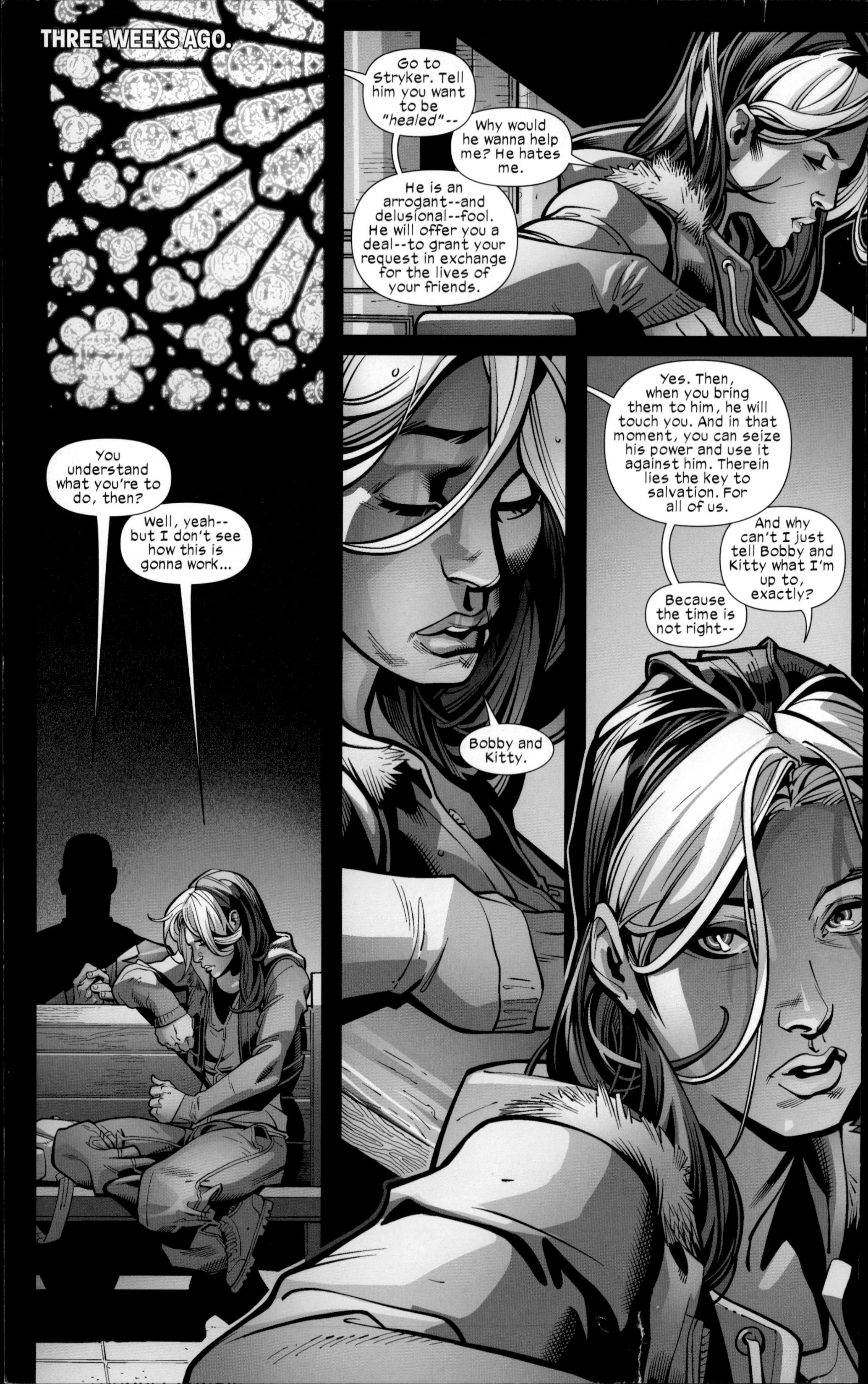
THREE WEEKS AGO.
Go to Stryker. Tell him you want to be "healed"--
Why would he wanna help me? He hates me.
He is an arrogant--and delusional--fool. He will offer you a deal--to grant your request in exchange for the lives of your friends.
You understand what you're to do, then?
Well, yeah--but I don't see how this is gonna work...
Bobby and Kitty.
Yes. Then, when you bring them to him, he will touch you. And in that moment, you can seize his power and use it against him. Therein lies the key to salvation. For all of us.
And why can't I just tell Bobby and Kitty what I'm up to, exactly?
Because the time is not right--

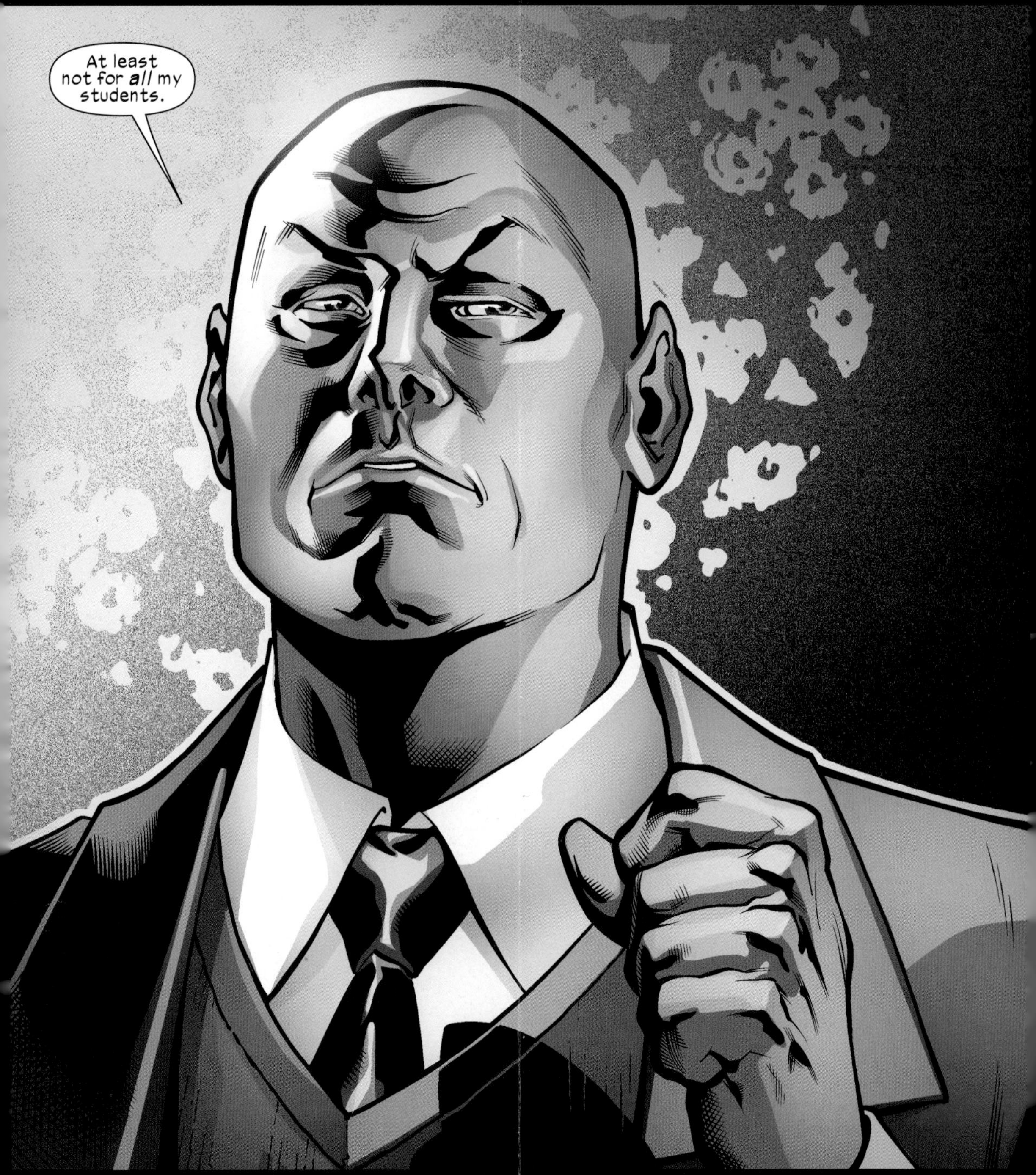
At least not for *all* my students.

TO BE CONTINUED...

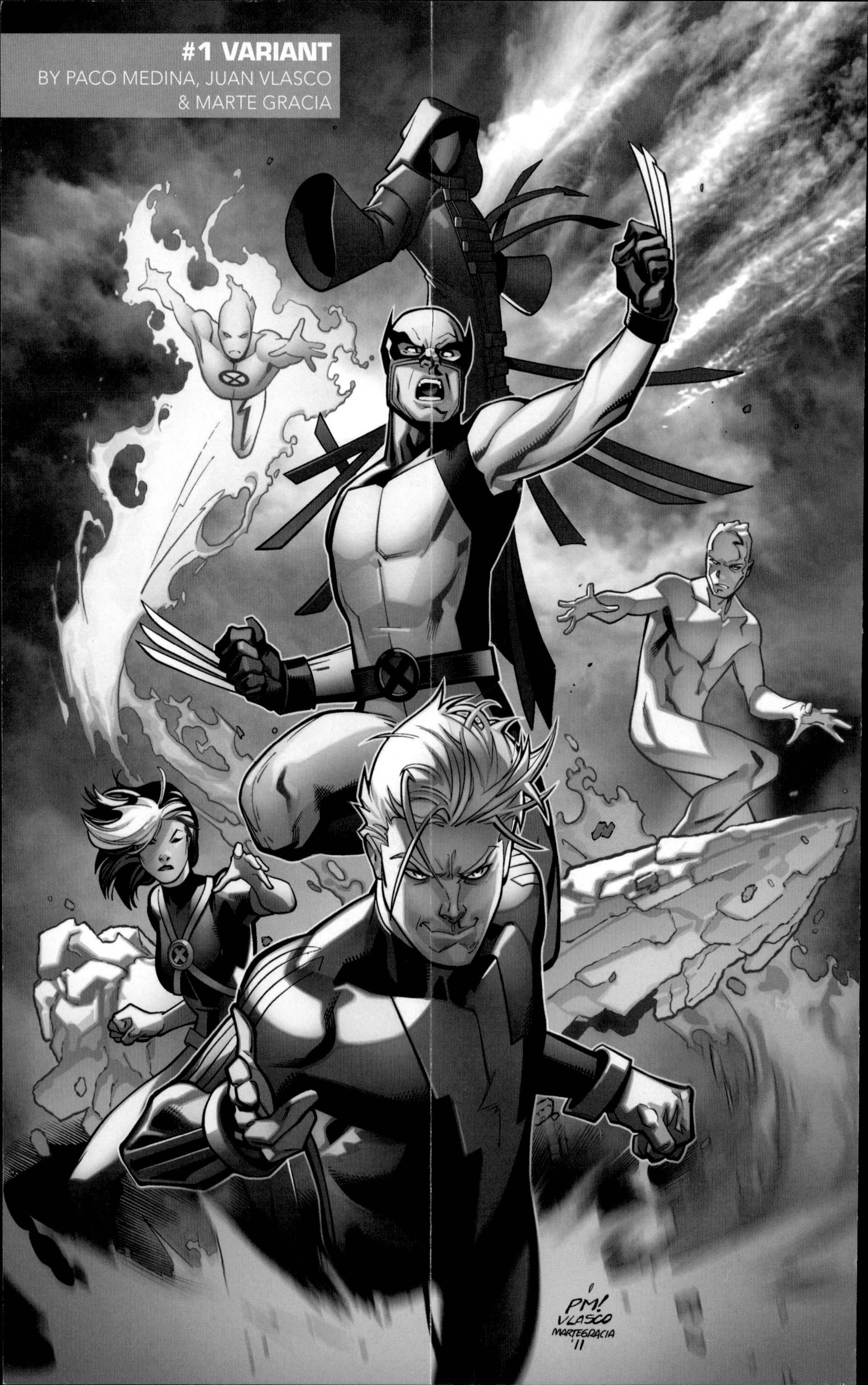

#1 VARIANT
BY PACO MEDINA, JUAN VLASCO
& MARTE GRACIA

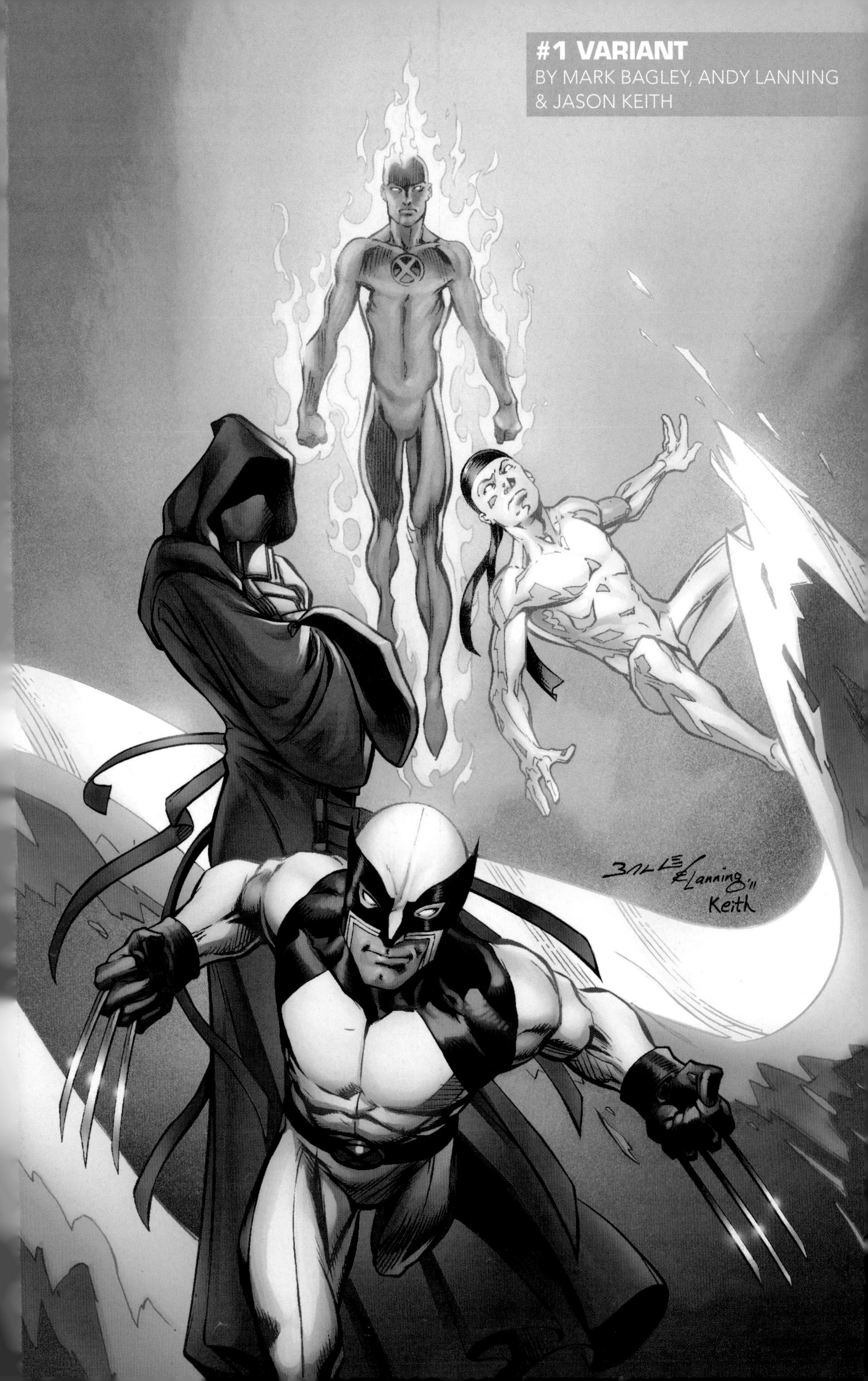
Lanning '11
Keith

#1 VARIANT
BY MARK BAGLEY, ANDY LANNING
& JASON KEITH

ULTIMATE COMICS

In the wake of Ultimatum, the Ultimate Universe was overhauled with comics top writers and artists bringing a new energy to Ultimates characters!

➤ Ultimate Comics Iron Man: Armor Wars HC/TP

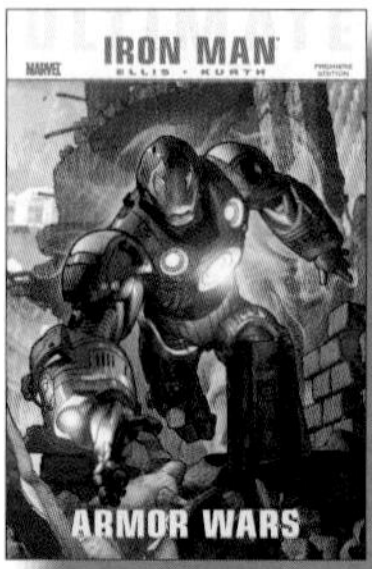
IRON MAN
ARMOR WARS

Collects *Ultimate Armor Wars* #1-4

By Warren Ellis and Steve Kurth

Tony's armor falls into the wrong hands in the wake of Ultimatum!

HC: JAN100637 • 978-0-7851-4250-8
TP: JUL100695 • 978-0-7851-4430-4

➤ Ultimate Comics Spider-Man Vol. 1: The World According to Peter Parker HC/TP

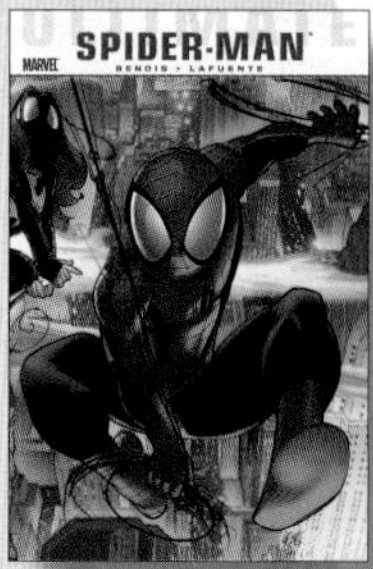
SPIDER-MAN

Collects *Ultimate Comics Spider-Man* #1-6

By Brian Michael Bendis and David Lafuente

Six months after Ultimatum, Spidey picks up the pieces on a new life!

HC: JAN100656 • 978-0-7851-4011-5
TP: APR100670 • 978-0-7851-4099-3

➤ Ultimate Comics Spider-Man Vol. 2: Chameleons HC/TP

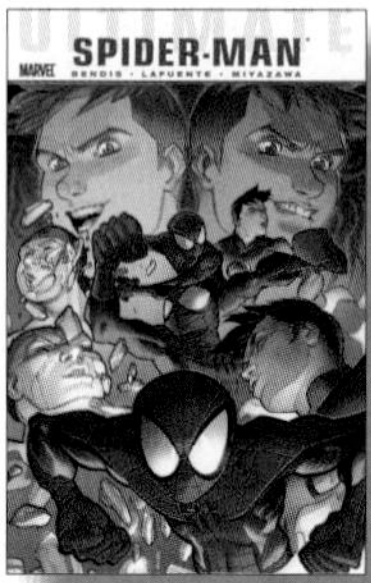
SPIDER-MAN

Collects *Ultimate Comics Spider-Man* #7-14

By Brian Michael Bendis, Takeshi Miyazawa and David Lafuente

Rick Jones has some crazy new powers…and might just be crazy!

HC: SEP100695 • 978-0-7851-4012-2
TP: MAR110801 • 978-0-7851-4100-6

➤ Ultimate Comics Avengers: Next Generation HC/TP

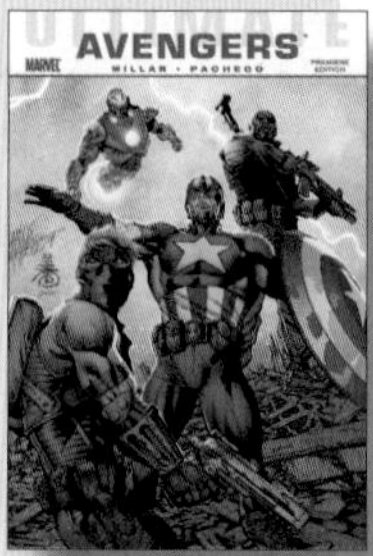
AVENGERS

Collects *Ultimate Avengers* #1-6

By Mark Millar and Carlos Pacheco

Classified secrets threaten Captain America and only Nick Fury can help!

HC: APR100654 • 978-0-7851-4010-8
TP: AUG100701 • 978-0-7851-4097-9

➤ Ultimate Comics Avengers: Crime & Punishment HC/TP

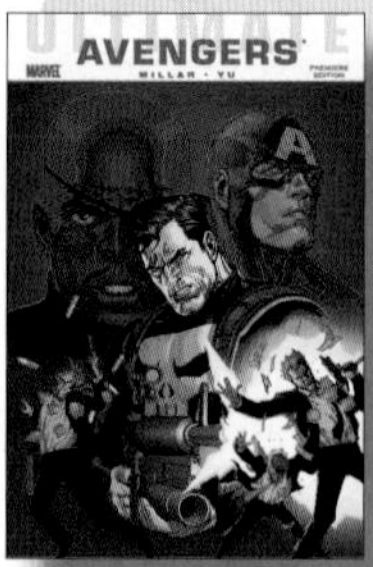
AVENGERS

Collects *Ultimate Avengers 2* #1-6

By Mark Millar and Leinil Francis Yu

When the job is just too dirty, Nick Fury calls in the Avengers!

HC: AUG100688 • 978-0-7851-3670-5
TP: FEB110685 • 978-0-7851-3671-2

➤ Ultimate Comics Avengers: Blade vs. Avengers HC/TP

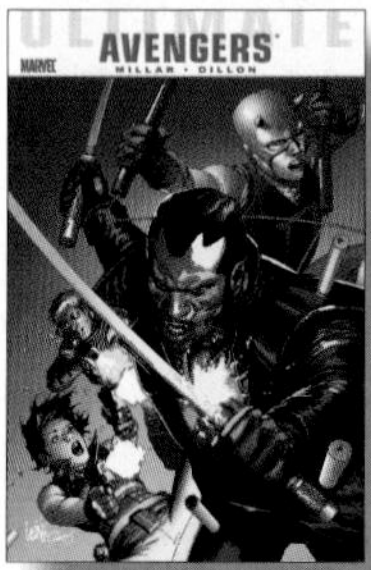
AVENGERS

Collects Ultimate Avengers 2 #1-6

By Mark Millar and Steve Dillon

Blade is back in a bad way, and that can only mean one thing: Vampires!

FEB110663 • 978-0-7851-4009-2

➤ Ultimate Comics X: Origins HC

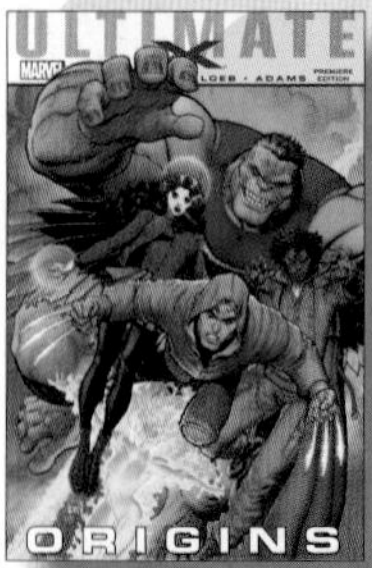
ULTIMATE
ORIGINS

Collects *Ultimate Comics X* #1-5

By Jeph Loeb and Arthur Adams

Who is Ultimate X? The character who will change the Ultimate Universe forever!

978-0-7851-4014-6

➤ Ultimate Comics Thor HC

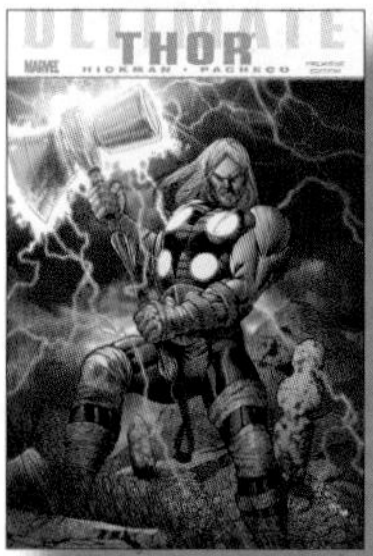
THOR

Collects *Ultimate Comics Thor* #1-4

By Jonathan Hickman and Carlos Pacheco

Origins revealed as Ultimates go back to the beginning of Thor, Loki and Asgard!

DEC100662 • 978-0-7851-5187-6

➤ Ultimate Comics New Ultimates: Thor Reborn HC/TP

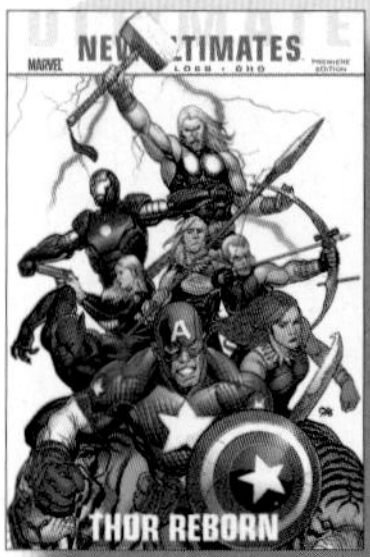
THOR REBORN

Collects *New Ultimates* #1-5

By Jeph Loeb and Frank Cho

Thor returns from the underworld ready to destroy Loki for good!

JAN110838 • 978-0-7851-3994-2